Women's and Gender Studies: An Interdisciplinary Approach

Women's and Gender Studies: An Interdisciplinary Approach

Daniel King

MURPHY & MOORE
www.murphy-moorepublishing.com

Murphy & Moore Publishing,
1 Rockefeller Plaza,
New York City, NY 10020, USA

ISBN: 978-1-63987-574-0

Cataloging-in-Publication Data

Women's and gender studies : an interdisciplinary approach / Daniel King.
p. cm.
Includes bibliographical references and index.
ISBN 978-1-63987-574-0
1. Women's studies. 2. Sex role. 3. Gender identity. 4. Women. I. King, Daniel.
HQ1180 .I58 2022
305.4--dc23

For information on all Murphy & Moore Publications
visit our website at www.murphy-moorepublishing.com

 **MURPHY & MOORE**

Contents

Women and gender studies is a field of academics which makes use of feminist and interdisciplinary methods to study the lives of women and their experiences. It is a multidisciplinary academic domain of literature, history, economics, political science, anthropology, media studies, etc., which is concerned with the analysis of gender identity and gendered representation. Gender studies include women's studies, men's studies and queer studies. It investigates the social and cultural constructs of gender, relationships between power and gender, and systems of privilege and oppression. Their intersection with various other identities and social locations such as race, sexual orientation, socio-economic class, and disability is also a key area of focus. Popular concepts that define the field of women studies include the standpoint theory, feminist theory, multiculturalism and intersectionality. The topics included in this book on women and gender studies are of utmost significance and bound to provide incredible insights to readers. Different approaches, evaluations, methodologies related to this field have been included herein. This book is a complete source of knowledge on the present status of this important field.

To facilitate a deeper understanding of the contents of this book a short introduction of every chapter is written below:

Chapter 1- The field of study which deals with gender identity and gendered representation is termed as gender studies. It encompasses women studies, sex and gender, and the different theories related to patriarchy such as Bateman's theory, concept of patriarchy and structures of patriarchy. This is an introductory chapter which will introduce briefly all the significant aspects of gender studies.

Chapter 2- The major concepts within the domain of gender studies are gender sensitisation, gender and language, gender and labour, gender and disability, gender stereotypes, and gender and media. Within media, films and video games are studied through a gendered perspective. This chapter discusses in detail these concepts related to gender studies.

Chapter 3- There are numerous theories which are studied under the discipline of gender studies. A few of such theories are psychoanalytic theory, sexism, sexual identity models and Hagan's power control theory. This chapter closely examines these key theories related to gender studies to provide an extensive understanding of the subject.

Chapter 4- The set of behaviors, characteristics and roles which are associated with boys and men is termed ass masculinity. The study of masculinity within the field of gender studies focuses on men's movement, toxic masculinity, hegemonic masculinity and machismo. This chapter discusses in detail these aspects of masculinity in gender studies.

Chapter 5- Feminism covers a range of political and social movements as well ideologies which are aimed at defining and establishing all sexes as equal in a political, economic, personal and social manner. The topics elaborated in this chapter will help in gaining a better perspective about the branches of feminism as well as feminist theory.

Chapter 6- LGBT is an acronym which stands for lesbian, gay, bisexual and transgender people. An important critical theory which is associated with LGBT community is the queer theory. It studies gender and sexual practices which challenge heteronormativity. The diverse aspects of LGBT community as well as the history of LGBT movement have been thoroughly discussed in this chapter.

Finally, I would like to thank the entire team involved in the inception of this book for their valuable time and contribution. This book would not have been possible without their efforts. I would also like to thank my friends and family for their constant support.

Daniel King

Gender Studies: An Introduction

The field of study which deals with gender identity and gendered representation is termed as gender studies. It encompasses women studies, sex and gender, and the different theories related to patriarchy such as Bateman's theory, concept of patriarchy and structures of patriarchy. This is an introductory chapter which will introduce briefly all the significant aspects of gender studies.

Sex and Gender

Sex denotes the biological characteristics of men and women expressed through physiology, anatomy, hormones, genes etc. The principles for categorizing sex are either genitalia at birth or chromosomal composition before birth, although it is important to remember that these do not necessarily conform with each other. Since the inception of the discourse on sex, only two socially legitimate sexual identities were 'male' and 'female'. However, at present our knowledge and understanding of sex has come a long way as we have come to appreciate other sexual identities as well. For example, "preceding ideas of sex presumed chromosomal provisions XX and XY as the representative character for woman and man, correspondingly, whereas we nowadays also understand that the configurations of chromosomes XXX, XXY, XYY, and XO do exist, besides XX males and XY females". Thus sex is now conceptualised in more than binary terms. Sexual variances lead to alterations in body form and mass, metabolism, hormonal and biochemical and hormonal outlines, muscle and fat delivery, functioning of organ, and structure of brain, amongst other variances. These alterations have reflective effects on state of health.

Although most often, sex is understood to be an invariant aspect of the male and female body, some researchers have contended that even sex is socially constructed in a manner that "determination of sex is made through the application of socially agreed upon biological criteria for classifying persons as females or males". Being socially constructed, sex, similar to gender, is also subject to change over time. For example, the intersex movement in recent years advocates that assessing the sex of babies at birth by visual assessment of genitals is insufficient for those whose reproductive or sexual anatomy is neither visibly male nor distinctly female. Thus the process of identification of sex at birth has evolved over the years and now includes genetic and chromosomal also.

Another issue that needs to be flagged here is that the ways we identify and understand the groupings man, woman, intersex etc. are "not biologically intrinsic but comparative to space and phase". Sex is not only conceptualised differently across different cultures, but such conceptualisations are also changing with time as different types of biological forms are getting recognized andthe ways of measurements/identification are being refined. In order to understand sex as a socially produced and culturally rooted part of identity, one needs to appreciate the concept of sex category. "Placement in a sex category is achieved through application of the sex criteria, but in everyday life, categorization is established and sustained by the socially required identificatory displays that proclaim one's membership in one or the other category". Thus, according to the authors, one's sex group which is externally discernible acts as a proxy for an individual's sex in many instances of life, although sex classification and sex may vary independently. That is, an individual may dress and behave like a woman (sex category) without having the necessary criteria for being biologically female (sex).

Gender

Similar to sex, gender is "a multidimensional construct that refers to the different roles, responsibilities, limitations, and experiences provided to individuals". Gender is built on the edifice of biological sex and categorise individuals as men, women, hermaphrodite, and hijra, amongst others, founded on sexual variances. These categories are socially constructed. Therefore, like sex, notions around gender are also culturally produced, specific to particular timeframes and subject to modification".

The analytical concepts of sex, categorization of sex and gender should be clearly understood for comprehending how gendered identities are produced through the interaction of these three concepts. "The labelling of individuals into categories such as "girl" or "boy," or "woman" or "man," is a cultural process which is not based on any definite set of standards that must be openly contented earlier to confirming membership to a particular gender category. Relatively, the submission of association categories depends on an "if-can" trial in daily communication". This test specifies that:

"If people can be seen as members of relevant categories, then categorize them that way. That is, use the category that seems appropriate, except in the presence of discrepant information or obvious features that would rule out its use. This procedure is quite in keeping with the attitude of everyday life, which has us take appearances at face value unless we have special reason to doubt".

It is extremely pertinent to understand how the process of gendering operates in the society i.e. how people are produced as 'appropriate' men and women through a range of social injunctions. Following are the approaches through which the engendering process operates in our societies.

Approaches to Conceptualizing Gender

Institutionalised Gender

In almost all societies across the world, men are accorded with much higher status compared to women and given greater power, opportunities as well as access to resources and public life. Institutions such as educational, medical, political, social as well as media and religion play an important role in shaping such hierarchical gender identities. Institutionalised gender denotes the "ways in which gender is rooted in and expressed through these large social systems, through the different responses, values, expectations, roles, and responsibilities given to individuals and groups according to gender". It also interacts with other markers of social identities such as race, class, sexual identity etc. to further systematically arrange individuals into hierarchies of privilege.

Gender as Constrained Choice

Gender is enacted by individuals through their everyday transactions in life. In doing so, they either consciously or unconsciously, take on identities and roles that are socially legitimate and appropriate with respect to their sex categories. However, such procedure of adopting specific gender attributes is a subtle strategy which becomes explicitly visible only through critical reflection about self and others.

"Becoming a gender is an impulsive yet mindful process of interpreting a cultural reality laden with sanctions, taboos, and prescriptions. The choice to assume a certain kind of body, to live or wear one's body a certain way, implies a world of already established corporeal styles. To choose a gender is to interpret received gender norms in a way that organizes them anew. Rather than a radical action of conception, gender is an implicit assignment to restart one's traditional antiquity in one's personal terms."

Thus gender is chosen, produced and reproduced by individuals. However, it must be remembered that such choice is not freely available to everyone and, in fact, can be quite constraining in many ways. People's "choices" in the context of gender identities are mediated by biology. For instance, those who inwardly identify themselves more as women may be forced to take on the identity of men in order to confirm to the social norms of legitimate gender identities that their sex categories thrust them into. Thus scholars have argued that those located in marginalised power position are often "choice-disabled" i.e. they are unable to make informed choices due to the gross inequalities of power and norms of social legitimacy. Viewing gender as a constrained choice enable us to address the countless restrictions we encounter at different stages (singular, family, society, community) and recognising that "choices are limited by these overarching and intersecting constraints".

Gender Roles

Society accords distinctly different tasks and jobs to men and women on the basis of their perceived gender characteristics (women as nurturing, caring, emotional and men as aggressive, risk-taking, rational etc.) These jobs and tasks are called gender roles which vary across cultures and locations, and change over time. "Gender roles structure the various 'parts' that individuals play throughout their lives, impacting aspects of daily life from choice of clothing to occupation". These are learned social behaviour that men and women come to accept as inflexible and 'natural' to the extent that they often fail to question such stereotypical gender roles, no matter how exploitative these may be. Traditional gender roles play the most crucial role in social organisation. For this reason, individuals unknowingly internalize these stereotypes irrespective of their particular chosen gender.

Gender Identity

Gender identity is a form of social identity. It is an expression of how people view themselves as well as how others view them with respect to gender. Gender identities are developed in compliance to the societal norms of "correct" and "corresponding" gender. In the event of non-conformation, individuals are susceptible to being subjected to various forms of violence.

Additionally, even within the 'progressive' societies where different types of gender presentations are considered acceptable, if it is not possible to readily identify and categorise the gender of an individual, it evokes considerable anxiety because human beings constantly try to "recognise and categorize individuals as per the dyadic model of gender." Individuals therefore internalize features of institutionalised gender and gender roles and confer their own gender identity as either male or female. Masculinity not only relates to the male body but also encapsulates a range of behaviours, practices, and characteristics such as rational, bold, strength, aggression, courage, independence, virility etc. Similarly, "femininity is connected with femaleness. It is not inherently attached to any particular bodies and instead is constructed and reproduced through individuals' practices and behaviours in their everyday lives".

Gender Relations

Gender functions relationally by "influencing our expectations and understandings of others, and the ways in which we relate to and interact with them". These refer to the manner in which the relationships between men and women are influenced by gendered expectations which in turn can restrict opportunities for the women while providing expanding spaces for men.

Women's Studies

Women's Studies are not exactly new. Despite public and professional neglect, for centuries there have been histories of women, anthologies of women's literary writings, and statistical and sociological studies of such topics as the working conditions of women and the organization of family life.

Women's Studies were born within or grew alongside the women's movement, and it began with a fruitful interaction between amateurs outside the academy and professionals within it. Those in universities were uninstructed about the study of women in psychology, sociology, history, or the humanities and the arts. Outside the academy, among women, there were activists founding magazines, publishing and even founding their own feminist publishing houses.

Women's Studies are not a narrow study about women or information about women but a critical instrument for analyzing the social reality so as to lead to the development of social sciences. The UNESCO Meeting of Experts on Women's Studies and Social Science in Asia held in New Delhi in October 1982 defined Women's Studies in terms of the objectives that such studies sought to achieve. It is the pursuit of a more comprehensive, critical and balanced understanding of social reality, whose essential components include:

- Women's contribution to the social process.

- Their struggles and aspirations.

- Women's perception of their own lives and of the broader social reality.

- The understanding of the roots and structures of inequality that lead to marginalization, invisibility and exclusion of women from the scope approaches and conceptual frameworks of most intellectual enquiry and social action.

Objectives of Women's Studies

The objectives of Women's Studies may be elaborated as:

- To conscientise both men and women by helping them to understand, recognize and acknowledge the multi-dimensional roles played by women in society.

- To promote better understanding of processes of social, technological and environmental change.

- To contribute to the pursuit of human rights.

- To investigate the causes of gender disparity analyzing the structural, cultural and attitudinal factors.

- To empower women in their attempts for equality; and for effective participation in all areas of society and development.

- To render 'invisible' women 'visible' in particular the women of the underprivileged strata.

- To help develop alternative concepts, approaches and strategies for development.

- To promote the construction of a better, more balanced society.

Defined thus, Women's Studies as an academic discipline, has its own identity, and autonomous existence. It has, over a period of time, developed its own theories based on feminist concepts, and evolved its own methodology that is distinguished from the varied precepts and methodologies adopted by "mainstream" disciplines. As part of the critical theory it is an instrument that questions the traditionally held premises, theoretical categories and methods in social sciences and has brought out the glaring absence of gender as a social category, in addition to class, ethnicity, colour, region and caste as tools of analysis and understanding of social reality. It has highlighted the role that patriarchy and gender bias have played historically in shaping the knowledge system. Thereby it has questioned the well-known ideologies of conservatism, liberalism and socialism and pointed out the need to re-examine the traditional and inherited knowledge from the gender/women's perspectives.

In a nutshell, Women's Studies may be defined as a body of knowledge that has grown out a felt concern for gender equality. Rooted in feminism, Women's Studies seek to explain the socio-historical, cultural, economic and political reasons for women's subordination. Additionally, it suggests measures by which these forms of discrimination may be countered.

As it provides an alternative viewpoint to the existing knowledge construction, Women's Studies enriches the various branches of social sciences and provides a more holistic understanding of human experience in society. Women's Studies is a critical instrument to examine those social processes that have so far favoured men and made invisible women's contributions. The driving force behind Women's Studies is feminism. The various schools of feminist philosophies represent a continuation of the humanist philosophical traditions since the age of enlightenment which placed the human being at the centre of its inquiry and was committed to the ideals of liberty and equality. The difference feminism introduces into this discourse is: it shows that human experience is gendered; an individual's life experiences, choices and entitlements in the family and society are determined by the biological accident of sex. Grappling with critical questions about the exclusion of women in all expressions of human knowledge, feminism has evolved new concepts and analytic frameworks that better encompass and explain social reality.

Women's Studies aims at promoting gender equality by sensitizing men and women about women's rights and entitlements. It goes beyond intellectual explorations of women's lives to translate itself into action. Women's Studies, therefore, is not just another academic discipline; rather it is an attempt to bridge the gap between the professed ideals and the existing social reality, by initiating social change.

Concepts describing the Historical Situation of Women

- Oppression of women is the term commonly used by women writers and thinkers and by feminists. The term "oppression," meaning forceful subordination, has also been used to describe the subject condition of individuals and of groups, as in "class oppression" or "racial oppression."

- Subordination of women has distinct advantages over oppression. "subordination" does not have the connotation of evil intent on the part of the dominant; it allows for the possibility of collusion between him and the subordinate. It includes the possibility of voluntary acceptance of subordinate status in exchange for protection and privilege, a condition which characterizes so much of the historical experience of women.

- Deprivation has the advantage of being objective, but it has the disadvantage of making and hiding the existence of power relations.

The Rationale for Women's Studies and its Growth

In the first days of Women's Studies, several issues were key to laying foundations and shaping debates. They have resonated ever since, so we need to understand them even though they are not front-burner concerns today. The first was posed in Simone de Beauvoir's The Second Sex, arguably the most influential book about women written in the twentieth century. Translated and read around the world, The Second Sex asked "What is a woman?" No one, the author claimed, would ever ask a similar question about men, nor would anyone really be puzzled about men's wants and desires. That was because men were taken to be the norm, the unquestioned human type, the universal category by which all else was measured. In contrast, women were the non-norm, the opposite and the other.

Simone de Beauvoir was a first-class French philosopher, and she lived at the center of a well-known philosophical circle of existentialists. This philosophical school claimed that biological life in itself was not true existence but merely a natural or biological condition. Existence was something one chose and acted upon in order to create freedom. Men, de Beauvoir claimed, lived out such an existence based on choice and action. Women, as the other, lived in an unfree state, following the dictates of nature to reproduce. Additionally, women made no rationale choices but rather lived as the "Other" by following the notions men had of them and all the rules and regulations for female life that society constructed. The "Other" as a concept became foundational to early Women's Studies and other fields such as post-colonial and cultural studies. It has only grown in importance, while continuing to evolve.

Betty Friedan's The Feminine Mystique picked up on de Beauvior's question. It described the dwindling intelligence of women who stayed at home to be housewives and mothers. Her contention that middle-class women's IQs actually dropped over their life course in the home was based on interviews with her college classmates and on statistical studies done of similar women. Moreover,

Friedan claimed, women who should have led sparkling lives of creativity that enhanced society, questioned the banality of their existence: "Is this all? She found them repeatedly asking. A woman was a trapped housewife.

Women's Studies has its roots in the women's liberation movement of the 1960s. The 1960s was a period of widespread protests. Participating in these various civil rights movements, women gained political experience; they also realized that none of the existing systems of progressive thought, which affirmed the values of freedom, justice and equality, addressed the question of women's subordination. The underlying assumptions being: 1) women's subordination is biological and determined by the natural order; 2) issues of justice, equality and liberty are the concerns of the public sphere, i.e. the realm of politics, economy and the military; and 3) these issues mediated the relationship of the individual or group with the State. Nevertheless, within this political discourse on the relationship of the individual with the State and society, the issues pertaining to man/woman relationships in the private sphere of the home were left out. As there was no scope within these systems of political thought to raise questions of women's subordination within the home and society, women who were part of these progressive movements found themselves alienated. They also found that the various forms of gender discrimination evident in the larger society were replayed even within these progressive movements; their contributions (unlike those of their male colleagues), were rarely acknowledged and they were usually assigned subordinate functions.

Participation in these movements, nonetheless, enabled women to gain political experience; women formed separate collectives and consciousness raising groups in which they explored their life cycle experiences. Gaining insights about the existing processes (which denied women their rights), they began to question accepted theories. Domestic violence, for instance, they realized was not an individual problem or an aberration of the existing social reality, but rather an expression of the power relationship that existed between the sexes. Therefore, instances of domestic violence could no longer be dismissed as sado-masochist relationships in which women participated; for such explanations were tantamount to blaming the victim. Invariably, the reason why women could not opt out of violent relationship was because of socio-economic constraints.

Increasingly integrated within academia in the 1970s, the roots of the discipline lie in its critique of existing scholarship and the fundamental questions it raises about the accepted theories and methodologies. As these theories failed to explain their own lives and that of other women, feminist scholars started to question the universal applicability of established theories. They pointed: these historically accepted theories, methods and systems of explanations were biased and only offered a partial world-view as perceived by men. Women's Studies, therefore, helps to complement and complete our understanding of social reality. Committed to tolerance and non-hierarchical modes of generating knowledge, it has no set rules and procedures; it consists of a set of open-ended questions about women and society. This explains the rich diversity of theories and explanations that have developed about women's lives.

Since its recognition as an academic discipline in the early 1970s, Women's Studies has evolved in many directions: it has helped to break many disciplinary grids; altered our understanding of the various branches of human knowledge, and questioned the universal applicability of the established theories. Specifically, it has underscored the politics of knowledge: 1) the questions raised from the point of view of women's experiences of powerlessness make evident that truth (as inscribed in theories) is not objective and constant; it is rescripted, modified and defined by those who have the power to assert truth; and 2) the accepted methods and technique of data collection do not necessarily prove useful in gathering information on the lives of those who have no say in the process of generating knowledge. Thus, identifying issues of power (as reflected and played out in the lives of women), Women's Studies helps to strengthen the discourse against all forms of inequality, injustice and oppression.

Pointing to the gendering of human experience, Women's Studies questions the assumptions in the dominant construction of knowledge that there is an objective reality which could be studied by individual scholars to establish universal truths. Western sciences and modes of inquiry evolved within the framework provided by Descartes, as such western modes of inquiry (both philosophical and scientific) into the nature of reality were premised on the assumption that there is an objective reality which could be explained by the methods of science to establish and explain universal truths. Within such a paradigm, the inquirer (i.e. the scientist, the philosopher and the researcher) was viewed as free of any kind of subjective response and capable of arriving at truth uncoloured by emotions or his subjective experience. These assumptions about the nature of truth were being questioned by many scholars who pointed out the relativity of truth – that truth was not only constructed socially in a specific historical and cultural locations but was also gendered. Further, that "truth" is established through various forms of power politics that influence the various modes of knowing, methodology and concerns. Therefore what is studied and why it is studied also informs the discourse. Feminist challenge to methodology questions the selection of certain techniques of knowing; also the artificial barriers between knowing and feeling.

The rationale for the growth of Women's Studies is premised as follows: 1) Women have been left out of codified knowledge; and 2) this exclusion has given rise to partial (often inaccurate) portrayal of women's lives by men. Both these issues require careful examination for they reveal the politics of knowledge generation. The first indicates that women's exclusion from the process of knowledge generation was deliberate and political; it was aimed at maintaining a patriarchal social order (wherein the social, political and economic powers remained in the hands of men), and ensured women's subordination. This explains the opposition throughout history to women's education and intellectual impulses. Denied the necessary intellectual space to conceptualize and create knowledge, few women (in proportion to men) could make significant contributions to the growth of knowledge. Other than that, women's contributions to art, literature and sciences were either appropriated by men (such as husbands, brothers, fathers or even male researchers with whom they worked) or allowed to die unrecognized, if they contradicted the prevailing (male-centric) world view. So pervasive was the prejudice against women of letters (they were derided as bluestockings), that they often adopted male pseudonyms while writing.

The second implies that the explanations offered about women's lives remain partial and inaccurate because women have not been part of the process of knowledge generation. Such a process was created out of a view of human nature as comprising two distinct halves and a socio-political and economic system which placed all forms of decision making powers in the hands of men. Arrogating for themselves the power of knowledge creation, men kept women out of areas of intellectual inquiry. But this does not mean that women have not been objects of study.

With gender as a category of social analysis, Women's Studies attempts to correct the excessive androcentric tilt of the various disciplines. In the process, crude assumptions of objectivity in the generation of knowledge stand dismantled. The delineation of the ways in which power relations operate to omit women's experiences as autonomous beings is the most significant contribution made by feminism. Furthermore, by asking questions in terms of women and not in terms of a particular disciplinary framework, feminists move beyond some of the limitations imposed by compartmentalization. It lays the groundwork necessary for a more holistic and egalitarian basis of knowledge production.

Feminist Perspectives on Interdisciplinarity

Another characteristic feature of Women's Studies is that it is interdisciplinary; women's lives cannot be split up into separate mutually exclusive halves without endangering the purpose of social research, which in this case is to understand the visible and the invisible indicators that influence women's lives. It uses collective modes of production of knowledge and non-conventional sources. For instance, in trying to reconstruct women's history one is forced to rely on non-documentary sources. This is because women's lives and experiences have not been discussed in the official accounts of the past. Therefore, while Women's Studies draws upon the existing knowledge base and methodologies, it does not exclude the more non-conventional methods. Such experimentation with research methods and theories has generated a rich variety of material in Women's Studies; this perhaps explains some of the seeming contradictions in the discipline.

From the field's beginnings, practitioners of women's studies have identified interdisciplinarity as a basic scholarly mission. Feminist scholars in many fields felt "impatience with the power arrangements of the university as an institution, and the way that the experience of women (was) devalued or excluded" in existing disciplinary frameworks. From the multidisciplinary handshakes around issues such as sexual harassment, the feminization of poverty, and women's health, to the construction of entirely new, transdisciplinary epistemological categories for the study of gender such as "visual and narrative cultures" instead of art, film and literature, interdisciplinarity has long been the hallmark of feminist research problems, questions and theoretical debates across the academy.

There is also evidence that transdisciplinary feminist conceptual frameworks, terminology, and "generative grammars" have transformed research and curriculum development in traditional disciplines. The insistence by pioneers of women's studies that women's lost contributions of history and literature be recovered and that the historical and literary canons and critical schools of thought be redesigned in the light of this recovery has been replicated in other fields, such as art and music. These developments may "add women and stir", but they still represent important new data points for disciplinary revision. In psychology, for example, transdisciplinary gender considerations have infused definitions of individual identity and mental health with a social analysis. Feminist transdisciplinary discoveries and analyses have also promoted or furthered the generation of numerous other interdisciplines, such as sexuality studies, disability studies, popular culture studies, and lesbian/gay studies. The transnationalization of gender studies has contributed to several disciplines and fields such concepts as the "global sex trade" and the key idea that women's rights are human rights.

From the standpoint of women's experiences, critical questions are posed to social science theories. In Economics, for instance, the concept of work is questioned. This question underscores the ways in which a patriarchal society dominates and controls women's reproductive and productive labour. Further, as proper conceptual tools have not been evolved to measure women's contribution to the survival of the household, it does not get computed as work in the GDP; the various tools of data collection exclude many women from the economically active population on the assumption that women have no economic activity. The result of such gender blindness implicit in the theory helps to reinforce the existing inequalities between men and women in society.

In Sociology, prescriptions of ideal gender relationships are treated as descriptions of social reality. These descriptions rarely correspond with women's lived experiences. The inexplicable question is that if the aim of social sciences is to understand and faithfully depict people's lived experiences, why do these explanations about women's lives remain so far removed from reality? For instance, despite the reality of various kinds of families, why did sociological theories continue to define the nuclear family with a male breadwinner as the norm? This fails to take into account the growing trend of female headed households, resulting from male desertion or migration.

Women and Christianity

Christianity is counted among the oldest religions of the world and Christians, spread all over the world, constitute a substantial part of the world population. But like the other major religions, institutionalized Christianity too has accorded women a secondary position both in the church and the family making leadership positions inaccessible to them. Traditional interpretations have claimed that this gender based hierarchy has been mandated in the scriptures and theology has placed woman under the man's authority — in the church, in marriage, and elsewhere. Historically, it has excluded women from important decision making positions that give them any kind of authority over men.

Much of early Christian thought was influenced by Plato and Aristotle, neither of whom were Christian thinkers. Aristotle believed that women were irrational in relation to men and not as virtuous. Some of the early Church fathers wrote with contempt and from positions of inherent bias regarding women. Augustine (354-430 CE) probably the most famous theologian in all of church history, believed that God did not create the woman for any reason other than procreation. Explicitly he said, "I cannot think of any reason for woman's being made as man's helper, if we dismiss the reason of procreation" Thus the potential equality embedded in Jesus' message often failed to pan out in the teachings and practice of the church. Interestingly, the situation in the early church was quite different and the history of Christianity of the first century offers definite evidence of the contribution of women and the leadership roles they played. Indeed, till the first four centuries women continued to hold important positions in the community. It was only later, as time went by, that women were excluded from any position of authority, and were systematically relegated to the background where they remained till recent times. But the status of women in Christianity has been looked at with a more critical perspective from the second half of the twentieth century, and more moderate views have begun to emerge.

In fact, Christian Egalitarians believe that Jesus Christ, the founder of Christianity did not subscribe to a gender hierarchy either in the Church or in marriage. They fall upon a particular verse, of the apostle Paul, sometimes referred to as the "Magna Carta of spiritual emancipation." to substantiate their claims. This verse is found in Galatians 3:28 and states, "There is neither Jew nor Greek, slave nor free, male nor female, for you are all one in Christ Jesus." This statement wipes away all hierarchies. In fact, Jesus can be described as a radical in the sense that he was different in his attitudes towards women in contrast to the prevailing cultural attitudes which treated them as inferior. He invited and encouraged them to follow Him. In other words, "Traditional Christian thinking is not the same thing as biblical thinking about women." Indeed, feminist theologians stress that women must try and unlearn the way and interdependence they have been taught to read the Bible and read without the lens that have been worn for so long.

Jesus Christ

Jesus Christ, the founder of Christianity, is believed to be the Son of God and his birth is celebrated as Christmas Day. He taught non- violence and preached the message of love for each other. He had the power to heal and perform miracles and the New Testament is an account of his life, sayings and actions. Jesus selected twelve disciples known as the twelve apostles to whom he entrusted the responsibility of carrying the message of God to all corners of the world. He was persecuted by the Jews although he was innocent and a Jew himself and was crucified. The day he died is known as Good Friday, a day that the Christians consider holy and a reminder of the supreme sacrifice that Jesus made. He rose again after three days and ascended to heaven. The day of his resurrection is called Easter. Jesus was not biased against women and his attitude towards them was fair. In fact many of his followers were women and they were granted both respect and honour by him. Mary, his mother, Mary Magdalene, Mary of Bethany, Martha her sister are women who hold a high place in Christianity. Joanna and Susanna who supported him with their money were among the other women disciples of Jesus.

Jesus disapproved of any kind of subordination of one of his followers over another. Instead, he expressly forbade it in any Christian relationship. Having issued his strong prohibition against subordination of others, he prescribed the Christian alternative to subordination as being the exact opposite: profound service to others, extending even to making the ultimate sacrifice of giving one's life if necessary.

The letters of St. Paul—dated to the middle of the 1st century AD—and his casual greetings to acquaintances, offer information about Jewish and Gentile women who were prominent in early Christianity. His letters provide clues about the kind of activities in which women were engaged. He specifically mentions Phoebe, a deaconess of the church at Cenchreae, Priscilla, Junia and Julia.

Position of Women in the Early Church

Many researchers have researched deeply, specially investigating resources vis a vis women looking into historical data and has found evidence about the elevated status of women in the early Christian Church. According to them "one of the best-kept secrets in Christianity is the enormous role that women played in the early church. Though they leave much unsaid, still, both Christian and secular writers of the time attest many times to the significant involvement of women in the early growth of Christianity".

Women as Priests

There are even a few scattered references connecting women to the priesthood" with a special reference to Theosebia, "the pride of the church, the ornament of Christ, the finest of our generation, the free speech of women, Theosebia, the most illustrious among the brethren, outstanding in beauty of soul. Theosebia, truly a priestly personage, the colleague of a priest, equally honored and worthy of the great sacraments." The walls of the Roman catacombs bear pictures showing women in authoritative stances, with their hands raised in the posture of a bishop. More evidence of the high position of women during the first centuries in the Church comes from an unexpected source-art.

A fresco Fractio Panis belonging to the early second century shows a Eucharist ceremony wherein all the participants including the one performing the ceremony are women. Another mosaic of a group of women found in a Roman basilica is inscribed with the words, Theodora Epicopa- the Latin Epicopa translating into the word Bishop in English i.e. Bishop Theodora. On the Greek island of Thera, one of the inscriptions found bore the title of Epiktas, a woman as a priest. The women who became Deaconesses were given a lot of honour as representatives of God. They could visit households where a male would be unacceptable. To them belonged the duties of visiting the sick, bathing those recovering from illness, and ministering to the needy. Deaconesses also assisted in the baptism of women, anointing them with oil and giving them instruction in purity and holiness. They could give communion to women who were sick and unable to meet with the entire church. The Apostolic Constitutions even specified that both male and female deacons might be sent with messages outside the city limits. While the ministry of the widow was largely that of prayer, fasting, and laying of hands on the sick, the deaconess, usually a considerably younger woman, undertook the more physically arduous tasks.

Status of Widows

Like the deacons and the presbyters, widows were respected. They were part of the ordained clergy, "had been appointed to bless" and came to be looked upon as "the altar of God". Their responsibilities involved such activities as teaching women and giving encouragement and guidance to those who wanted to lead a better life. They assumed pastoral responsibilities such as instructing the ignorant, gathering those who desired to live a pure life for prayer and encouragement, rebuking the wayward, and seeking to restore them. They were often given gifts by the wealthier people. Widows were clearly part of the ordained clergy.

Christian Maidens were very Numerous

In its early days, there were more women than men who were Christians. In the 2nd century Bishop Cyprian of Carthage stated that sometimes there were not enough Christians men for them to marry. There could be several reasons for this. Unlike the others, Christians did not abandon their female babies to die. Consequently they had a larger number of grown women. Also many of the upper class women, but not their husbands, converted to Christianity. Fear of the loss of their official status prevented the men from doing so. This too contributed to the church being disproportionately populated by women. These wealthy and educated women made a serious study of the Bible and Hebrew and Greek. In fact, Augustine in the early 400s is supposed to have said that "any old Christian woman" was spiritually more educated than any number of so called philosophers. Many of them gave away their money liberally for helping those in need in the face of much opposition from their family members.

The Legend of St. Thecla

The legend of St. Thecla has endeared itself to modern women as well as to their earlier counterparts.

Considered one of the early Christian heroines, Thecla was a wealthy woman belonging to the nobility who was inspired by the teachings of Paul and converted to Christianity. She faced extreme hostility and many dangers but overcame them because of her strong faith. She journeyed with Paul through Asia Minor and finally settled near Seleucia. There are historical references to her and a description by a pilgrim Egeria who visited the place in 399 A.D. He mentions the monasteries, convents, hospital and activity centre that she built there. A German excavation team discovered in 1908 beautiful mosaics, two chapels and several large containers of water in a site as large as a football field. Apparently the place had functioned for at least a 1,000 years. More than anything else, this is testimony of the fact of an extremely strong Christian female leader in Asia Minor.

The Beginning

In order to understand the core tenets of the religion, it is necessary to trace the origins and the growth of Christianity over the centuries. The Bible, the sacred book of the Christians, is divided into two parts – the Old Testament and the New Testament. The Old Testament pertains to Judaism while the new Testament contains the description of Jesus Christ, his birth, his life, teachings and death. The two books, however form a composite whole. The very first book of the Bible is called Genesis, meaning creation, and contains an account of how Creation took place and how man and women were created. According to it, God created the world in six days and rested on the seventh day, which is why Sunday is generally considered a day of rest. After the heavens, the oceans, animal and plant life were created, God created man in his own image. "So God created man in his own image, in the image of God created he him; male and female created he them." The Biblical translation of the line God created man in his own image does not denote a male person but may be understood as meaning humankind or human beings. Both the sexes equally reflect God's image. This is what the Bible teaches. The first man and woman were called Adam and Eve, were made for each other, therefore they do not achieve their full realization until they are together.

The Story of the Garden of Eden

The story proceeds with God creating a beautiful garden with wondrous fruits and plants, called the Garden of Eden or Paradise and inviting Adam and Eve to enjoy it. However, there is a single instruction that He gives them. And that is that they are not to eat the fruit of a particular tree. This is the tree of knowledge. However, Satan, who is the personification of evil, taking the form of a snake and finding the right opportunity, approaches Eve and persuades her to eat an of that particular fruit. The gullible Eve is taken in by the words of Satan and eats the forbidden fruit. She then asks Adam also to eat the fruit and he does. When God discovers of the disobedience of the two, he is very disappointed with them and turns them out of the Garden of Eden.

Temptation, Sin and Gender Concepts

Perhaps no Bible story has been more misinterpreted than the story of Eve and the forbidden fruit. Traditions observed by the elders regarding the temptation of Eve may or may not lead to a clear understanding of the Biblical truth. In many cases such ideas, more than the Bible, have influenced views on gender and few characters have been more criticized than Eve. Tertullian (155-225 CE) an influential teacher of the early centuries calls Eve. "The unsealer of that forbidden tree" and "she who persuaded him whom the devil was not valiant enough to attack." In fact he calls all women Eves "the devil's gateway." However, the Biblical text states that Adam was with Eve, and he also ate the fruit. They were tempted together, yielded together and ate together. The Scripture never mentions their being apart from the time of Eve's creation and clarifies that the blame for the Fall into sin cannot be imputed to Eve alone, but also equally to Adam. Eve was the first to eat the forbidden fruit, but Adam undeceived also knowingly broke God's commandant not to eat of the tree of knowledge of good and evil. When called to account, Adam blamed God and Eve, for what he himself had done. Interestingly, Eve did not ascribe the blame to him or the snake.

Equal Partners

Contemporary interpretations claim that Eve should be regarded as an equal partner of Adam. In Genesis 2:18 the contextual meaning suggests mutual assistance in the marriage relationship by one who corresponds and is equal to man. The Hebrew word for helper (ezer) is not indicative of a subordinate or inferior, it can actually indicate a superior and most often refers to God himself as helper. According to the teaching of the Bible, authority is not to be granted according to gender, but according to the spiritual gifts of the individual and Christ-likeness.

Some Aspects of Gender in the Old Testament

The Hebrew Bible, called the Old Testament by the Christians, was written by writers from a male-centered culture. Men dominated both society and religion, especially religion. Nonetheless, female imagery is used in the Bible in several instances. God is referred to as a mother figure who taught Israel to walk, who healed him, and fed the hungry child. Likewise, the Book of Psalms, speaks of God as a midwife, and the prophet Isaiah also speaks of God as a mother figure. The Apostle Matthew, in the New Testament, speaks of a sheltering presence and the image of a hen gathering her chicks safely under her wings.

Christian Marriage

Marriage is seen as a sacred bond as well as a partnership of mutual respect and support. Insights into marriage and the marriage relationship come from the New Testament where several Books contain advice and instructions regarding it. The Book of Corinthians clearly states that husbands and wives must fulfill their marital duties towards each other and to be mindful of fulfilling each other's needs. "Nevertheless neither is the man without the woman, neither the woman without the man, in the Lord. For the woman is of the man, even so is the man also by the woman; but all things of God". The Book of Ephesians refers to the fact that there must be love and respect between husband and wife. The husband is called to love his wife as much as he loves himself and the wife is asked to respect her husband. "So ought men to love their wives as their own bodies. He that loveth his wife loveth himself.

Divorce – Some Scriptural Insights into Divorce

There were stringent laws against divorce in Christianity, but these have been relaxed with time. The Holy Bible says 'therefore what God has joined together, let no man separate.' Furthermore in the New Testament Jesus clearly states, that God has given the divine command that wives and husbands must not separate or be divorced and that the only permissible cause for divorcing a woman, is sexual immorality and divorce for any other reason, makes the woman a victim of adultery.

Patriarchy

Origins

The origins of patriarchy are closely related to the concept of gender roles, or the set of social and behavioral norms that are considered to be socially appropriate for individuals of a specific sex. Much work has been devoted to understanding why women are typically thought to inhabit a domestic role while men are expected to seek professional satisfaction outside of the home. This division of labor is frequently mapped onto a social hierarchy in which males' freedom to venture outside of the home and presumed control over women is perceived as superior and dominant. As such, rather than working to destabilize the historical notion of patriarchy, much literature assess the origins of patriarchy or a social system in which the male gender role acts as the primary authority figure central to social organization, and where fathers hold authority over women, children, and property. It implies the institutions of male rule and privilege and entails female subordination.

Though less popular in modern academic circles, there has been a traditional search for biological explanations of gender roles. Before the nineteenth century, this conversation was primarily theological and deemed patriarchy to be the "natural order." This took on a biological trope with Charles Darwin's ideas about evolution in The Origin of Species. In this work, Darwin explained evolution from the biological understanding that is now the accepted scientific theory. Biologists such as Alfred Russel Wallace quickly applied his theory to mankind. To be clear, though, the line of thought called Social Darwinism, or the application of evolutionary principles to the development of human beings and our social practices, was never promoted by Darwin himself. With the popularization of the idea of human evolution, what had previously been explained as a "natural order" for the world morphed into a "biological order?"

The modern term for using biological explanations to explain social phenomena is sociobiology. Sociobiologists use genetics to explain social life, including gender roles. According to the sociobiologists, patriarchy arises more as a result of inherent biology than social conditioning. One such contemporary sociobiologist is Steven Goldberg, who, until retirement, was a sociologist. In 1973, Goldberg published The Inevitability of Patriarchy, which advanced a biological interpretation of male dominance. Goldberg argued that male dominance is a human universal as a result of our biological makeup. One evolutionary sociobiological theory for the origin of patriarchy begins with the view that females almost always invest more energy into producing offspring than males and, as a result, females are a resource over which males compete. This theory is called Bateman's principle. One important female preference in selecting a mate is which males control more resources to assist her and her offspring. This, in turn, causes a selection pressure on men to be competitive and succeed in gaining resources in order to compete with other men.

These sociobiological theories of patriarchy are counterbalanced by social constructionist theories that emphasize how certain cultures manufacture and perpetuate gender roles. According to social constructionist theories, gender roles are created by individuals within a society who choose to imbue a particular structure with meaning. Gender roles are constantly toyed with and negotiated by actors subscribing to and questioning them. Since the feminist movement in the 1970s and the flood of women into the workforce, social constructionism has gained even greater traction.

Bateman's Theory

In biology, Bateman's principle is the theory that the sex which invests the most in producing offspring becomes a limiting resource over which the other sex will compete. Typically it is the females who have a relatively larger investment in producing each offspring. A single male can easily fertilize all a female's eggs: they will not produce more offspring by mating with more than one male. A male is capable of fathering more offspring than any female can bear, if he mates with several females. By and large, a male's reproductive success increases with each female he mates with, whereas a female's reproductive success is not increased nearly as much by mating with more males. This results in sexual selection, in which males compete with each other, and females become choosy in which males to mate with.

Bateman's observations came from his empirical work on mating behaviour in fruit flies. He attributed the origin of the unequal investment to the differences in the production of gametes, sperm are cheaper than eggs. Animals are therefore fundamentally polygynous, as a result of being anisogamous.

"A male can easily produce sperm in excess of what it would take to fertilize all the females that could conceivably be available". Hence the development of the masculine emphasis on courtship and territoriality or other forms of conflict with competing males.

"In most animals the fertility of the female is limited by egg production which causes a severe strain on their nutrition. In mammals the corresponding limiting factors are uterine nutrition and milk production, which together may be termed the capacity for rearing young. In the male, however, fertility is seldom likely to be limited by sperm production but rather by the number of inseminations or the number of females available to him. In general, then, the fertility of an individual female will be much more limited than the fertility of a male. This would explain why in unisexual organisms there is nearly always a combination of an undiscriminating eagerness in the males and a discriminating passivity in the females."

Sex-Role Reversal

The most well-known exceptions to Bateman's principle are the existence of sex-role reversed species such as pipefish (seahorses), phalaropes and jacanas in which the males perform the majority of the parental care, and are cryptic while the females are highly ornamented and territorially aggressive.

Other Examples of Violations to Bateman's Principle

Some modern evolutionary biologists believe Bateman's principle is often not correct. The formulation of Bateman's principle was limited by such things as short observation time in his experiments.

Observation of many species, from rabbits to fruit flies, has shown that females have more children if they have sex with more males. This is in contradiction to Bateman's theory that "a female's reproductive success is not increased by mating with more males."

Research has also shown some species in which males will guard one female and mate only with her, attempting to prevent her from mating with any other males. Examples include stick insects and Idaho ground squirrels. These observations seem to challenge Bateman's theory that "a male's reproductive success increases with each female he mates."

The assumption that females have a relatively larger investment in producing offspring is also often false. In animals that spawn into the sea, for example, each sex's investment is approximately equal. In animals with internal fertilization, many sperm must be produced for every egg - so even though it takes less energy to create one sperm than one egg, males of many species spend more energy making gametes than do females.

The statement that the sex that invests the most in producing offspring will become a limiting resource is not always true. In flowers, for example, the female part of the flower invests more energy into making seeds than the male part of the flower does. The reproduction of most flowering plants, however, is limited by delivery of the male gamete - pollen - not by production of the female gamete.

Bateman's statement "there is nearly always a combination of an undiscriminating eagerness in the males and a discriminating passivity in the females" and his assumption that anisogamous species would be polygynous is false. Actually, females of many species mate with several males.

Concept of Patriarchy

The concept of Patriarchy itself is not a contribution of feminist theories. Many social scientists in the nineteenth century wrote about it as a more civilized or complex form of organization compared to the primitive matriarchies. Engels referred to it as the earliest system of domination establishing that Patriarchy is "the world historical defeat of the female sex. In this sense, it is said that Patriarchy was a form of political organization that distributed power unequally between men and women to the detriment of women. The Royal Academy of the Spanish Language Dictionary defines Patriarchy as "A primitive social organization in which authority is exercised by a male head of the family, extending this power even to distant relatives of the same lineage."

Feminist theories updated and expanded the understanding of Patriarchy in the second half of the twentieth century. In fact, the social sciences had left it behind precisely because it was considered only to apply to and characterize ancient civilizations. But for many feminists, Patriarchy is much more than civilizations that existed in the ancient past and goes beyond "the unequal distribution of power between men and women in certain aspects of our societies", as many dictionaries still define it. On the contrary, most forms of feminism characterize Patriarchy as a present day unjust social system that subordinates, discriminates or is oppressive to women, "The patriarchal construction of the difference between masculinity and femininity is the political difference between freedom and subjection." the concept of Patriarchy includes all the socio-political mechanisms, which we call Patriarchal Institutions, which reproduce and exert male dominance over women. Feminist theory typically characterizes Patriarchy as a social construction, which can be overcome by revealing and critically analyzing its manifestations and institutions.

Fixating on real and perceived biological differences between the two recognized sexes, men justify their domination on the basis of an alleged biological inferiority of women. Both feminist and non-feminist thinkers recognize that Patriarchy has its historical origins in the family, the leadership (legal and practical) of which is exercised by the father and is projected to the entire social order – an order that is maintained and reinforced by different mechanisms/institutions, among them the Institution of Male Solidarity. Through this institution, men as a social category, individually and collectively oppress all women as a social category, but also oppress women individually in different ways, appropriating women's reproductive and productive force and controlling their bodies, minds, sexuality and spirituality mainly through "peaceful" means such as the law and religion. However, often these peaceful means are reinforced through the use of physical, sexual, and/or psychological violence. Combining all of these elements of Patriarchy, we define it as:

"Patriarchy is a form of mental, social, spiritual, economic and political organization/structuring of society produced by the gradual institutionalization of sex based political relations created, maintained and reinforced by different institutions linked closely together to achieve consensus on the lesser value of women and their roles. These institutions interconnect not only with each other to strengthen the structures of domination of men over women, but also with other systems of exclusion, oppression and/or domination based on real or perceived differences between humans, creating States that respond only to the needs and interests of a few powerful men."

By "gradual institutionalization" we refer to a historical process that proves Patriarchy is not natural, has not always existed, and is not identical in all cultures and in all generations. This, in turn, means that although men have power over women in all institutions considered important in each society, it does not mean that women do not have any power or rights, influence or resources, nor does it means that all women have or exert the same power. Moreover, as Patriarchy becomes more sophisticated, more women of specific groups are allowed access to certain institutions, although they are almost never the most powerful people within those institutions.

By "sex-based political relations", we mean, that sexual and other relations between the two sexes recognized as such by Patriarchy, are political relations, through which men dominate women.

By "consensus on the lesser value of women", we refer to a tacit and subconscious agreement between each member of a community that women and everything relating to women is worth less than men and everything relating to men. We see this reflected in the Institution of Sexist Language, which establishes the feminine as "the other" and the male as the norm and that which represents or contains the feminine. By "consensus", we also make reference to an ideology and its expression in language that explicitly devalues women, assigning them, their roles, their work, their products and their social environment less worth and/or power than that assigned to men.

By "patriarchal institutions", we refer to the set of mechanisms, practices, beliefs, myths and relationships organizing relatively stable patterns of human activity with respect to the distribution of resources, the reproduction of individuals, and the type of societal structures within a given Patriarchy. These institutions are closely linked with one another, creating, maintaining and transmitting inequality from generation to generation. Most sociologists recognize as institutions such social structures as governments, the family, human languages, universities, hospitals, business corporations, and legal systems. We prefer to rename these recognized institutions with more appropriate names such as the Institution of Androcentric Law, the Institution of Misogynist

Religion or of Sexist Language, of Male-stream Media or Male-centered Science, etc. But we also like to make visible other institutions which patriarchal sociology does not recognize as such, like the Institution of Male Solidarity, of History with Capital H, of Erotic Violence, of Woman-Blaming Myths, of Male-heteronormativity, of Dichotomous Sexual Beings, etc.

Many feminists, while not speaking of institutions per se, argue that Patriarchy exists not only in the family but in all structures that allow for control over women, their work and reproductive force. we call these structures patriarchal institutions, because aside from being mechanisms for the perpetuation of Patriarchy, they are also a set of beliefs, practices, myths, relationships, etc. which make sure that Patriarchy is invisible even to those women which suffer the most exclusion or at the most, make sure it is perceived as natural or simply as the way things are and always will be for women.

The "appropriation of women's reproductive force" and the control of their bodies and their sexuality comes from radical feminism. For example, how human reproduction, which happens in women's bodies, is legally appropriated and controlled by men and is used to benefit men or to keep women at the mercy of men. Women can be considered as a social and economic class, insisting that it is the father and/or husband who enforce the appropriation. Many feminists, have spoken of the productive relationship between husband and wife in the modern nuclear family, which is similar to the relationship between a supervisor and a subordinate in the workplace. This subordination occurs in the private space of family because whatever the husband's produces enters the market (the privileged area of capitalist Patriarchy), while the wife´s production is not. In this way, all of the wife's work in the non-privileged private space of the nuclear family is invisibilized. Some aspects, elements or characteristics of modern Patriarchy are the following:

- Patriarchy had a beginning and therefore can have an end. Even if we still do not know how exactly it came into being we do know it came about after millenniums of different more egalitarian human organizing. The earliest forms of Patriarchy only began at the most 6 millenniums ago.

- We also know that there are different models of Patriarchy at different times and in different cultures and places but the lower value given to women and their roles as compared to men and their roles remains constant in all models. In other words, Patriarchy co-exists with very different forms of government and socio religious political organizing such as empires, kingdoms, theocracies, republics, democracies, etc. and can co-exist very well with capitalism, socialism, etc. However, due to the globalization of neoliberal capitalism, almost all existing Patriarchies today can be categorized as capitalist Patriarchies.

- In all known Patriarchy negative meanings are attributed to women and their activities through symbols and myths (not always explicitly expressed). These symbols and myths are different in different cultures but within each culture they attribute negative meanings to women or the feminine.

- Patriarchy is made up of structures or institutions that exclude women from participation in, or contact with, spaces of higher power, or what are believed to be the spaces of greatest power economically, politically, culturally and religiously.

- Despite the above, women are not treated identically in Patriarchy, nor are all women excluded in the same way from spaces of power. In fact this different treatment is a mechanism by which the lack of solidarity and competitiveness among women is promoted. This lack of solidarity and competitiveness among women sometimes escalate to outright contempt for each other, thus ensuring their loyalty to men and male values.

- Patriarchy is produced by and at the same time promotes, a mind-set based on dichotomous, hierarchical and sexualized thinking. This mind-set divides reality into two dichotomous categories placing all of perceived reality either into things and acts associated with nature or things and acts produced by culture. Furthermore, everything placed within the category "culture" is overvalued while everything associated with nature is undervalued. By situating men and the masculine under the higher category of culture, and woman and the feminine under the less valued category of nature, "man" and masculinity become the parameter, model or paradigm of humanity, while the subordination of women is justified based on their alleged inferior "natural roles".

- In Patriarchy, gender roles and stereotypes may be different in each social class, age and culture but through the mechanisms, structures and institutions mentioned previously, it makes these roles and stereotypes seem natural and universal.

- In any given Patriarchy all men will not enjoy the same privileges or have the same power. Indeed, the experience of domination of men over women historically served for some men to extend that domination over other groups of men, installing a hierarchy among men that is more or less the same in every culture or region today. The male at the top of the patriarchal hierarchy has great economic power; is an adult and almost always able bodied; possesses a well-defined, masculine gender identity and a well-defined heterosexual identity, adding a few more features by region. For example, in Latin America, for a man to be at the top of the patriarchal hierarchy, that man has to be white and Christian, in addition to the other characteristics shared with Patriarchy's counterparts across regions.

- Across Patriarchy's different models, women are exposed to different degrees and types of violence, some common to all and others specific to each cultural, religious or economic model adopted by the Patriarchy.

- Patriarchy was the first structure of domination, subordination and exclusion which is recognized as such by History with a capital H (recognized patriarchal history) and still remains a basic system of domination. Ironically, while being the most powerful and enduring system of inequality, it is hardly ever perceived as such even by women themselves. In fact, precisely because the invisibilization of Patriarchy is one of its institutions, even some feminists deny its existence.

Structures of Patriarchy

Scholars define patriarchy as a system of social structures where men are in the dominant position to exploit and oppress women. They talks about six structures of patriarchy:

- Patriarchal Mode of Production.

- Patriarchal Relations in Paid Work.

- Patriarchal Relations in the State.

- Male Violence.

- Patriarchal Relations in Sexuality.

- Patriarchal Relations in Cultural Institutions.

It is seen that structures of patriarchy have formed the basis of our society since ancient times. The way and the level at which patriarchy manifests itself may have changed, but the underlying domination remains the omnipresent. So, patriarchal structures operate through modes of domination and suppression. It defines and structures the opportunities available to all human beings by creating a distinction between masculinity and femininity. It creates ideas and perceptions that explain our social surroundings. The basic ideology through which structures of patriarchy continue to rule human relations is by devaluing of female roles and valorisation of masculine roles. So, patriarchy is maintained through a system of hierarchy.

Women's subordinate status is attributed to their lack of control over resources such as land, lack of access to instruments of labour, such as plough, which according to custom women are disallowed to wield, kin networks that dictate how a woman should marry and where they ought to live, household rules that privilege the eldest man as the head of the family, lack of mobility and finally, a culture of self-effacement which women appear to practice willingly. Women are expected to subordinate their interests to their husbands and children. There are certain formal structures like family, motherhood, school, religion, etc. that support and extend these structures of patriarchy along with certain informal structures which operate as social norms that provide guidance to people. Now, let us study some of these institutions, practices and norms that maintain patriarchal set up of the society.

Family

"Patriarchy's chief institution is the family". Family is the main agent of socialization where young children learn the values and norms of society. It is with in the family that young boys and girls first encounter patriarchal power. The institution of family often internalise beliefs that lead to an unequal upbringing of women. For instance, in terms of food also, it is thought that women do not need that much nourishment as compared to men as the latter have to do all kind of laborious and tough work.

Family as an institution ensures reproduction and proper socialization of children. Man is the head of the family who controls women and other younger men. Apart from being considered as the protector of the family, father is also the inheritor of property in the family who also controls economic resources. Sexual division between labour begins with the family and the legacy continues to the public sphere, where both sexes invest equal amount of labour but the returns are different in terms of economic resources, respect and dignity of labour. However, most women are confined to the private sphere that furthers their economic dependency and exclusion from decision-making both in public and private. Betty Friedan in "the feminist Mystique" has called the family to be a 'comfortable concentration camp' Lack of adequate education opportunities for women have been the main reason behind it. They also lack confidence and zeal to fight patriarchy. Generally, whatever is taught by the patriarchal ideology running in the family is accepted as natural and unchallengeable.

Feminist Perspectives on Family

- Liberal feminist believe that family imposes impediment to gender equality. This is done through processes of socialization, reproduction etc.

- Radical Feminists believe that family is an embodiment of patriarchy.

- Marxist Feminists are of the opinion that family exists as economic units that benefit patriarchal system and are linked with patriarchy.

However, some feminists believe that family signifies female unity where women can show respect and love for each other labour and foster sisterhood based on women's need for dignified lives. stable family life is an essential pre-requisite for civilised society where women with feminine values nurture their children and other domestic skills. Today, divorced parents, unwed mothers and homosexuals adopting children have totally changed the social outlook of parenthood.

School

Women need to go the schools to receive education, in order to achieve freedom in true sense. The patriarchal belief system rests on the assumption that there is no need to enrich women with higher levels of education as they just have to remain inside the four walls. As it is believed that their primary job is to just look after their family. By providing them knowledge is just the waste of resources and time. It is believed that girls can be trained at home by other elder women in the family, with all the necessary information on activities like cooking, cleaning clothes and utensils, looking after the children. Patriarchy favours strict and limited roles for women and any kind of change in roles is not welcomed. So, it may be observed and claimed that by restricting women in the private sphere and not allowing them to receive education, patriarchy is able to make women ignorant of her capabilities and makes them highly dependent on the menfolk.

Family and Feminism

Feminists are of the opinion that women should have equal access to education. Good education can help women in providing them with good jobs. Then jobs can provide women with requisite economically resources and would help them getting independent and removing their dependency from others. If women are able to pursue better professional careers, they would get better salaries. Education not only makes women economically independent but also provides them with better sensibilities to be able to deal with problems. For instance, education makes women aware of their right and so no one can exploit or misuse them in any way.

They says because of lack of education women have remained invisible from the process of history writing. The actions of women were always guided by men. The agents of socialization never allowed women to know her history and her 'self. It was always felt that women are intellectually inferior to men. This was due to the fact that patriarchy always entered women's consciousness and became part of her being. It kept women in ignorance and positioned her in a way that they remained outside the dominant discourse. As a result, our history has been androcentric. In order to break away from this, they says, it is very important that for us to re-write our history without any biases and presumptions.

Marriage

Marriage is practiced and institutionalised in our society keeping in mind the patriarchal ideology and its structure. It is an institution that has supported the traditional arrangement of man's power over woman. It is the mainstay of patriarchy and symbolises and personifies female subordination.

Our society has put forth certain norms and values that a man and woman have to follow to make their marriage acceptable by people at large. For instance, in the marriage between a man and a woman and man should be elder to woman. However, in the present times, some countries have legalised the marriage between homosexuals. But, the patriarchal ideology does not accept it and puts forth many issues against it. Also, the age difference between the husband and the wife is another matter of concern.

In India, there have been cases of child marriages even though it was declared illegal since colonial times. In present times also, young girls have been married off old men because of the many problems faced by the families of the girls. Poverty has been seen as a major cause for this wrong done to girls. Marriage has become a sort of contract/agreement between families where primarily the family of the girl is exploited. For instance, the family of a good and capable boy with good earning capacity makes sure that the family of the girl fulfil all their demands and wishes. They have desires of getting a girl who is tall, thin, fair, well-educated and apart from this who gets good loads of dowry in addition to well organised marriage functions. As the family of the girl has to bear the cost of the marriage, this has become one of the main reasons as to why the birth of a girl child is not welcomed.

After marriage, the structures and ideology of patriarchy continues to direct the lives of married women. Wife's happiness is dependent on the whims, wishes and benevolence of her husband and many a times, the fate of marriage is also dependent on the latter. After marriage, men as husbands have more authority in decision-making. They become legally sanctioned masters of their wives. Unfortunately, for some women, the marital home becomes a prison, women are not allowed to move out of the house and her going out is seen with doubt and suspicion. Then, women are also supposed to observe purdah (veil) that seeks to maintain the private/public divide. So, the private is implicated not only through the four walls of the house, but also the purdah (veil) that is raised around woman's immediate self.

However, patriarchy in control of women's sexuality is not limited to their prohibited movement from private sphere to public sphere or the legitimacy provided to bride price (dowry) by society at large. Patriarchy also renders men with reproductive and sexual rights over women. It is believed that marriage must be consummated through sexual intercourse. Wife has to fulfil the sexual desires of her husband and the purpose of marriage gets fulfilled when they gives birth to a male child.

In most societies, talking about sex is taken up as a taboo, but marriage provides legitimacy to sex to the extent, that even marital rape is acceptable by societies. In most countries, marital rape has not been taken up as a legal crime. In the similar vein, some feminists have even gone to the extent of calling marriage as legalised prostitution.

So, we see that society values marriage. Individuals are given no alternative, but to marry. For women, marriage becomes an utmost priority and to get married within a prescribed age to avoid unwanted issues. Other issues related to marriage are dowry, divorce and widow re-marriage. At the time of marriage, family of the bride has to give money/gifts to the bridegroom and his family. In most communities, the better the bridegroom's prospectus, the more dowry (bride-price) the bride's family has to give. Dowry which is given at the time of marriage is not the end of everything. Many families are either not satisfied with the amount of resources given at the time of marriage or they demand an extra dose of resources as there is no end to their greed and desires. However, later if the bride's family is not able to fulfil the needs of the opposite family, the latter start torturing the bride. Both the husband and his family ill-treat, torture, disrespect, harass the wife and put psychological pressure on her demanding for more and more resources. Many dowry deaths have also taken place in this regard. Either the husband or his family kill the wife, or out of depression and psychological pressure, in need of some relief, the wife commits suicide.

If for some reason, the marriage does not work out well, then divorce becomes a huge difficulty. The divorced woman is considered as a burden and responsibility that is thrown out of the wedlock. The reason and cause behind divorce always rest on the shoulders of the woman and it is her incapability that is pointed out. At times, when the divorced woman goes to her native home for help and shelter, they is blamed, rejected and seen as an extra burden on the family. The responsibility of the children, if any, also rests with the woman. Divorce is not the opposite of marriage but the very transformation of it as the divorced women continue to look after the children from marriage and men are exempted from the same responsibility. For re-marriage also, the woman has to face a lot of problems as then the issue of her chastity, children from earlier marriage, and her incapability to survive the earlier marriage arise. All the blame for the divorce rests on her. It is because of these problems and issues; there is high probability that the woman would not get the groom of her choice or would have to make many compromises.

In another case, if the wife loses her husband and becomes a widow, then her life becomes really miserable. Apart from the loss of her husband, there are other issues that add to her pain and agony. Since ancient times in India, widows used to practice sati i.e. the practice in which the widow used to burn herself on the funeral pyre of her husband. The practice of sati rests on the patriarchal ideology according to which after the death of the husband, his wife has no reason left to live. Sati confers her sacrifice and her desire to end her life after her husband's death. Till date, the word sati is still present in the existing vocabulary that often connotes a good wife.

Sati

In India, in 1813, non-voluntary sati was made illegal by the British government. The latest case of sati was seen in the state of Rajasthan in the year 1987, when an 18 year old girl named Roop Kanwar died on the funeral pyre of her husband. Many people attended the sati event. After her death, Roop Kanwar was hailed as sati-mata and was seen as equivalent to goddess sati.

Widow-remarriage has its worst forms as patriarchal structure makes it really difficult and unbearable for the widows, irrespective of their choices, to marry or not to marry. It is very rare when widows express their wish for re-marriage and even if they do, it is frowned upon and socially rejected. Also, it goes against their socialisation especially in societies where widows used to practice sati. In other cases, widows are forced to re-marry their brother-in-laws as it may solve the problems that may arise like issues related to property, custody of the children etc. and would also serve the purposes of patriarchal ideology.

Recently, the institution of marriage has been challenged by both same-sex marriages and live-in relationship. Live-in relationships have taken the place of religiously solemnised marriages. It is believed that these kinds of marriages have gone against the patriarchal cultures and liberated human relations in some way or the other. Primarily, they have challenged the various forms of hierarchy that come along with a man and woman wedlock. These institutions of collaboration are based on the notion of equality where by both the individuals are at equal footing. However, the patriarchal society does not accept this collaboration and looks at it with disgust and rejection as it is against the natural norms of reproduction.

Motherhood

The practice of motherhood is basically considered a 'feminine' attribute as even if the father is responsible for taking care of the whole family, he is not directly associated with the nurturing of his children. Patriarchy absolves men from major social responsibilities. Researchers talk about the practice of motherhood in two forms - as an experience and as an institution. The experiential feeling of motherhood is natural and intrinsic, whereas the institutional aspect of motherhood is a forced one which coercively induces maternal attributes in women. This institutional aspect of motherhood constructs the experiential feeling. Institutional motherhood works to induce maternal "instinct" and selflessness in every woman. They says, "The experience of maternity and the experience of sexuality have both channelled to serve male interests; behaviour which threatens the institutions, such as illegitimacy, abortion, lesbianism, is considered deviant or criminal".

They also explain how forms of birth control and abortion are considered as "genocide" by the patriarchal norms. Thus, by putting forth this distinction, they say that the social role of being a mother induces characteristics which may not comply with her intrinsic nature. This is because of the immense love a mother is conditioned to shower over her children whereby they may lose her identity as a separate individual. It is seen that the pride of being a mother has been internalized by majority of the women. According to the patriarchal norms, a woman is incomplete till they gives birth to a child. Bearer of male child is given more value than who has only borne female children. Women who have problem in bearing children are considered "barren". The notions of barrenness and incompleteness are introduced into the dominant discourse in order to have compulsory re-production by the female body.

However, while looking at the construct of motherhood, one can see that there exists a contradiction in the patriarchal norms whereby there is a common contempt for woman on the one hand but on the other hand, there is respect shown for mother to the extent that metaphors of motherhood are used to glorify their values of love, care, nurture etc.

Therefore, we see that motherhood is culturally constructed as a norm. Also, motherhood as a concept is relational as women are not treated as individual in themselves but 'in relation' their families and children, as mothers and daughters. Women are socialized in such a way that their 'being' is incomplete without the relational aspect. Therefore, we see that patriarchal societies control their women in all sorts of ways.

Labour: Domestic and Work Place

Women's labour that is readily acceptable by the patriarchal structure is that of the household work and social reproduction; whereby in both jobs women are restricted to the private sphere. The patriarchal structure turns most of the women's labour as 'invisible' as according to patriarchal ideology, it serves almost nothing in terms of market criteria. Patriarchal ideology makes sure that women's labour, often quoted as "leisure work", and does not hold importance. And the social norms, rules and values should aim to prove women's labour as inadequate and unreliable. Also, whatever work women do, it is always underpaid, unrecognised and exploited.

Feminists have pointed out that the patriarchal structure supports a strict sexual division of labour between a man and a woman. And, this sexual division of labour is not only limited to the household but also extends to the market place. Within the household, women have to take care of both the domestic responsibilities like rearing children, cooking, cleaning etc. and also social reproduction. Men are responsible for getting money and other resources that necessary for the running of the household. In this regard, men's contribution is considered prime for running of the household and women's contribution is just another support structure. Their work neither gets paid nor achieves any acknowledgement. Men blame the women and believe that they do nothing and just sit idle at home. Their work is always considered secondary and negligible. So, we may say that there is no dignity of labour as far as women are concerned.

What is 'Double Burden'?

It is also called as 'double-shift'. It refers to the dual oppression that women have to bear both as paid worker in the public sphere and unpaid home-maker in the private sphere. Private sphere is the prime site of women's oppression and this oppression doubles up when women are forced to face additional burden in the public sphere as well.

Many radical feminists see domestic labour as a source of oppression as all kind of house work is unpaid. Marriage is a labour contract whereby men exploit women's labour and this exploitation takes place outside the capitalist mode of production. Also, domestic labour is seen as 'unproductive' and this is how patriarchal structure devalues the kind of work women perform.

Women as Reserve Army of Labour

According to Marx, capitalist economies had fluctuating demands with regard to labour. The demand of labour increased during the economic booms and reduced during economic slumps. So, this was implied in the employment levels that corresponded to the economic fluctuations. However, whatever may be the level of fluctuations in employment, there always existed a reserve army of labour i.e. women. According to Veronica Beechey, women were a significant part of the reserve army of labour who were easy to deal with as they could be taken part time or full time according to the needs/requirements of the employer and could also be dismissed during the economic depression/slumps.

Women are also sexually vulnerable at work place outside the household. Men consider them to be weaker section that can neither form trade unions nor fight for their rights. They are paid minimal and are given low profile jobs. The reason often quoted for less money is that they are not the bread winners but just add to the basic income of the family. Women are not on the bargaining position also as the whole market thinks of them in the same way i.e. women are low on intellect and physical strength. Some of the other generalisations made while taking them up for employment is that women have nimble fingers which are good for the textile and electronic industry. And for the same reason, they are often taken up by beedi rolling companies. For all these reasons, women have to rely on men for financial support.

Unfortunately, the patriarchal structure has put so many restrictions on women, that their sphere of action has become very restricted. For any kind of women's empowerment, it is very necessary to provide them the freedom of opportunity to express their competence in regard to all kinds of jobs that the men are already doing. But, this can only happen when the patriarchal ideology accepts women's equality and dares to treat them on equal grounds.

Rape

Rape is also a patriarchal construct which is used to dominate women. Patriarchal ideology seems to provide spaces to mothers in terms of their action in mainly domestic sphere, but they also take away the very basic individual autonomy in case of raped women. 'Being a mother' is considered to be a celebration; 'to be raped' is a shame. Rape is considered as a weapon of domination and coercion in the hands of men which is used against women. It is an act of violence and it symbolizes male domination. It gives men the power to brutalize women. Rape is understood as normal expression of male sexuality. To define an act of rape, the concept of 'consent' is used to differentiate it from sexual intercourse. There are no categories to define women's position in both cases of rape and sexual intercourse. "Treating rape as a sexual offence and not as an offence of violence has hardened the rule that lack of consent on the part of woman has to be proved beyond reasonable doubt. If there are no visible marks of resistance, which often are absent, the judges have tended to doubt that the victim did not give her consent". Therefore, patriarchy fails to provide space for women's subjectivity. This is because the dominant discourse produces concepts and categories which are androcentric.

Also, we see that rape as domination is not only physical but is psychological too. Researchers talk about the fear of rape which shapes a woman's psychology and guides her movements and actions. They say, "Even if they have never themselves been raped or attacked, the fear still inhibits them. Such women are made unfree by such power and fear it generates; the existence of power against, though not actually exercised at a given moment, has translated into a generalized and constant power over, rape 'is nothing more or less than a conscious process of intimidation by which all men keep all women in a state of fear'. Therefore, through rape, patriarchy challenges the autonomy of a women and her as a being. Rape signifies intrusion of one's self honour and dignity. So, through the practice of rape, we may see that women are the objects with which the patriarchal society determines their being.

References

- The-origins-of-patriarchy, cochise-sociology-os: lumenlearning.com, Retrieved 05, July 2020
- D-Facio-What-is-Patriarchy: learnwhr.org, Retrieved 24, March 2020

Concepts of Gender Studies

The major concepts within the domain of gender studies are gender sensitisation, gender and language, gender and labour, gender and disability, gender stereotypes, and gender and media. Within media, films and video games are studied through a gendered perspective. This chapter discusses in detail these concepts related to gender studies.

Gender Sensitization

One of the major lacunae in our social organisation is the prevalence of gender based discrimination in different walks of life, be it social, economic or political. Gender discrimination refers to biased treatment of women/girls and men/boys which in turn is a consequence of deep-rooted normative beliefs about the 'usual' traits, behaviours and roles of women and men. Such beliefs are learned since childhood and passed down through generations such that people come to recognise these as given and obvious facets of gender identities. For instance, the fact that women have typically performed the task of rearing children have resulted in the stereotype that women are by nature nurturing and caring and hence the only "appropriate" role for them is care-work. In similar manner, people tend to develop inflexible ideas about 'what is feminine' and 'what is masculine.' Eventually such stereotypes get implicated in all forms of social institutions and organisations- family, community, state. Indeed such stereotypes can be observed anywhere- educational institutions, workplaces, religious institutions, sports and cultural events etc.

The Need for Gender Sensitisation

A major concern in the context of gender stereotypes are that these often operate in a subtle manner, because these are considered as obvious truths, to the extent that it becomes extremely difficult, if not impossible, to even reckon and decode these stereotypes. Most often, these are practiced unconsciously and unknowingly. For example: Unequal wages given to women for doing equal and similar work as done by men is a common practice in labour markets the world over. Often such unequal wages are justified on the grounds that women lack the requisite skill, they prioritise family over work/career, they are suited for soft jobs compared to men, their earnings are secondary source of income for the household, so on and so forth. Such stereotypes are underlain by the assumption that women are home-makers and men are the bread-winners for the family which actually place women in a secondary position in the labour market. Although women are mostly the victims, individuals of any gender stand disadvantaged in the face of such overwhelming stereotypes.

In order to address these stereotypes, one needs to be gender sensitive which basically means being informed about the gender equality concerns and act accordingly. To this end, gender sensitisation is an important tool which help in raising awareness about such stereotypes and inequalities, and cultivate a disposition to behave in a gender-sensitive. Thus, sensitization of gender "is about changing behaviour and instilling empathy into the views that we hold about our own and the other genders." It assists people in "analysing their personal point of view and opinions and questioning the 'actualities' they believed they know.

Needless to mention that gender sensitisation is an imperative for not only the development of sensitive individuals but also of a society that is devoid of sexist biases. It is however important to mention here that gender sensitivity does not pit women against men. Rather, it inculcates an open-mindedness which allows an individual to unpack the unseen nuances of gender constructions, determine the validity of such generalised constructions and widens the horizon of life choices for both women and men.

Importance of Gender Sensitisation

- By enabling us to decipher the gender stereotypes that are subtly entwined into all forms of social organisations, gender sensitisation helps us to critically view what is otherwise considered as 'natural' and obvious, thus leading the pathway towards development of informed individuals.

- It helps to generate respect for all individuals irrespective of sex.

- It enables us to see human rights as intrinsic to the attainment of gender justice and appreciate the worth of the women and other genders as human beings.

- It helps to address the hurdles that thwart any attempt to reduce gender gaps in family, community, education, employments and all other spheres of life.

Gender sensitisation enables people to critically review their personal beliefs and opinions they have been socialised into. That said, it is important to flag few gender issues which one should be conscious about for being an informed and gender sensitive individual. These are as follows:

- Sex and gender,

- Gender ideals and stereotypes,

- Gender roles.

Role of Family

A progressive society must be built on the edifice of social justice, gender being an important parameter. This basically means that there must not be any denial of equality, opportunity and rights on the basis of gender. Family being the primary unit of social organisation, any effort to inculcate gender sensitivity must begin here. In the Third World countries in general and India in particular, gender discrimination within the families is rampant and is manifested through son preferences, denying the girls of the right to proper food, nutrition, education and health, unequal access to economic resources based on gender and inflexible gender roles whereby men are seen as the primary bread-winners and women as mothers, home-makers and caregivers. Such forms of discrimination operate at different scales and at different levels across the societies the world over. The socialisation process of children begins from their families first and the gender ideals and messages they pick up from their immediate surrounding environment contribute towards shaping their persona and approach towards gender ideologies. Girls/women come to accept their position as inferior to that of the boys/men while the latter begin considering themselves as superior to the former.

The persuasion experienced at home along with the previously existing social disparity between men and women lead to re-entrenchment of patriarchal ideologies in the society. Several studies on violence point out that child who had experienced gender-based violence being committed in the home in their childhoods are more likely to consider violence against women as 'normal'. Thus, men learn to behave brutally against women and women learn to tolerate it. Intimate partner violence, therefore, is learned social behaviour. Hence, the familial context is the most important site for gender sensitisation because the children learn whatever is practiced at home.

Gender Sensitivity in Education

Gender stereotypes are mostly learned through socialisation processes and perpetrated by the education received since childhood. Schools, colleges and institutions of higher education play important role in reproducing the gender stereotypes which boys and girls have already imbibed from their familial environment. The learning materials, text books etc. often underscore subtle biases in favour of asymmetric gender roles and characteristics. Often, in most disciplines, knowledge is produced by man and sometimes for male readers. Male writers tend to select examples from their everyday experiences. The illustrations, examples, case studies, presentation of role models etc. used to substantiate the study content are frequently rooted in cultural stereotypes of gender. As discussed earlier, the content of curriculum and the manner in which it is produced is of extreme relevance in this context. Several studies analysing the content of school text books point out that gender stereotypes are perpetuated by the portrayal of women in school books as only low-status workers, mothers and wives which do not reflect the contemporary social realities. The nurses and teachers in the text books are consistently depicted as women, while drivers, carpenters, postman, doctors, farmers, pilots, soldiers are shown as men. These text books, thus, reinforce the stereotypical notion that men have much wider access to public sphere while women's access is limited and is merely a reflection of their care-giving roles.

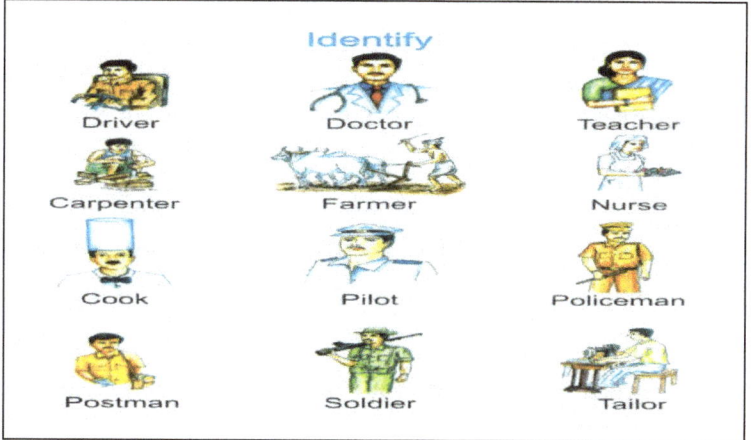

Also, it has been highlighted that the language in which the contents are written, sometimes, does not cater to the call for gender inclusivity. In fact such language frequently hinges on perpetuating gender stereotypes. Some eco-feminists while exploring the symbolic association between women and nature which is rampantly visible in art, literature, religion etc. observe that there are subtle linguistic connections between the two. In fact many literary critics claim that patrilineal concepts of women and nature warrant "a two-pronged rape and domination of the earth and the women who live on it". Some eco-feminists have highlighted the typical connections between naturist and sexist articulation, i.e., language that inferiorizes women and non-human nature by "naturalizing women and feminizing nature".

Gender and Language

Language is used by both men and women but somewhere in its course of development it gets divided (unknowingly) between two parts – male and female – as per social and cultural norms. Language mirrors, records and transmits differences. These gender differences can be marked in various ways.

Men and women are socialized to express themselves in appropriate social language that teaches and reinforces differentiated gender roles. Following three questions can lead us to clarify our point:

- Do men and women speak different languages? The answer is No and yes. No, because it is the same language they speak. In this case, let us say English. Yes, because their phrases, expressions and intonations are so different that they appear to be speaking different languages.

- Do they use language differently? Yes. Men have many expressions peculiar to them which women understand but do not use. On the other hand, women have words and phrases which men know of but never use for fear of being scorned at. That is the reason, the language of men and women appears different.

- Is there gender bias in English language? Yes. This bias is obvious in the manner in which language uses women. Women are ignored when words such as 'he' or 'man' signify women too. For example, "everyone must do his duty." Here the pronoun 'his' denotes woman also. "Man is mortal." In this sentence 'man' also means 'woman'. In both these sentences her presence is ignored. These are known as 'masculine generics' and are widely accepted.

Language also defines women's status vis-à-vis men's and by inference gives them secondary position. Let us look at the titles of respect, Mrs or Miss. These terms show the presence/absence of man in a woman's life whereas the appellation Mr is independent and does not need woman's presence.

Feminine nouns of some words are derogatory like 'dog-bitch', 'wizard witch'. Similarly, words like 'lady doctor', 'lady lecturer' specify gender unnecessarily. Terms of endearment used by men for women like 'chick' or 'babe' highlight how language devalues women. Now we will look into the factors influencing language.

Biological Factors

The biological factor can be studies from three angles – voice, phonology and intonation.

- Voice: Women have a thin voice as compared to men's gruff voice and their voice-frequency is almost twice as high as that of men. Psychologists say that speaking in high-pitched voice is their physical limitation but socially it is associated with their timidity.

- Intonations: There are two types of basic intonations – rising intonation and falling intonation. Women usually answer a question with rising intonation which suggests their docility and gentleness, besides lack of self-confidence.

- Phonology: Pronunciation comes under phonology. Women pronounce words in a better manner than men do. For example, women pronounce the letter 'r' softly as in 'chair' which sounds like 'chaise'. In English, the ending "...ing" as in running, walking, writing is pronounced fully by women while men miss the last 'g' and pronounce these words as "runnin", "walkin". Women's pronunciation denotes use of proper formal language, compliance to accepted social expectations and politeness. Men's pronunciations suggest their assertion and informality.

The above example drawn from the situation of language use is in the American context.

Cultural Factors

Culture is a dominant factor in maintaining language identity. Culture is a blanket term; within it several diverse groups live and operate, which are called subcultures. There is a sub-culture of men and also sub-culture of women. Men and women belong to their respective sub-cultures and these sub-cultures mould their behaviour pattern, language use and conduct.

As per the expectations of their sub-culture women use language that is not aggressive or adventurous. In larger groups they remain silent but speak in smaller groups. Their conversation aims to build friendship, loyalty, equality and such other traits. They usually speak of simple domestic or personal matters which Gender and Language men consider ridiculous. On the contrary, men choose to work in larger groups. They want power, control and status. They like to compete and win; and they dominate the conversation. These cultural differences in the male and female groups lead to the different ways in which they converse.

Two examples from literature would illustrate the above points. In William Golding's novel Lord of the Flies, we get a fine example of how boys can be aggressive for power. Their language and games drive them unwittingly to frenzy and murder. In To Kill a Mocking Bird, the girl protagonist's aunt always upbraids her to speak proper lady-like language and criticizes her for tomboyish activities.

Power and Domination Factor

In the patriarchal system women are seen to be in a subordinate position. The male members of the society use patronizing language when conversing with them. This is called male language which is the language of power and authority. Therefore, interaction between the males and the females has always been male dominated.

Language also shows social inequality. Women's speech is considered unimportant; therefore, they use linguistic forms that are associated with their low status. These forms included tag questions, intonation, hedges, politeness strategies and others. Conversely, men's speech becomes a tool of patriarchal power through gender-role training. They learn to dominate the conversation through interruption and cross-talk.

Gender Difference in Vocabulary

Men use hard and aggressive expressions like damn, shit to express anger or frustration, women would never use these tabooed words that are rated as slang. They usually go for harmless expressions like oh, ah. Tabooed words and slang are found more in men's speech than in women's though they may be of same educational level or social class. For example, when a woman is frightened, she will shout, "Oh, how frightened I am!" But a man would only say, "damn it!" and rarely admit that he is frightened. The difference in vocabulary is shown in the following five aspects:

- Color words: Women use color words like blue and lavender and azure more frequently but men would not.

- Adjectives: Women use adjectives such as adorable, charming, lovely more often. When a woman leaves a restaurant, she will remark, "It is a nice meal." If a man wants to express the same idea, he will use the word "good". Using more adjectives to express their feelings or to describe things is because women are sensitive to the environment.

- Adverbs: Women tend to use adverbs like pretty, terribly, vastly, quietly etc. more freely than men do. Men, on the contrary use, really, very, utterly. Women like to use so quite regularly. Like "She is so pretty" or "The play was so interesting."

- Swear words and Expletives: Swear words are considered dirty and impolite and women do not use these like damn, shit, hell. Women pay more attention to their manners and social propriety. In order to express their sudden and deep feelings they may say, O God!, oh dear or dear me! Let us examine the following example:

  Woman: Dear me! Are we going to be late again!

  Man: Shit! The train is on the platform and we have to run.

- Modulation: When a woman talks, she often takes what others think into consideration. She uses tag questions such as, "It is cold, isn't it?" and hedges like well, you know... I think... I suppose, ... kind of,.... maybe I am wrong but...

Interrogative Sentences

Compared with men, women are more likely to use an interrogative sentence to express their ideas, and they use tag questions, because the tag questions can make the tone less tense. Some linguists researching in this area collected many couples' conversation tapes, and found that women used three times more interrogative sentences than men. Women do this because they are less sure about themselves and their opinions. They lack the confidence to use direct and firm statements. On the other hand, this style shows politeness and gentleness.

Imperative Sentences

Imperative sentences give command or order. Since women hold a subordinate position in the patriarchal society they are trained to not to order about. A study showed that in conversation women use the "let us" pattern of sentence, such as "let's go out for a long drive." A boy/man may say it directly, "Today we are going for a long drive." This sentence has the sense of giving order. Some other examples are:

Man: Give me that pen.

Women: Would you give me that pen, please?

Man: It's time to go

Woman: Let's go.

Difference in Attitude Towards Language

Language is constantly changing. It evolves. It grows. Both men and women have helped in the development of language but their approaches have been different. Women instinctively shrink from gross and rough expressions. They prefer refined and indirect expressions whereas men use direct and often coarse expressions.

Men find women's language too delicate and feel that if this style is adopted, the language will become weak and insipid. It will lose its vividness and strength. Men renovate the language by adding new words. In the beginning these words may appear slang but later they are accepted into the main language.

On the other hand, women are conservative by nature and they prefer to use Gender and Language traditional language. Thus, they help in preserving old language. It may look comical today but it is a fact that women used to avoid words like vulgar, indecent in their routine conversation. They preferred to use common for vulgar and would break half way through a sentence if they were supposed to use the word indecent, like "this book is a little … um h … Isn't it?"

Difference in Nonverbal Language

We can see that women do not like to patronize any conversation or discussion; they like to listen and then reply. Men on the other hand interrupt other's talk. Men do not like to be silent in conversation/discussion. When a conversation involves both sexes, women are at the receiving end. They play the role of patient listeners.

Difference in Choosing Topics

In social interaction, men and women have different interests in choosing their topics. Men are more likely to discuss politics, sports, economics and current news; women prefer cooking, domestic chores, clothes, fashion, children etc. Women talk more in informal situations but they play a secondary role in the formal meetings. They speak less.

Reasons behind these Differences

Biological difference between the two sexes cannot explain the reasons behind the different ways of communication. But gender difference plays a great role in creating these differences. The causes behind the difference can be understood as under:

- **Different Psychology:** It is an accepted idea that women are more careful, sensitive and considerate than men. Before a woman speaks she usually thinks of the effect her words may have on the listener, so she often appears to be hesitant or more polite. On the contrary, men are rash, they do not bother much for public opinion and they just say what they want to say and seldom care what others think. So man's speech is usually blunt and solid.

- **Different Social Status:** Of the social causes of gender differences in speech style, one of the most significant is level of education. Studies show that the greater difference in the educational level of boys and girls, the greater is the difference in their speech. The gap between men's speech and women's speech has reduced considerably with improved and equal educational opportunities for girls. But even then women display care and caution in the appropriate use of language.

- **Different Social Roles:** Language use also depends on the social roles of men and women. Linguistic studies carried out in the 1970 reveal that in almost all countries men hold higher job positions that give them opportunities to dominate everything, including women. Men can order about freely while women are not so confident of giving order even when they hold higher position today. Women have had very less power in the society and this lack is obvious in their language. Women's social status makes them submissive to men.

Gender and Labour

With the earliest development of agriculture and the subsequent settlements around which it was pursued, more complex social and family structures evolved. Private property was primarily owned by man and gradually production for exchange obscured production for use by the household. Women's work got relegated to private maintenance for family use and became a mere appendage to men's work of producing exchangeable surplus. Private property created its possessor the leader of the family, i.e., recognized men's control over women within the household as well as outside it. Women's role came to be: 1) hearth activities including cooking, feeding and care of infants; 2) Courtyard activities including production of food, crafts etc. 3) Field activities including gathering and collecting of fruit and nuts, clearing, planting, cultivating and harvesting food, animal rearing, collecting material for building, fuel for hearth etc. women combined these with their role of nurturing children.

Gradually special agriculture became more developed. Productivities increased which could sustain larger population densities. Consequently, trade developed and people with higher status withdrew from maintenance of basic activities and wielded superior power and greater access to basic resources through administrative roles. Since women did participate in this whole process of distribution of roles, their right to access resources narrowed down thereby reducing their status and opportunities. Over and above this, their new status implied their withdrawal from productive roles. In brief, women failed to specialize when agricultural villages began to be more and more specialized. Consequently, all subsidiary activities were left to women. Thus, women's denigrating status arose when clan structure of society was overtaken by the public sphere. Women, being less skilled and specialized lost out with the growing pre-eminence of public sphere which demanded greater political bonding.

The process of sex segregation of labour further got amplified with the emergence of industrial capitalism. Most researches on women's contemporary universal subordination are based on the supposition of an essential historical transition in female's labour force participation in the 18th and 19th century co-terminus with the rise of industrial capitalism. Marxists have typically contended that the expansion of capitalism had lead to a deterioration of women's status through separating the household from waged work. The "family economy" was overtaken by the "family household system" which is a combination of a household structure based on dependence of the family members upon the paid labour of the fathers or husbands and the unpaid work of mother/wife in household tasks and the ideology of the family-"the private sphere beyond the public realm of community and individuals."

Earlier, men and women worked in family industries. In general men preformed the more skilled works while women did most of the processing of raw resources or finishing end produces. After industrialization, the family-industry system started to break down due to the demand for increased productivity. The capitalists structured production on a larger scale and production became disconnected from the home. Consequently women got excluded from the production process and became increasingly dependent on men. These developments in mid 19th century forced women into the basis for a sexually segregated labour market which in turn form the basis of socially constructed gender differences. However, some women did seek work, driven by necessity, in the capitalist-owned factories as wage labourers. Even then women were placed at the receiving end.

- Firstly, they continued to receive lower wages as in agriculture.

- Secondly, women were less skilled than men and therefore mostly engaged in low-paid and less desirable jobs.

- Thirdly, they appeared to be less organized than men.

The hierarchical division of labour between men and women and its dynamics forms an integral part of the dominant production relation in society throughout history.

Public-Private Contradiction

The sexual division of labour is manifested in the form of a spatial organisation of the society in terms of the public and private realms. The public realm is shared in common with the others and is characterized by such activities as participation in productive or paid work, enjoying civil and political rights, under the State's jurisdiction. On the contrary, the private domain is the personal space of the home, family and intimate relationships, comparatively free from the state jurisdiction. As ordained by the sexual division of labour, the public sphere has come to be appropriated by men while the private sphere is the territory of the women. Within the contemporary society, the private and the public exist as a perception with "powerful material and experiential consequences".

As per the liberal political perspectives, the beginning of the public-private dichotomy can be traced back to the writings of the social contract theorists which explored the legitimacy of government and the state. According to this school of thought, the social contract ushered in a new social order comprising of two domains: firstly, political and public and secondly, private and separated from politics. In traditional social contract theory, these domains were gendered. The public realm necessarily emerged as a masculine one because only men were reckoned as capable of being informed citizens. On the other hand, women were essentially viewed in terms of their sexual identities such that they were considered as unfit for active participation in political life. Therefore, the private sphere was deemed as appropriate for women. Thus, according to the classical social contract theorists, the ideological functions of public – private in conjunction with gender served to develop and maintain hierarchical social relations between men and women.

Gender and Disability

 Simply put, disability is a state or condition of mind or body that affects an individual's functioning and interferes with their ability to participate in the activities of day to day life. Disability is not just an individual, medical problem, but a social one. For instance, a person may have lost her ability to see. That is her 'impairment'. But because the environment around her makes it difficult and dangerous for blind people to function, she becomes 'disabled' and thus her quality of life suffers. Thus, there is both a medical as well as social dimension to the issue of disability. Disabled persons represent the largest minority group in society after women. Disability can affect a person anytime in the life-span; as health care improves and persons live longer, the chances of developing an age-related disability increase as one grows older. Furthermore, accidents and injuries are a major source of injury and disability. It is rightly said that we are all 'temporarily able-bodied'. Thus, disability is not a unique experience of particular individuals labelled as disabled but of each one of us at some point in our lives.

Disabled persons differ from one another in terms of the type and degree of disability. Moreover, gender, class, caste, race, ethnicity, sexuality, residence, and other such social, economic, political and cultural factors determine how disability is experienced and understood. For instance, in a rural, agricultural community, the loss of a limb may be seen as a severe disability because it affects the ability to work in the fields and earn a living. A person with intellectual disability who can do farm work may not be considered disabled at all, but may be teased for being a simpleton. But in an urban society, having an intellectual disability or mental retardation, may be more of a problem because so much importance is given to academic performance and getting into a profession.

But what is a disability and what does it mean to be disabled in the first place? Disabilities may be present from birth (congenital). For instance, developmental disabilities like mental retardation and autism are believed to be congenital. Malnutrition and micronutrient deficiencies may result in disabling conditions in children in the form of stunted physical and mental growth. Certain kinds of disabilities are acquired later in life due to accidents, injuries or advancing age, as mentioned above. A disability may be static such as the loss of limb due to an amputation; or 'progressive' in which a person's condition may deteriorate with time. The commonly known disabilities include blindness, deafness, locomotor disability, mental retardation, cerebral palsy and mental illness. Recently, autism and learning disabilities like dyslexia have also become more familiar.

Historically, persons with disabilities have always been regarded with a mixture of fear, horror and disdain, almost as if they were sub-human. They have been portrayed as freaks, helpless victims and a lifelong burden for family and society. Even in religion and mythology, negative traits have been attributed with form of deformity. Indeed, the law of karma decreed that being disabled was a punishment for past misdeeds. Such constructions of the disabled by the non-disabled leads to the marginalisation and disempowerment of a whole population group. At the same time, such negative stereotypes are internalised by the disabled people themselves. This leads to passivity, dependency, isolation, low self-esteem, and a complete loss of initiative. Pity, segregation, discrimination, and stigmatisation became normalised in the management of persons with disabilities.

This reflects in social policies which are based upon charity and welfare. Medical rehabilitation including distribution of assistive aids and appliances such as braces, crutches, hearing aids etc., special schools, vocational training in low-end occupations and sheltered employment have been the pillars of state policy for the disabled right from the colonial period. Furthermore, they have never been regarded as a politically significant group and hence their issues and concerns have not been taken up seriously by the political class. As many of them are hidden away from public view and denied access to education and social experiences, they have not been able to come together in a big way and make their presence felt in public life.

The plight of women with disabilities is far worse than that of men, as they suffer on account of being a woman in a male-dominated society, and disabled in a world which considers the healthy, able body as 'ideal'. How a person with a disability experiences the condition and is perceived by others is Gender and Disability largely dependent on whether s/he is male or female. For instance, Michelle women with disabilities experience 'sexism without the pedestal' i.e. they are doubly disadvantaged. Not only do they experience disability- linked discrimination but they experience sexism and are denied the consideration and social status that non-disabled women may claim as wives and mothers. Men with disabilities also experience a similar assault on their masculinity and may be shamed or bullied as 'not being man enough' or dependents and burdens upon the family. This can be very bruising and damaging to their self-respect, as traditionally, men are expected to be the providers and decision makers of the family.

Marriage and Family Life

A disabled woman is considered incapable of fulfilling the normative feminine roles of homemaker, wife and mother. Then, she also does not fit the stereotype of the normal woman in terms of physical appearance. Since women embody family honour, disabled girls are kept hidden at home by families and denied basic rights to mobility, education, and employment. They are less likely to be given in marriage than disabled men.

The capacity of women with disabilities to be sexual partners, homemakers and mothers is questioned and doubted. They are not considered capable of performing household chores efficiently, having meaningful sexual relationships or producing and rearing healthy children. Under these circumstances, they may be married off to older already married or men in poor health. In short, women with disabilities do not have the same options of marriage and motherhood as non-disabled women. Being nurturing and caring are important aspects of female identity and cultural expectations of 'proper' womanhood, but women with disabilities are themselves in need of care. Thus, they are not regarded as complete women.

Violence and Abuse

Being powerless, isolated and anonymous, women with disabilities are extremely vulnerable to abuse and violence. In addition, help in activities of daily living like dressing, eating, and other bodily activities makes them more vulnerable to abuse both at home and in institutions. She will be less able to defend herself in a risky situation because she may not be able to run or shout for help. Then, persons with developmental disabilities may be too trusting of others and hence may be easier to trick, bribe or coerce. They may not understand differences between 'good touch' and 'bad touch'. Many cases are known of mentally or intellectually disabled girls and women who are sexually abused by people responsible for their safety and care because they are sure that the victim will not be able to report what has happened to her, and the abuser can escape scot-free. Persons with speech and hearing difficulties may have limited communication skills to report abuse. Furthermore, since disabled persons are often taught to be obedient, passive, and to control their behaviour, this may make them easy victims.

Physical Access and Mobility

Women in general in our country find it difficult to move freely from one place to another for work or leisure. So we can well imagine the condition of women with disability. Poor public transport, bad roads or no roads, lack of proper lighting and safety on the streets all make it very difficult for women with disabilities to move from one place to another without assistance or help. You may have seen women with disabilities in public places facing great hardships because the built environment (roads, buildings, toilets etc.) are so difficult for them to negotiate. Conditions in public buses and the railways are also very unfavourable for persons with disability in general and women in particular. Lack of proper toilet facilities is a major problem. Public toilets are filthy and unhygienic and usually at ground level (Indian style toilet) making it very difficult for loco-motor disabled women who often get around by crawling on all fours.

Many women with disabilities have narrated their experiences of not eating food or even drinking water for long periods while they are out of the house for fear that they may need to use the toilet. This has a bad effect on their health. Due to these difficulties in moving from place to place, families often prefer to keep their disabled daughters confined in the four walls of the home. Many such girls never get the opportunity to interact with the outside world; go to school, make friends or visit relatives or neighbours. This leads to feelings of depression, isolation and worthlessness.

Education, Training and Employment

Many disabled girls never go to school. There is a lot of social stigma attached to their condition and families may want to hide them from the eyes of the world for fear of bringing a bad name on the family and affecting the marriage chances of other girls in the family. Special schools or vocational centres that are equipped to deal with their needs are usually only found in urban centres and travelling daily to these centres becomes a burden on the family.

Lack of hostel facilities and proper care if such hostels exist further worsens the problem. Many families consider their disabled daughters to be unfit for education and are unwilling to invest any money for the purpose because the girls are already considered a burden. Needless to say women with disabilities also find it very hard to secure employment because of their lack of education and training. This poses a serious problem for their futures especially after their parents die leaving them without financial support or independence.

Health Care

Girls and women with disabilities may suffer from several health problems which may be related to their disability and which may require prolonged and costly medical care, rehabilitation, occupational therapy, physiotherapy, special diets etc. Assistive devices like hearing aids for the deaf, wheelchairs or artificial limbs for those with loco-motor disabilities may prove prohibitively expensive for poor families. Women find it very humiliating when they go for health check-ups because health professionals often treat them in an insensitive and callous way. Many women neglect their health because they do not want to burden their families more and consider themselves worthless. Health is directly related to nutrition and a good quality of life. Many women with disability also suffering from poverty and neglect do not get adequate nutrition, fresh air, exercise and a wholesome atmosphere in which they can be healthy.

Leisure Activities

Girls and women with disability are often confined within the house because of stigma, shame and practical considerations like mobility issues. This gives them little opportunity to socialise with their peers, make friends, attend family events, religious ceremonies etc. This further isolate them and makes their lives dull and drab. Our public spaces are not at all accessible for persons with disabilities. Leisure activities like going out for a meal or for a film become potentially embarrassing and humiliating encounters. A woman with a disability may have to be physically carried because there is no lift or ramp; or made to sit at a distance from her companions because there is not adequate space for her wheelchair.

Thus we see that women with disabilities face violations of their rights at every level. They are considered a financial burden and social liability by their families; they are denied opportunities to move outside the home, and have access to education; they are viewed as asexual, helpless and dependant; their vulnerability to physical, sexual and emotional abuse is enormous; their aspirations for marriage and parenthood often denied; they grow up isolated and neglected within the walls of home or special institutions with no hope of a normal life.

Although a rights-based approach has entered the disability rights movement, the specific concerns of women with disabilities have not yet found a place neither in the government policies and programmes nor in the voluntary sector.

Gender Stereotypes

Gender stereotyping refers to 'normalization' of beliefs and perceptions about gender based attributes and roles. These stereotypes are so inflexibly ingrained into the minds of the individuals that they come to accept the stereotypes as 'normal' and universally applicable. For example, 'men are rational and women are emotional' is a very common stereotype that pervades the social organization of our everyday lives. Internalization of gender stereotypes since childhood through several socialization channels- such as family, educational and religious institutions, workplaces, media etc. rob the people of their ability to question and challenge these stereotypes. They consider these as obvious truths. Persistence of gender stereotypes lead to production and reiteration of gender based inequalities including violence.

Across different cultures, stereotypes about ideal masculine characteristics include "competent, stable, tough, confident, strong, accomplished, nonconforming, aggressive, leadership" while ideal feminine characteristics include "warm, emotional, kind, polite, sensitive, friendly, fashionable, gentle, soft, follower".

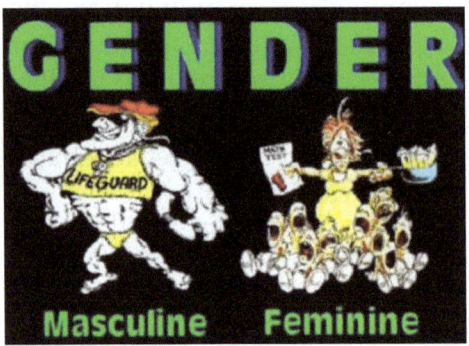

Table: Cultural Stereotypes about 'appropriate' attributes and roles of women and men.

Women	Men
Attributes	
• Dependent • Weak/fearful/fragile • Emotional • Implementers • Home-makers • Supporters • Soft • Risk-averting • Nurturing • Patient • Cooperative	• Independent • Powerful/brave/protectors • Rational • Decision makers • Breadwinners • Leaders • Aggressive • Risk-taking • Assertive • Impetuous • Competitive
• Women are beautiful who should be looked at and pursued. • Women's roles are home-bound and interior. The ideal women are stay at-home moms. • Women are naturally better caregivers than men. • Women are supposed to be earning less money. • Women are expressive and cry easily. • Girls naturally want to play with dolls. • Girls have a natural knack for music and dance. • Women are less intelligent, so they lack the skills of being politicians and engineers.	• Men need not be good looking, but powerful, rich and aggressive. • Men's roles are superior and befitting for public domain. • Men do not do housework and they are not responsible for taking care of children. • Men are breadwinners and protectors of family. • Men's earnings must exceed that of their female Partners. • Men are less emotive and never cry • Boys naturally want to play with cars and balls.

• 'Cleaner' and 'safer' jobs requiring less technical expertise such as secretaries, receptionists etc. are more suitable for women.	• Boys have a natural knack for maths and science.
• Women are nurturing, so they can be goodnurses, not doctors (which requires specialised skills).	• Men are intelligent and understand politics better than women.
• Women are not interested in sports.	• Men do "dirty jobs" such as construction and mechanics.
• Women are meant to be the damsel in distress who need to be protected by men, they can never be heroes.	• Men are not nurses, they are doctors.
	• Men love sports and outdoor activities such as camping, fishing, and hiking.
	• 'Real' men are more forthcoming in courting women.
• Women can never be good leader or decision makers.	• Men are in charge; they are always at the top.

These stereotypes, when internalized, significantly limit a person's life-choices. For example, those women who may not naturally develop motherly instincts might be obliged to be mothers while men despite not having aggressive traits might be compelled to act belligerently to uphold socially acceptable norms of womanhood and manhood in respective cases. Inculcation of gender stereotypes begin since the time of birth. The identification of babies as boys or girls at birth (which itself marks a gross oversight of the existence of other sexual/gender identities) immediately typecasts everything about the former as 'blue' and that of the latter as 'pink'.

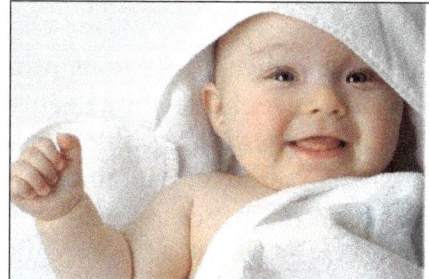 

Boys wear blue and girls wear pink.

The first picture of figure shows a baby, although it is not possible to identity whether it is a boy or a girl. The second picture of figure would immediately enable the readers to identify the baby in blue as a boy and that in pink as a girl. Gender stereotyping starts from such a mundane level indeed. Although this is nothing more than intelligent market strategy, yet through our robust acceptance and practice, we have managed to establish this gendered colour schemes as a natural desire- an obvious fact of life.

The colour-coded world of girls and boys.

Gender Stereotypes in Media

Even though the media is a very dominant dynamism of socialization, educators can have influence as to how youthful children right from the beginning visualize the gender stereotypes as propagated by television as well as advertisements in the print. As young children do not possess the clarity of thought they are essentially vulnerable to the ideas propagated by the media and fail to distinguish between the real life and the reel life. They fail to identify the manipulative ideas and notion of the media which subtly propagates gender stereotypes.

This in turn hinders the holistic development of the young individuals of society. Thus they tend to develop a misogynist outlook towards women which is often a narrow characterization based on incorrect preconceived notions.

Several studies have observed that gender stereotypes are as much part of children's animation films as much as those of the adults. Even in the Disney films and fairy tales, the popular myth which gets reiterated is that women are helpless souls who need to be rescued or they are beautiful and must be pursued by men. These stories have disturbingly high content of gender stereotypes. For example, the story of Cinderella propagates the message that if a woman is beautiful enough, she may be able to come out of her deplorable living conditions by finding a wealthy man who would fall for her beauty.

In most stories, there is an evil woman who tries to harm the godly and virtuous princess namely Ursula (The Little Mermaid), Lady Tremaine (Cinderella), Maleficent (Sleeping Beauty), the Queen (Snow White and the Seven Dwarfs) to name a few. These villainesses are seductive, self-obsessed with their own beauties, practice witchcraft and ruthlessly exploitative. Such indomitably wicked female villainesses are almost always killed by male heroes. The princes, on the other hand, are showed as rich, handsome, charming and always coming to the rescue of the fragile princesses. It is needless to mention that the age-old practices of gender stereotypes resonate through such depictions.

Messages Communicated by Few Popular Disney Princesses' Stories.

In contemporary mainstream media also, women are frequently depicted in very formulaic ways. Children are instilled with sexist concepts about conventional roles of men and women and more likely, boys are to exhibit aggressive behaviour. Through its different channels, media highlights women as sex symbols who live principally to serve men, who are extremely defenseless to protect and protest against social dogmas and are victims of sexual harassment, assault and domestic violence.

While speaking of daily soap operas, one can relate to the antiwoman sentiments present in the family setting in the structure of the narrative. The stories often center around the manifestation of recurrent adversities on women, which apparently articulates feminist concerns about patriarchal space but in actuality side-lines the realities about women on the whole. The Daily soaps provide a clear cut demarcation between 'the good woman' and the 'bad woman'. As opposed to reality, there are no mixed characters. The 'good woman' is the one who is portrayed as passive and submissive, the one who is often tormented in the hands of her in-laws but suffers in silence and never questions her miseries.

The 'bad woman' although shown as an independent woman is often demonized. She is cunning, sly, conniving and plotting against the 'good woman', thus adding onto her miseries. Such instances are so common in the television and film industry that the audience almost accepts every details shown to them without posing any challenge. In most of the Bengali television serials, women are depicted as homemakers who have or are on the verge of giving up their professions no matter how lucrative they are to fit into their familial settings. The female characters are often "side-lined, trivialized, sexualized and stereotyped and of course there exist a clear employment imbalance".

In the world of media, the perception of female characters as sex objects is nothing new. Equality has been an issue of debate ever since the media came into being. Gender bias in popular films is a common feature. While male characters have had variety of roles, their female counterpart has not much evolved. She has always and continues to play either 'femme fatale' or more often than not ' a damsel in distress' waiting for the 'hero' to rescue her. These aspects remain absent from public view.

The relentless bombarding of differentiated messages on gender has a vital unsociable effect on the youth. The media at times champions aggressive behavior against women. When society is struggling to avoid violence against women, media through its passive- aggressive messages often lead young children to believe in the reel life drama where the extreme polarization of the sexes is in vogue.

Education is the only measure which can neutralize the effect of media led gender stereotypes. If inculcated at an early age children can counteract the effect of media stereotypes. One has to make them understand that gender stereotypes is often a media construct —which does not reflect – reality. They should also be educated in the fact that media communicates through both explicit and implicit messages thus affecting their social outlook and personal values. These are vital lessons towards achieving a gender neutral society where one needs to be treated as per their intellectual merit and not discriminated against because of their gender.

The media's inclination to connect sex and viciousness is alarming. Gender neutral socialization at an early age, resolving gender conflicts at home, letting children engage in imaginative play inculcating gender neutral social values might help resolving gender bias. A few measures to neutralize the effect of gender stereotypes:

- Investigating the media in order to define how definite professions are depicted, and then questioning people from those professions to establish how accurate depictions are. Type-casts frequently limit our observations.

- Fairy tales to be re-written from the point of view of a woman where she is not playing the role of 'damsel in distress'.

- Viewing literature-based films. Comparing those films with the prevailing books to assist and examine gender roles.

- To question the existing way of portrayal of women in media and crafting games for girls and boys that is not stereotypical or violent.

Gender and Media

Media is considered as a "mirror" of modern society, In fact, it is the media which shapes our lives and perspectives. Society is influenced by media in so many ways. It is the media for the masses that helps them to get information about a lot of things and also to form opinions and make judgments regarding various issues. It is the media which keeps us updated and informed about what is happening around us and in the world. There is a need to learn to access, analyze and interpret media messages, as well as to create our own media. Thus it is important to understand the role of media in our life which begins with understanding the concept of media along with its functions, types and genres.

Media is the plural form of 'medium', understood as something in a middle position; a means of effecting or conveying something (as a channel or system of communication); a condition or environment in which something may function or flourish ('media'). The concept of media has grown enormously and the term is used in the modern sense to reference the agencies of mass communication. At one time missing, but desperately desired, the concept has become commonplace in our society. It has become so common, that in terms of communication it has become known as any tool used to store or deliver information or data, such as advertising media, electronic media, hypermedia, mass media, social media and multimedia.

Media has been defined as "means of communication designed to reach and influence very large numbers of people". Media is the communication channels through which news, entertainment, education, data or promotional messages are disseminated. Media is an umbrella term that includes all types of print, broadcast, out-of-home, and interactive communication. It includes all channels that carry brand messages. It includes newspapers, magazines, television, radio, cinema, billboards, mail, telephone, fax and now, the internet.

Thus media refers to the means of delivering and receiving data or information. In other words, media is a form of dispensing information. The term is also commonly used in place of mass media or news media. Media consists of the various means by which information reaches large numbers of people, such as television, radio, movies, newspapers, and the Internet. Mass Media has been defined as "means of communication designed to reach and influence very large numbers of people". Media are those means of communication which help:

- Transmit messages to large, heterogeneous, anonymous masses living in different regions of a locality, nation or the world.

- Transmit messages rapidly and instantaneously.

- Large group of people in different locations to receive same information in the same language, although translations of the main points can simultaneously be displayed in subscripts.

Classification of Media

The mass media comprise different kinds of communication means which is designed to reach a large audience. Mass media can be categorized according to physical form, the technology involved, nature of the communication process, etc. given below are the major categories of mass media:

- Folk Media (Puppetry, Folk Theatre, Street Theatre).

- Print (books, pamphlets, newspapers, magazines, etc.)

- Electronic (Radio, Cinema, Television).

- New Media (Internet, Mobile).

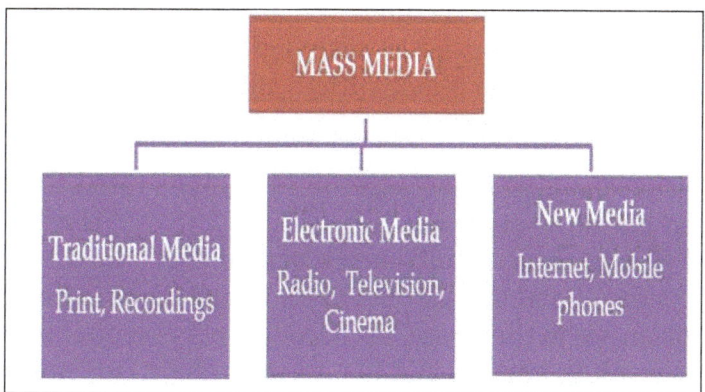

Folk Media

Folk Media or Traditional Media is an excellent tool to enhance communication and promote dialogue at the grass roots level of any society. Puppetry is a popular form of folk media that is entertaining and informative. Ancient philosophers have paid the greatest tribute to puppeteers. They have likened God Almighty to a puppeteer and the entire universe to a puppet stage.

Street Theatre is another form of traditional media which is being used widely to propagate socio political messages and to create awareness for social issues. Street plays are short, direct, loud, and over expressive since they perform in places where there are huge crowds. They are known to propagate strong message about social reforms and are considered as powerful tools to mobilize crowds towards a certain matter.

Print Media

Print media encompasses mass communication through printed material. It includes newspapers, magazines, booklets, periodicals etc. The printed word are a carrier of knowledge, information and news stories.

One of the chief characteristics of Print media is that they offer extensive news coverage and in depth treatment of themes. They provide a large variety of coverage, through different kinds of writings. The main weakness of the print media is that they can be read only by literates.

Electronic Media

Another very popular means of social interaction and propagation that has emerged along with the print media is the rise of Electronic Media. Electronic media are media that use electronics or electromechanical energy for the enduser (audience) to access the content. The birth of electronic media took place with the invention of Radio when a single voice a mile away thrilled millions across the continents who marveled at this miraculous hearing of a voice.

Radio

One of the most dramatic developments of the 20th century has been the invention of the radio waves. Radio has become a means of communication of unparalleled immediacy, intimacy and power as it is highly effective and found everywhere. Radio broadcasting in its reach, power and impact, constitutes the most significant medium of mass communication. Radio has an inherent advantage to overcome three major hurdles to meaningful communications- such as mass illiteracy, lack of efficient means to reach the remote places and poverty which prevents access to mass media.

In 1926, Scottish television pioneer John Logie Baird demonstrated the first television system since then Television has played a very important role in our lives. Television is considered one of the greatest inventions of man. It is a multi-media system predominated by the visual medium. T.V can transport the Gender and Media viewers to the actual scene of action to see things as they happen. Having a television set in the home has become very essential in today's society. We depend on it to entertain us with its sitcoms and to inform us about current world issues.

A T.V broadcast directly affects two senses simultaneously i.e those of hearing and seeing. It is more effective than radio because of its visual components which has a greater influence on the minds of the viewers.

With the help of satellite technology, T.V has reached all corners of the globe. According to Marshall Mc. Luhan the T.V has turned the world into a global village in which ideas, information and images can be exchanged with people spread all over the globe. Television is a medium of immediacy as it captures images of events as they are happening, that is why we have headlines like 'breaking news' that present events exactly as they are unfolding, hence, T.V is also called the medium of 'here and now'.

New Media

New Media is also known as new media or global media. New media are those that are recent in origin. The most important feature of the new communication technology is interactivity. While in the case of television, radio and other electronic media, communication is only a one-way process; their interactive capabilities are very limited because feedback is delayed. However, in new communication technologies we can get immediate responses and feedback because of advanced techniques of communication.

Modern media transmits signals instantly from one source to any destination in the whole globe by modern electronic technology. The new communication technologies are based on 5A'a "Anyone can transfer any information at any time at any place to anyone". The media or the global media are capable of a much higher degree of interactivity than those offered by traditional communication technology. The use of computers in one form or the other is an integral part of most of the modern communication technologies.

Effect of Media on Society

Media effects human mind and the way we behave and act in society. The degree of influence depends on the availability and pervasiveness of media. All of the traditional mass media still have great influence over our lives.

Books once were supremely influential because they came first before newspapers, magazines, radio or television. Newspapers and magazines became great influencers after they were developed. Sound recordings and film were and still are influential. Radio and then television were very influential. As the 20th century closed, TV exposed us to untold numbers of images of advertising and marketing, suffering and relief, sexuality and violence, celebrity, and much more. New and influential media-distribution channels have appeared in the 21st century. Delivered via the World Wide Web across the Internet, we are influenced daily by blogs, wikis, social networks, virtual worlds and myriad forms of content sharing.

The media permeates almost every part of our lives. Whether it's TV news, web content, books or anything in between, the information we receive from the media plays a major role in everyone's everyday life. Something this large and ubiquitous is bound to. The impact of media on the society extends to both social and political sectors. There are a variety of elements in each and media touches on both sectors and each element. Media has both positive and negative effects on society.

Positive effects of media on Society such as access to information, improved access to education, independent nature of social media, media can play a positive role in children's learning and development, it gives current news and information about what's happening in the world.

The major areas of negative effects of media are presented here: Invasion of privacy; perversion of truth by electronic trickery; violation of security (Governmental and institutional); Impact on the democratic process; Isolation of people; and Information overload.

Women in the Media

Women are also the potential victims of media's influence over society. The portrayal of women as sexual figures in popular culture is also a threat to the well-being of our society. Frequently women are depicted or portrayed in some form of sexual representation. This portrayal has created a standard for the ideal female image that women are compared to by themselves or others. Research claims that the sexualized images of women in media serve as 'models of femininity' for females, especially young girls who are still developing their sense of self. Young girls exposed to these models may face future problems in mental and sexual development. Research also links exposure to sexualized female ideals with lower self-esteem, negative mood and depressive symptoms among adolescent girls and women.

Objectification of Women in the Media

Objectification is the representation of women in media as an object rather than as a whole human entity. This happens in many contexts including advertisements and cinema. Feminist scholars say that the objectification of women involves the act of disregarding the personal and intellectual abilities and capabilities of a female; and reducing a woman's worth or role in society to that of an instrument for the sexual pleasure that she can produce in the mind of another. Media often portrays women in vulnerable and easily overpowered situations. Some images will focus only on a part of the body, a leg, a neck or a headless torso that constitutes objectification and introduces the concept of Fetishisation. It intends to reduce women to disembodied parts of their anatomy.

Gender and Print Media

Print media and electronic media continue to enjoy as widespread a reach. They also leave their impression on both general readers and policy makers. Events rather than processes make news. Most issues of special concern to women do not fit into the traditional concepts of what constitute news.

Women's empowerment should bring about a situation where women can use their fullest potential and capacity to construct a better human society for all and media has a critical role to play in responding to these processes. Media commitment and support are seen as necessary for effecting social reform and initiating various movements towards achieving a better quality of life for women.

Gender and Electronic Media

The tremendous popularity of television and its ability to reach a vast audience with illiteracy being no barrier led to the idea of using television as a channel for information on development among several governments/administrators. From the mid- seventies television began to be used to promote development oriented messages among the Indian population. But there was no exclusive focus on women's problems and their development. In the absence of a comprehensive media policy, television content emphasizing entertainment has grown to such an extent that today all television channels are oriented towards commercialization.

Gender Roles in Advertisements

Advertisements are yet another prominent and integral part of television viewing. Due to its persuasive power, advertising is the best known and most widely discussed form of promotion. Advertising persuades and motivates consumer about the advertised products, service or ideas. Advertising plays an important role in persuading the public to change their attitudes towards a product, service or idea. The constant flow of advertising images of gender, types of persons, social classes, and other groups influence our social learning process.

Men and women are portrayed in advertisements according to the constructed definition of femininity and masculinity. To be a woman is to be feminine and to be a man is to be masculine. There is little room for variation or a reversal of roles, except within the smaller frame of: niche marketing.

In the world of advertising, men and women have consistently been portrayed in stereotypical ways. Men are portrayed as more autonomous than women, with men portrayed in many different occupations as compared to women being shown as housewives and mothers. Men were far more likely to advertise vehicles, or business products, job website while women were found mostly in advertisements for domestic products. Some common sights of women as seen in advertisements show them cooking in the kitchen, washing bucketful of clothes bandaging wounds of their husbands and children. Men were far more likely to be shown outdoors or in business settings while women were shown primarily in domestic settings.

Women are alternately displayed as stay at home mothers whose only purpose in life is to please their family, ravishing sex-idols who are as objectified as they are seductive, and independent, strong-willed, intelligent go getters. Women are usually shown in advertisement of household products. They are seen washing utensils, clothes or cooking for family. In the advertisements, women are predominantly employed to promote products and services. In every item they are utilized whether it requires their presence or not. Even in masculine accessories women are presented. From these advertisements a desirable value can be discerned. Women are portrayed as sex objects who are probably cast to titillate the viewers by exposing their body parts. Women are shown wearing revealing clothes and adopt leaning and yearning postures - signs of incompleteness or lack of security. Even in commercials of the products consumed mostly by men- male perfume/deodorant, briefs, male soaps etc. women are used as models exposing their bodies.

Fair complexion, tall, slim and beautiful looking women are the ideal ones and dark complexion is propagated as a major hindrance for self-development even marriage. Utmost care is taken to manipulate the minds of young women that overweight, dark complexion are the disqualification for their self-development. Fairness cream and beauty soap, shower? promises to make their dreams come true.

Film and Gender Stereotypes

Film is the most influential medium since its invention and impact of cinema is visible in almost all culture and society. Film's role in society is not only as a medium of entertainment but also in cultural, social, political, religional, lingual and psychological levels. This makes films different from other medium of mass communication. There are enough literature which states that the film has always been a powerful medium and its portrayal of society brings out the harmonic patterns of social structure in any society. This is true especially of mainstream popular cinema which reflects the dominant culture codes that shape the sensibility of a social being. As we move on to the building of identity, Culture Studies stress the impact of these prevalent codes of behavior and social structures in every society.

The understanding of identities in films are very important as it represent the corresponding culture. The motive of filmmaker or producer can also be uncovered by observing on the identities represented on films. For example, the representation of Indian slums in the film Slumdog Millionaire had been considered as problematic. Both film critics and reviewers keep an eye on representation of identities in cinema in order to examine the achievement, distinctiveness, and quality of a film or lack of it. The identities are portrayed in films in many ways. Cultural, national, religional, regional, racial, gender and lingual are prominent ways of portraying identity. "Identities are theoretical constructions that enable us to read the world in specific ways. In them, and through them, we learn to define and reshape our values and our commitments, we give texture and form to our collective futures".

Film as a medium of great coercive power enjoys the status of being the mouthpiece to the dominant social groups and hence remains problematic as a narrative. The signification process involved in this narrative style exposes the deep structural hierarchies running through the social system. Film interpellates its heavily coded structure opens the possibility of multiple readings. Interpellation when it happens, aims at building identities by hailing the individuals towards the dominant ideologies perpetuated in a society. The understanding and studying on gender representation and portrayal in film is very crucial as it works on society on three different levels.

- The popular films which gratifies audience of all catagories intake notions of gender portrayal through the films.

- The gender portrayal in art house films takes inspiration for its subjects from real life situations and alive circumstances in the society.

- A film represents a culture or nation, thus a film becomes the media text for that particular nation which will be used for orientation for further studies.

Gender and Cinema

From its day of commencement, films were criticized and argued as dominated by male thoughts and gaze. Be it production or viewership, the pleasure of a man was considered as focal point. But these arguments were countered by films itself to an extent. "Le Voyage dans la Lune (A trip to Moon)" is a 1902 French silent film directed by Georges Méliès which is considered as the first narrative film. If we closely watch gender portrayal in this film, the story mainly revolves around male astronauts who are reaching Moon. On other hand, females were shown as passive audience who witness the departure of astronauts. But once significant findings state that the role of marines who triggers the rocket to moon is played by women's sailors. This argues that attempts were from early days to represent women in spaces.

Gender Studies in Film

The gender studies came as result of several women's liberation movements during 1960s to 1970s and it entered into the realm of film studies around same time. Huhn and Westwell in Oxford Dictionary of Film Studies notes that "gender issues have been prominent in film studies since the 1970s, when roles, image and stereotypes of women, men in films began to be seriously addressed". Since a large portion of this work was considered under the aegis of feminist politics, it viewed itself as prevalently with women. They extend the argument that "feminist work on images of women and female stereotypes quickly morphed into theorizations of women as spectacle, and the view that in classical Hollywood films the female figure on the screen is constructed pre-eminently as an object to-belooked-at". There is no surprise that gender studies is dominated by feminist studies. In any case, the questions into man and manliness, and films started in early 1980s, these drew for most part on the ideas and strategies for cultural studies. In the course of developments in the field, the gender studies in cinema carried over with other traditions of film studies like psychoanalytic film theory, poststructuralist film theory, queer theory and reception theories.

The gender studies in films are considered as important area in any film or media studies course. The need and importance of gender studies in film text can be understood from following points:

- Understanding the social development of sexual orientation and the connection amongst sex and emotional ideas, for example, part, performativity, generation, portrayal and execution.

- Information of significant history and flow in gender orientation.

- Learning of the historical transformation of gender specific portrayals on the screen.

- Learning of gender specific working conditions in films.

- Understanding the connection between sex, sexual orientation and execution, the positive as well as subversive measurements of this relationship, and its association with power connections and orders.

- Comprehension of the transaction amongst theatre and society as to the (re)presentation and (re)production of sexual orientation, sex relations and their assessment.

- The interdisciplinary way of gender studies.

Same as academics, the popular media and critics also give decent space for gender disclosures in films. Film studies scenario, it is important to understand the difference between popular commercial cinema and art house cinema. Because the representation and portrayal of various identities are socially, politically and aesthetically constructed. When art house films focussed on politically correctness of portrayals, popular masala films tried to reproduce popular belief and stereotypes of gender identities.

Judith Butler, in her work The Psychic Life of Power spoke of female experience and the oppressive patterns evolving out of the female identity as conceived and operated by the patriarchy. "Accepting identities is same as accepting dominant scripts and performing roles prescribed by them. Identities cannot be accurate representation of real self, when interpellation happens by hegemonic structures, people respond to it, especially oppressed ones perhaps because it recognizes them as a group". Butler's concept of performativity elucidates the identity conceptualized, created and perpetuated by society. Performativity is not a singular act but a repetition and a ritual which achieves its effects through its naturalization in the context of the body understood in part as a culturally sustained temporal duration.

Women Portrayal in Cinema

The works of feminist film theoretician Claire Johnston is considered as an important work in studying women in cinema. She remarked that "despite the enormous emphasis placed on woman as spectacle in the cinema, woman as woman is largely absent". The critics feel that the true representation of women in film will be sensed when the film is made from subjectivity of a woman. Laura Mulvey is another important figure in feminist film studies whose works are popular in contemporary film studies. Her work concentrated in female image, mage gaze and complex understanding of cinema as a social technology of gender.

There were only very few women film directors in early stage of film who sustained with critical and reflexive accounts on women portrayal. Dorothy Arzner was an early American film director who made her films like Fashions for Women, Sarah and Son, Working Girls, The Bride Wore Red, Dance, Girl, Dance. Fatma Begum was the first Indian women director who made her films during silent and talkie era. Her films notable were Bulbul-e-Paristan and Goddess of Luck. She also established Victoria-Fatma Films in the times when the film production were owned by male dominant studio system.

The mainstream films or conventional films are considered as male oriented where female is represented through male gaze. This tradition is visible in any mainstream film of world cinema. The Hollywood started a tradition of hero centric film formula where a man controls the plot and heroine is just placed with the hero for his narrative and voyeuristic enjoyment of the female object of the gaze. With rare occurence, the mainstream cinema continued with its formula where they generated popularity and economic profits.

The experimental cinematic tradition Avant-garde in 1970s brought changes in gender roles and representation in world cinema. Its reflection was also found in Indian parallel film movement. The creative liberation from studio and big production house gave film writers and directors to pave their camera to true vision of social structures. The women characters were given freedom and space to perform rather than skin show.

Films like Breakfast at Tiffany's, Flashdance, and The Sound of Music had strong and appropriate women rendering. The shift from realistic women characters in male dominant films to women centric films also became popular after these movements. The Indian mainstream film tradition of women portrayal also followed the classical Hollywood placing women in objectified version. The efforts from Satyajit Ray and other pioneers of Indian parallel film moment portrayed women as they were. This is not to say that women got much importance or came center of focus but women portrayal found meaningful outcomes.

Video Games and Women Characters

The story of the development of video games is as interesting as some of the most popular video games themselves are. A brief account is necessary to have a better perspective for the issues discussed. Video games began their journey in the post-war years in the science laboratories of leading academic institutions in Europe and America like the Cambridge University and the Massachusetts Institute of Technology. The early games were in the form of simple simulations on analogue machines that were based on the technology developed during the Second World War. Not surprisingly the credit for designing arguably the first interactive video game, Tennis for Two, goes to William Alfred Higinbotham, American physicist, who also helped build the first atomic bomb.

None of these early video games were sold to the public because of their huge sizes and high cost. It was not before the 1970s that video games started to be produced commercially and attained a popular status in the form of what were called arcade games. From amusement arcades and other public places the video game entered into the homes of people in 1972 as Odyssey, the first commercial home game console. By the late 1970s several companies like Magnavox, Atari, Coleco had ventured into the US video game market and launched gaming consoles one after the other. By early 1980s, the American market was flooded with home gaming consoles.

A coin operated arcade machine for Nintendo's Donkey Kong game.

In 1981 Japanese company Nintendo released the game Donkey Kong that eventually evolved into the iconic arcade game Mario Bros. It was one of the earliest games to have a storyline. The saturation of the video games market led the market to crash in 1983. Atari and other gaming companies suffered huge losses. The slump prevailed for almost two years before Nintendo made waves in UK and USA with its Nintendo Entertainment System (NES) that was launched in 1985.

Gaming consoles based on optical drives entered the markets in 1995. With the internet becoming popular and cheaper towards the end of the millennium, companies started shipping gaming systems with inbuilt modems. First console based massively multiplayer online game was released in the year 2000. In terms of superior graphics and immersive game-playing experience, video games had come a long way from their pixelated past.

Father of Video Games

Ralph Baer with a prototype of his console Brown Box in 2009.

For his diverse and significant contributions that helped establish the video game industry and culture, engineer Ralph Baer is called the father of video games. In 1967 he demonstrated the fully functional ping-pong game that went on to become one of the most iconic games of the arcade age. Two years later, he developed the Brown Box, the first video games console that allowed the users to attach it with television. In 1972, home gaming console Odyssey designed by Baer was released by Magnavox.

Why Study Video Games

Video games had already established themselves as part of the popular culture in the 1980s. Ever since, scholars have tried to understand video games variously as extension of traditional games, or even of toys, which are understood to be cultural artifacts that represent and shape popular consciousness. Further, due to the fact that video games incorporated myriad technologies during the course of its development, its historic study often overlaps with studies of films, television, computers, graphic design, and human-machine interaction.

In a recent study researchers contended that "[Video] games are significant part of contemporary culture; as part of our culture, they are a part of what makes us human, and by learning from them, we can better understand ourselves." They further describe how video games were significant as history, property, products of design process, an art form, and a source of joy.

Recognising the cultural and historical significance of video games, a consortium made up of the Stanford University, the University of Maryland and the University of Illinois submitted a proposal to The United States Library of Congress in 2006 for preserving and studying video games as cultural artifacts.

Subsequently, a committee consisting of Henry Lowood, curator of the History of Science and Technology Collections at Stanford University and three other members announced a game canon, a list of 10 video games that they considered to be the most important of all time.

Sl. No.	Game	Year	Importance
1.	Spacewar!	1962	First multiplayer, competitive game, and the first action game.
2.	Star Raiders	1979	Established many of the conventions of the first-person space simulator genre.
3.	Zork	1980	Introduced adventure game.
4.	Tetris	1985	Influenced generations of puzzle games.
5.	SimCity	1989	Helped establish the genre known as god games.
6.	Super Mario Bros. 3	1990	Nonlinear play.
7.	Civilization I/II	1991	Turn-based strategy game.
8.	Doom	1993	Popularised and highly influenced the first-person shooter games genre, pioneered 3d game worlds and networked multiplayer.
9.	Warcraft series	beginning 1994	Introduced real-time strategy overlaid on a narrative.
10.	Sensible World of Soccer	1994	Inspired the genre of sports games.

However, with its strands attached to the traditional forms of entertainment and media, video games also inherited some of their long criticised aspects. The video games continued the replication of racial and gender stereotypes as other forms of media had been doing. Again, as with the development of any new form of media, there has been a section of the public who see video games as inherently evil, having tremendously bad impact on its users.

Books and articles based on studies about the impact of video games had started appearing as early as the first half of the 80s. In order to understand videogames, academicians have predominantly taken the conventional approach of analysing storytelling devices like in the case of dramas and narratives.

More recently, an emerging school of video game theorists have argued that the nature and structure of video games is radically different from earlier objects of study (like books, newspapers, magazines, drama, films, or television). This makes existing approaches (most arguably the above mentioned storytelling model or Narratology) unsuitable to explain everything that constitutes the video game and the playing experience. This school of thought that calls for a novel approach treating games more as abstract rule based systems than as narratives has come to be known as Ludology.

Ludology can be defined as a discipline that studies games in general and video games in particular. Its proponents, Ludologists, while not rejecting the narrative aspect of video games, claim that unlike drama and stories (as in short stories and novels) video games are not held together by a narrative structure.

As a discipline still in its infancy its proponents are still working to develop a domain and answer questions like how to study video games. Ludology does not disdain this dimension of video games but claims that they are not held together by a narrative structure.

The difference of video games from other traditional forms of media stems from the fact that video games are not just based on narrative and representation but on an 'alternative semiotical structure known as simulation'. Traditional media are representational, not simulational and games are just a particular way of structuring simulation, just like narrative is a form of structuring representation.

Besides, being an interactive medium, video games allows the players not only to see events but to actually choose to actively participate in the events. As such, representation and treatment of any character in general and female characters in particular takes on a whole new meaning. The players no longer remain the spectator of objectification of female characters and the consequential violence against them but are given the freedom to perform dehumanising acts that are often incentivised in many popular games. In the light of the immersive and interactive nature of video games, it is pertinent to study their role in dehumanising women and perpetuating the dominance of heterosexual male.

Video Games as New Media

As a medium of mass consumption that emerged in the 1970s video games as we know today is still in its infancy. Starting with entertainment as their sole function, video games have increasingly been used to serve several diverse functions owing to its versatility, inclusivity and customisability. As a form of new media, video games are finding application in political and social activism, scientific experiments, medical applications, marketing, education, and military training, among others.

With online streaming of video gameplay competitions attracting millions of viewers, both males and females, big corporations not linked directly to the industry have also started taking interest in the popularisation of these events recognising it as a significant online media force.

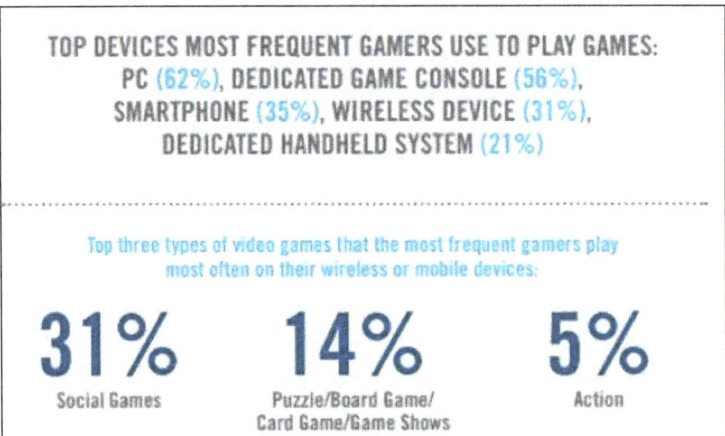

Over the last couple of years the exclusive place once enjoyed by dedicated gaming consoles has been challenged as young gamers increasingly opt for smartphones and tablets as their preferred gaming platform. These mediums come with the added perk of large number of freely available games.

Women in Video Game Design Industry

Video games development took a leap in the 1980s with the arcade culture and then with the onset of home computers. The early creators of the games hailed from the traditionally male dominated areas of computer science and engineering. This in part explained the dearth of women in these fields of study. To this date, reports by several industry bodies have found that the percentage of women in the industry is small. Their presence at positions of power is more dismal. The recruiters often blame it on the low and declining number of women taking up engineering and computer science courses. Women have spoken about the presence of glass ceiling in the industry as in most other areas.

It is also observed that majority of women in the industry are employed in the public relations and marketing rather than the design and development – where the actual content generation takes place. As the fastest growing consumer segment of video-games, women constitute close to 50 per cent of the total number of gamers in major markets including the UK and the USA. This scenario has brought in a need for gaming companies to think afresh about the content of video games. This includes fair representation of females in the games. In order to be just to the need, companies realise the need to bring in female viewpoint into the content. Recruiting more female developers is considered to be one measure in that direction.

Representation of Women in Video Games

Video games, like any other visual media, act as cultural sites that construct and reinforce traditionally established and socially prescribed gender norms and behaviour. Right from the formative days of video games in the 1970s, gaming companies have been accused of catering almost exclusively to the stereotypical heterosexual male gamer. This is reflected in the content as well as the marketing campaigns that target only the male gamers. Even in games targeted to female players, gaming companies base the representation and gender roles based on stereotypical notions of femininity. Mattel's Barbie games are a good example of this approach.

Content laden with both subtle and overt sexism have existed in video games ever since the nascent years. To this day, most of the top-selling videogames are found to carry mature content, intense violence, sexual imagery and degrading depiction of women. Very few of the top-selling video games feature females as the main character. And more often than not, female characters are hyper-sexualised.

Nintendo's 1981 release Donkey Kong was the first game with a storyline. The reason we evoke the game in this section again is that besides being the earliest video game to have a storyline it also pioneered the use of the classical sexist 'damsel in distress' theme or trope. Since then the trope has been used in innumerable video games of almost every genre.

Feminist media critic Anita Sarkeesian defines the damsel in distress trope thus: "As a trope the 'damsel in distress' is a plot device in which a female character is placed in a perilous situation from which she cannot escape on her own and must be rescued by a male character, usually providing a core incentive or motivation for the protagonist's quest.": She asserts that the trope objectified the women by portraying them as passive disempowered victim, the distressed damsel who is 'reduced to a prize to be won, a treasure to be found or a goal to be achieved.'

Criticism of sexism in video games is not new to the industry. In 1983 a company called Mystique released Custer's Revenge that went on to become one of the most despised games of all times for being misogynistic, pornographic and racist at the same time. The game sparked protests by women and Native Indian organisations across America. Consisting of crude pixelated graphics, the game required the player to assume the role of General Custer who is featured naked. He dodges arrows to get to a Native American woman who is tied naked to a pole in the desert. Women against pornography criticised the manufacturers for making "rape a game." The then president of the New York unit of National Organisation for Women, Denise Fuge, remarked that sexist video games pushed teenage boys closer to our culture's acceptance of recreational violence against women.

Activity

Flyers published in 1981 for the promotion of Video Game Donkey Kong.

Analyse the flyers of the popular video game Donkey Kong released in 1981 and study the roles attributed to the male and the female characters of the game. Take into account the imagery as well as the words.

Feminist critics of video games often point out towards the representation of women as 'background decoration'. This representation is a 'subset of largely insignificant non-playable female characters whose sexuality or victimhood is exploited as a way to infuse edgy, gritty or racy flavouring in game worlds. These sexually objectified female bodies are designed to function as environmental texture while titillating presumed straight male players."

Of late, accused of catering only to predominantly male gamers, game developing companies have started offering option for the players to customize the protagonist as male or female. It is interesting to note that in academic as well as industry sponsored studies it has been found that given the choice, a significant proportion of male gamers often choose to play as a female character. Released in 1996, action genre game Tomb Raider broke from the traditional depiction of female characters as passive or secondary by featuring an active female heroine. The game and characterisation of its protagonist Lara Croft had critics and academics debating over her possibly being a role model. Among the players, the game received unprecedented response from both males and females.

The game and its female central character defied the typical norms of video games on several counts. In Lara Croft the players got a strong female lead who rejects norms of femininity and breaks the patriarchal values while overcoming dangers and hurdles in 'masculine' spaces in a genre that is typically male-dominated. In another positive departure, the storyline is devoid of any romantic subplot. The makers of the game were successful in providing the increasing number of female gamers in the 1990s with a character they could identify with. However, as critics would point out, the character of Lara Croft was coded with markers that strengthen the conventional stereotyping of the female body as an 'eroticized object of the male gaze and the fetishistic and scopophilic pleasures which this provides for the male viewer.' In an obvious bid to appeal to their primary market of male gamers, the creators of Lara Croft give her the typical sexualised female body with accentuated curves and provocative form-fitting clothes.

Jade, the protagonist of the 2003 action adventure game Beyond Good & Evil, is one of the very few relatable positive female character in a video game that have been critically acclaimed for her realistic portrayal.

Female Video Game Players

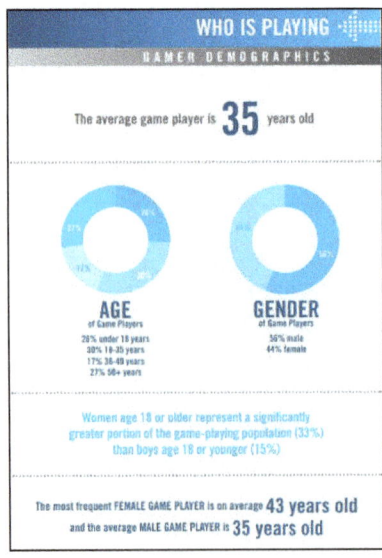

Ever since the video games became a cultural phenomenon in the 1980s, several scholars have conducted studies to ascertain if there was any relation of gender with gaming behaviour. These studies have established gender differences ranging from time spent playing video games to game preferences.

It is largely held that in general females spent less time playing video games. Consistent findings from several research studies verified the assumption as true. The situation saw little change over the course of initial decades of development of video games. The reasons for this include the embedded masculinity within the game structure as well as the male dominated physical contexts in which games were played.

Female gamers often describe their experience of playing video games as if they were treading a male-created virtual space. Analysts have found that most of the times both male and female characters in video games cater to the fantasies of the male gamers. While in the case of male characters it is what the male players want to be and in the case of female characters it is how they want the female body to be.

For example, many of them showed that males played violent video games more frequently than females. The underlying reasons pointed out by these studies differ from as simple as late entry of girls into gameplay to complex psychosocial factors like negotiations between societal expectations and personal ambitions.

Gender and Psychology

Gender is a social and cultural construct. The basic difference between sex and gender, is that while sex is a biological construct which is identified immediately after birth, gender involves the construction of biological sex into a social form. The biological sex includes external organs, chromosomes, hormones and other secondary sexual characteristics. The physical and sexual characteristics make for the identification of male and female sex. Biological and physical conditions thus determine the sex of a person as male or female whereas, the main assumptions of the Gender system are based on social and cultural perceptions of masculinity and feminine traits.

It takes Biological identifiers (physical/sexual differences of male & female) as the criterion for male & female characters, roles and duties, access to resources i.e. determinants of power & position. Gender is learnt through a process of socialization and through the process of acculturation in a particular community/society. Though there can be minor differences in gender ideology among different societies/communities, but broadly speaking they all are marked by inequality and power relations. Within the patriarchal system, Institutions such as family, community, society, religion, mass media etc. all promote the socially accepted gender differentials.

Across cultures and societies there are various norms, beliefs and practices associated with the male and female sex. Different cultures approve or disapprove certain sets of behavior for the male and female sexes. The socially determined differences of male and female sexes are actually the accepted concepts of gender in any society. Gender can be considered as social codes, attributes and opportunities associated with the male and female sex. These social codes and attributes are also the reflection of masculine and feminine behavior. In any culture, people are prescribed distinct codes of masculine and feminine qualities which they are expected to fulfil. Masculinity and Femininity are socially produced but embodied ways of being male and female.

Construction of Gender

One of the important aspects of any societal process is socialization. Gender, as has been just explained, like all social identities, is socially constructed. A general definition of socialization makes us understand it as one of the processes in which culture is transmitted and how human beings in a society are adapted into that organized life. It is a fundamental sociological concept which prepares individuals to live a social life as per the societal norms and expectations. In the very broadest terms, we can say that socialization in any society changes human beings from animals into social actors which includes the learning of knowledge, skills, motivations, and identities that make our genetic potentials interact with our social environments.

The specific content of the socialization, its learning, depends on the place, situation, and context and varies as per the social class, caste, religion etc. Socialization also plays a very important role in development of gender identity and 'doing gender'. Gender norms, i.e. the socially acceptable ways of acting out gender, are learned from birth through childhood socialization. We learn what is expected of our gender from what our parents teach us, as well as what we pick up at school, through religious or cultural teachings, in the media, and various other social institutions and thus one can say that gender experiences will evolve over a person's lifetime and is therefore always in flux. We see this through generational and intergenerational changes within families, as social, legal and technological changes keep influencing social values on gender.

The prevailing notions of gender identities like masculinity and femininity, the essential norms, expectations and behavior considered to be appropriate for the sexes are taught and learnt through the process of socialization. This learning process also includes rewards and punishment to support or criticize a particular behavior and enhancing the practice of appropriate behavior. The process begins in infancy and the basic assumptions of those roles and duties are linked to the social systems which are played by all the different agencies within the social system like family, school, communications, media, peer group etc. The socializing agencies constantly convey consistent messages about masculine and feminine roles within that particular social system. These normative behaviors within the social system create roles of males and females of that society.

As we have discussed that gender roles are taught, learnt and reinforced within the complex socialization process of each society, one can say that "People are born male or female but learn to be Girls or Boys. During the socialization process they are gradually taught about the appropriate behavior, attitudes, roles and activities for them and how they should enact their roles in society. This learned behavior is what makes up gender identity and further determines gender roles.

In the majority of societies, women need to follow the stereotyped feminine roles of Mother, Daughter, Sister and Wife and develop suitable temperamental characteristics like being subordinate to the male sex, nurturing ,committed to are to family and domestic work, having poor self-esteem, restricted mobility, suitable dress codes, lower level of educational opportunities, health and nutritional aspects. In human society the family is the primary provider for its members, including the basic needs of the children in it. Human society also has various social norms, rules, regulations, values, taboos as also social institutions like, marriage, family, and religion. The child has to learn and adopt the social and the family norms to become a full fledged member. This learning – teaching process happens in very non-formal way within the family and society in the day to day life of all children. They are taught and prepared for their future roles and duties according to the gender perception of each society.

From the formative years – early childhood, childhood, adolescent till adult phase the socialization process continues so that they can perform effectively in their socially assigned roles and duties with appropriate behavior, dress, temperament, attitude as also with skilled management and productive work. Whenever needed there are provisions for reward and punishment as prescribed in the society. This total process is technically called "Socialization Process" for building Gender Identity (Man & Woman) as per particular societal norms. By this informal system of teaching and learning one can say that a biological female turns into a woman and a biological males turns into a Man. Along with family other societal members like distant relations, Peer group members, Political and Religious leaders, folk media etc all contribute in the formation of gender Identity, as also moral values, faith, taboo etc. are imparted.

One of the important issues in understanding gender has been historically linked to discussion related to inequality and discrimination among males and females. Various literature in psychology, sociology & anthropology indicates the discriminatory practices in societies in gender relations and females vs males roles. The theories related to feminist theories are deeply linked to patriarchal structures. The on-going discussion will see how in different behavioural sciences like Psychology, Sociology & Anthropology correlates with gender aspects.

Psychologists use human behaviour as their main data source and examine how the human mind functions. It is virtually impossible for an individual to read his/her own mind and thus, the mind is not readable directly. Indeed, our actions, feelings and thoughts are influenced by the functioning of our minds and that is why psychologists use human behaviour as the primary data for testing various psychological theories on how the mind functions. Thus, psychologists study human behaviour. Some psychologists would interpret 'behaviour' to mean both overt responses and conscious experience, that is, actions and thoughts or feelings; while others would be more restrictive, omitting thoughts and feelings because they cannot be observed directly. Similarly, some psychologists include the behaviour of other species, while some are concerned only with human behaviour. As a whole, psychology, as an integral part of the behavioural science, seeks to understand the physiological, emotional, and mental processes that drive and influence human behaviour.

Psychologists when they look into the issues related to gender are actually going into the details of the development of male and female psychology which results in human action. Deep seated reasons for acquisition of male and female roles in society and understanding the mental processes, emotions, motivational factors of individuals are some of key areas where psychologists work in understanding of gender. The psychological aspects of gender also look into intra- psychic processes surrounding gender development, cognitive construction of gender conception, styles of behavior in family transmission of roles. The psychoanalytical theories on gender basically treat gender development primarily as a phenomenon of early childhood and cognitive theories emphasizes the role of the thinking process and making sense of information about gender. The gender schema theory reflects first the formation of basic gender identity and development of gender schemas which are based on a child's interaction and observation of his/her environment.

Sociology and Gender

The study of the subject of sociology has considerably gained its space in the academic world as it deals with various social problems, social relationships and social interactions. Prior to the emergence of sociology in the 19th century, the study of society was carried on in an unscientific manner and society had never been considered as the central focus of any scientific study. It is through the study of sociology that the scientific study of society has been possible. Thus, sociology is a study of human society and more specifically, it is a systematic study of social behaviour and human groups. It seeks to provide an analysis of human society and culture with sociological perspectives and also analyses the factors and forces underlying historical transformations of society. The discipline has developed extensively its own methodology, scope and approach. While understanding social problems, and interactions in society, sociologists have frequently come across the gender domains i.e. to understand and classify the concepts in comparison to males and females. This has led to the understanding of gender discrimination and inequalities, values assigned by society in male female roles.

The major focus of Sociology is on the study of primary units of social life. In this area, it is concerned with social facts and social relationships, individual personality, groups of all varieties, communities, associations, organizations and population. It is also concerned with the development, structure and function of a wide variety of basic social institutions such as the family and kinship, religious, economic, political, legal, educational, scientific, recreational, welfare, aesthetic and expressive institutions. While understanding the social groups and institutions it is interesting for a sociologist to understand the perspective from a gender point of view. Within different communities, groups, classes, strata and castes, the socialization of males and females are different and thus gender roles are also identified in a varied manner.

The subject extensively focuses on the influence of social relationships upon people's attitudes and behaviour and on how societies are established and change. As a field of study, sociology deals with all the social issues including families, associations, communities, gangs, business firms, computer networks, political parties, schools, religions, and labour unions and so on. It is also concerned with various important dimensions like poverty, discrimination, health, alienation, over population, education etc. Gender remains a cross cutting in these fields and it is interesting for a sociologist to interpret the data on genders and understand the comparative figures.

Sociology also tries to understand the gender dimension per se i.e. how in one type of society the picture of male and female differs. It also looks into the complexities of social institutions, factors and its correlation with the gender inequality and discrimination process. The subject sees how in different caste, class, race ethnic groups categorises how the male and female sex is transformed into the masculine and feminine identities. It correlates how societal factors are responsible for shaping gender roles and how these become acceptable in society. It would be of interest to sociologists to understand how gender construction and development varies across societies and which societal factors are influential in shaping gender roles. The differences in various subgroups of society also take us into the deep understanding of the causative factors of gender differences. Understanding of this also help us to explain gender inequalities and discrimination.

Anthropology and Gender

Anthropology is the study of man from every aspect. However, a major aspect of the discipline deals with human behaviour. It explores human from wide ranges – from the study of culture and social relations, to human biology and evolution, to languages, to music, art and architecture, and to vestiges of human habitation. As a holistic discipline, anthropology delves deep into the matter related to human behaviour and considers questions like how peoples' behaviour changes over time, how people move about the world, how the human species has evolved over millions of years, and how individuals understand and operate successfully in distinct cultural settings, etc. Anthropology includes four broad fields—social-cultural anthropology, linguistics, physical anthropology and archaeology. Each of the four fields teaches distinctive skills, such as applying theories, employing research methodologies, formulating and testing hypotheses, and developing extensive sets of data. Over the years, these four fields have developed many subfields that cater to the challenges of modernization, globalization and the impact of technology, etc. Among scholarly disciplines, anthropology stands out as the discipline that provides the cross-cultural test.

When anthropology looks into gender it gives a huge emphasis to the culture constructs and how the male and female sex is categorized. Comparison with other cultural setting gives an understanding of masculinity and femininity across the cultures. While undertaking studies anthropologists depend heavily on ethnographic studies, participant observation and holistic approaches. While studying the ethnographies anthropologists have documented male female roles in various cultural settings. Understanding kinship patters in culture is yet another important area of anthropological investigation where detailed family relationships can be understood and role of males and females are highlighted in that. Some of the important issues where the understanding of gender was conceptualised in anthropology were marriage and family patterns and practices in various rituals.

If an anthropologist has to understand some of the gender issues like domestic violence she would try to understand its evolutionary aspects and the causes of such issues. She will investigate how societies in the primitive times looked at domestic violence, from when it started getting prominence in society and how the whole issue has changed over the years.

Correlation of Gender, Psychology, Sociology and Anthropology

All the three subjects are important in understanding the behavioural aspects of human beings. The subjects are correlated. However they use different research methodologies to understand the behavioural aspects of human beings. In the context of gender all three disciplines have developed the theoretical dimensions and have been using them to understand the problems and issues of gender.

Psychology focuses more on individual behaviour, personality traits, mental processes, perceptions etc. while Sociology focuses more on group behaviour and societal institutions. The behavioural aspects from the psychological point of view focus more on a person's emotional and cognitive states and its psychological influence on behaviour and the person's inner experience. Sociology would closely look at behavioural aspects from the point of view of societal institutions, cultures, traditions, beliefs, practices etc. in shaping human societies. Social Psychology would also link the role of society in shaping individual behaviour. Anthropology relies heavily on culture, customs, and traditions and tries to understand the why's of human activities and actions. All three subjects would apply their fundamental principles in understanding gender.

Let's try to understand any issue related to gender in context of three subjects. An issue like domestic violence is something which involves the pattern of behavior on violence or other abuse by one person against another in a domestic setting, such as in marriage or cohabitation, intimate partner violence by a spouse or partner in an intimate relationship against the other spouse or partner. Domestic violence affects men, women and children though a wife or female partner is more commonly the victim of such abuse. The subject of psychology would try to understand the domestic violence by understanding the perception on violence, the thought process of the violent partner which is usually a destructive one, personality traits of individuals, negative thoughts which usually surround around such feelings like "She/he is controlling you. Don't let her/him act like you are weak." She/he is making fun of you. Who does she/he think she/he is? "How dare he/she treat you this way! If he/she really loved you he/she would".

Sociology, in such a matter, would categorize the information according to social strata, community background, understanding the marriage pattern, societal influence, socialization process and how in a particular society the gender roles are perceived i.e. male to be supreme and female subordinate and to be suppressed. The role of important social institutions in developing the perception in a society as well at individual mind would be correlated. Similarly, when an anthropologist looks into the above subject, she would also look into how the domestic violence was perceived in primitive communities and how over a period of time these social institutions change. She will delve into how, in a primitive society this kind of violence was existing, its different forms and will try to see the evolutionary mechanism of this social practice. This would help in understanding how any social practice evolves, changes over a period of time and how human beings become adaptable to such practices.

On the whole we can see that if one has to understand the problem of domestic violence holistically and in order to have a complete understanding, one may try to merge the research outcomes in a particular topic from all three subjects. Gender is a subject which has numerous dimensions and the Psychological, Sociological and Anthropological aspects are crucial in its understanding.

References

- Gender-representation-and-media-52988: ac.in, Retrieved 17, June 2020

- Gender-and-disability-58094: ac.in, Retrieved 26, February 2020

- Gender-and-media-61300: ac.in, Retrieved 02, May 2020

Theories in Gender Studies

There are numerous theories which are studied under the discipline of gender studies. A few of such theories are psychoanalytic theory, sexism, sexual identity models and Hagan's power control theory. This chapter closely examines these key theories related to gender studies to provide an extensive understanding of the subject.

Psychoanalytic Theory

Psychoanalysis is a type of therapy that aims to release pent-up or repressed emotions and memories in or to lead the client to catharsis, or healing. In other words, the goal of psychoanalysis is to bring what exists at the unconscious or subconscious level up to consciousness. This goal is accomplished through talking to another person about the big questions in life, the things that matter, and diving into the complexities that lie beneath the simple-seeming surface.

Concepts of Sigmund Freud

It's very likely you've heard of the influential but controversial founder of psychoanalysis: Sigmund Freud. Freud was born in Austria and spent most of his childhood and adult life in Vienna. He entered medical school and trained to become a neurologist, earning a medical degree in 1881.

Soon after his graduation, he set up a private practice and began treating patients with psychological disorders. His attention was captured by a colleague's intriguing experience with a patient; the colleague was Dr. Josef Breuer and his patient was the famous "Anna O.," who suffered from physical symptoms with no apparent physical cause.

Dr. Breuer found that her symptoms abated when he helped her recover memories of traumatic experiences that she had repressed, or hidden from her conscious mind. This case sparked

Freud's interest in the unconscious mind and spurred the development of some of his most influential ideas.

Models of the Mind

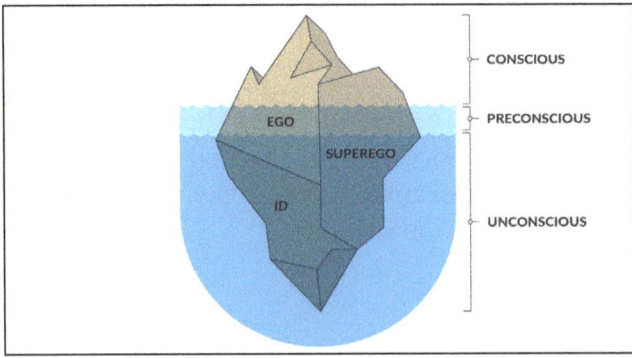

Perhaps the most impactful idea put forth by Freud was his model of the human mind. His model divides the mind into three layers, or regions:

- Conscious: This is where our current thoughts, feelings, and focus live.

- Preconscious (sometimes called the subconscious): This is the home of everything we can recall or retrieve from our memory.

- Unconscious: At the deepest level of our minds resides a repository of the processes that drive our behavior, including primitive and instinctual desires.

Later, Freud posited a more structured model of the mind, one that can coexist with his original ideas about consciousness and unconsciousness.

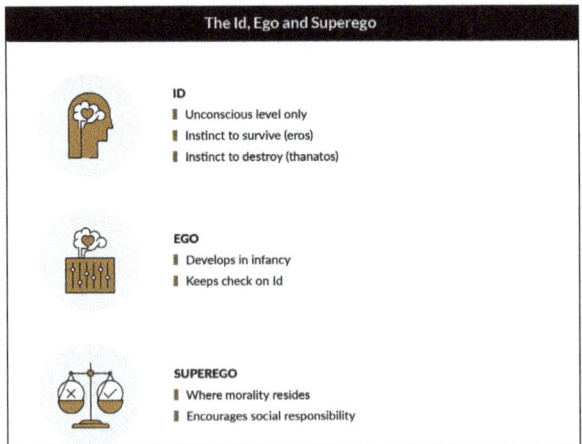

In this model, there are three metaphorical parts to the mind:

- Id: The id operates at an unconscious level and focuses solely on instinctual drives and desires. Two biological instincts make up the id, according to Freud: eros, or the instinct to survive that drives us to engage in life-sustaining activities, and thanatos, or the death instinct that drives destructive, aggressive, and violent behavior.

- Ego: The ego acts as both a conduit for and a check on the id, working to meet the id's needs in a socially appropriate way. It is the most tied to reality and begins to develop in infancy.

- Superego: The superego is the portion of the mind in which morality and higher principles reside, encouraging us to act in socially and morally acceptable ways.

The image above offers a context of this "iceberg" model wherein much of our mind exists in the realm of the unconscious impulses and drives. If you've ever read the book "Lord of the Flies" by William Golding, then you have enjoyed the allegory of Freud's mind as personified by Jack as the Id, Piggy as the ego, and Ralph as the superego.

Defense Mechanisms

Freud believed these three parts of the mind are in constant conflict because each part has a different primary goal. Sometimes, when the conflict is too much for a person to handle, his or her ego may engage in one or many defense mechanisms to protect the individual. These defense mechanisms include:

- Repression: The ego pushes disturbing or threatening thoughts out of one's consciousness.

- Denial: The ego blocks upsetting or overwhelming experiences from awareness, causing the individual to refuse to acknowledge or believe what is happening.

- Projection: The ego attempts to solve discomfort by attributing the individual's unacceptable thoughts, feelings, and motives to another person.

- Displacement: The individual satisfies an impulse by acting on a substitute object or person in a socially unacceptable way (e.g., releasing frustration directed toward your boss on your spouse instead).

- Regression: As a defense mechanism, the individual moves backward in development in order to cope with stress (e.g., an overwhelmed adult acting like a child).

- Sublimation: Similar to displacement, this defense mechanism involves satisfying an impulse by acting on a substitute but in a socially acceptable way (e.g., channeling energy into work or a constructive hobby).

The five Psychosexual Stages of Development

Finally, one of the most enduring concepts associated with Freud is his psychosexual stages. Freud proposed that children develop in five distinct stages, each focused on a different source of pleasure:

- First Stage: Oral – The child seeks pleasure from the mouth (e.g. sucking).

- Second Stage: Anal – The child seeks pleasure from the anus (e.g. withholding and expelling feces).

- Third Stage: Phallic – The child seeks pleasure from the penis or clitoris (e.g. masturbation).

- Fourth Stage: Latent – The child has little or no sexual motivation.

- Fifth Stage: Genital – The child seeks pleasure from the penis or vagina.

Freud hypothesized that an individual must successfully complete each stage to become a psychologically healthy adult with a fully formed ego and superego. Otherwise, individuals may become stuck or "fixated" in a particular stage, causing emotional and behavioral problems in adulthood.

The Interpretation of Dreams

Another well-known concept from Freud was his belief in the significance of dreams. He believed that analyzing one's dreams can give valuable insight into the unconscious mind. In 1900, Freud published the book "The Interpretation of Dreams" in which he outlined his hypothesis that the primary purpose of dreams was to provide individuals with wish fulfillment, allowing them to work through some of their repressed issues in a situation free from consciousness and the constraints of reality.

In this book, he also distinguished between the manifest content (the actual dream) and the latent content (the true or hidden meaning behind the dream). The purpose of dreams is to translate forbidden wishes and taboo desires into a non-threatening form through condensation (the joining of two or more ideas), displacement (transformation of the person or object we are concerned about into something or someone else), and secondary elaboration (the unconscious process of turning the wish-fulfillment images or events into a logical narrative).

Freud's ideas about dreams were game-changing. Before Freud, dreams were considered insignificant and insensible ramblings of the mind at rest. His book provoked a new level of interest in dreams, an interest that continues to this day.

Jungian Psychology: Carl Jung

Freud's work was continued, although in altered form, by his student Carl Jung, whose particular brand of psychology is known as analytical psychology. Jung's work formed the basis for most modern psychological theories and concepts.

Jung and Freud shared an interest in the unconscious and worked together in their early days, but a few key disagreements ended their partnership and allowed Jung to fully devote his attention to his new psychoanalytic theory. The three main differences between Freudian psychology and Jungian (or analytical) psychology is related to:

- Nature and Purpose of the Libido: Jung saw libido as a general source of psychic energy that motivated a wide range of human behaviors—from sex to spirituality to creativity—while Freud saw it as psychic energy that drives only sexual gratification.

- Nature of the Unconscious: While Freud viewed the unconscious as a storehouse for an individual's socially unacceptable repressed desires, Jung believed it was more of a storehouse for the individual's repressed memories and what he called the collective or transpersonal unconscious (a level of unconscious shared with other humans that is made up of latent memories from our ancestors).

- Causes of Behavior: Freud saw our behavior as being caused solely by past experiences, most notably those from childhood, while Jung believed our future aspirations have a significant impact on our behavior as well.

Lacanian Psychoanalysis: Jacques Lacan

In the mid to late 1900s, the French psychoanalyst Jacques Lacan called for a return to Freud's work, but with a renewed focus on the unconscious and greater attention paid to language.

Lacan drew heavily from his knowledge of linguistics and believed that language was a much more important piece of the developmental puzzle than Freud assumed. There are three key concepts of Lacanian psychoanalysis that set it apart from Freud's original talk therapy:

- The Real,

- Symbolic Order,

- Mirror Stage.

The Real

While Freud saw the symbolic as being indicative of a person's unconscious mind, particularly in dreams, Lacan theorized that "the real" is actually the most foundational level of the human mind. According to Lacan, we exist in "the real" and experience anxiety because we cannot control it.

Unlike the symbolic, which Freud proposed could be accessed through psychoanalysis, the real cannot be accessed. Once we learn and understand language, we are severed completely from the real. He describes it as the state of nature, in which there exists nothing but a need for food, sex, safety, etc.

Symbolic Order

Lacan's symbolic order is one of three orders that concepts, ideas, thoughts, and feelings can be placed into. Our desires and emotions live in the and this is where they are interpreted, if possible. Concepts like death and absence may be integrated into the symbolic order because we have at least some sense of understanding of them, but they may not be interpreted fully.

Once we learn a language, we move from the real to the symbolic order and are unable to move back to the real. The real and the symbolic are two of the three orders that live in tension with one another, the third being the imaginary order.

Mirror Stage

Lacan proposed that there is an important stage of development not covered by Freud called the "mirror stage." This aptly named stage is initiated when infants look into a mirror at their own image. Most infants become fascinated with the image they see in the mirror, and may even try to interact with it.

But eventually, they realize that the image they are seeing is of themselves. Once they realize this key fact, they incorporate what they see into their sense of "I," or sense of self. At this young stage, the image they see may not correspond to their inner understanding of their physical self, in which case the image becomes an ideal that they strive for as they develop.

The Approach: Psychoanalytic Perspective

In the psychoanalytic approach, the focus is on the unconscious mind rather than the conscious mind. It is built on the foundational idea that your behavior is determined by experiences from your past that are lodged in your unconscious mind. While the focus on sex has lessened over the decades since psychoanalysis was founded, psychology and talk therapy still place a big emphasis on one's early childhood experiences.

Methods and Techniques

A psychoanalyst can use many different techniques, but there are four basic components that comprise modern psychoanalysis:

- Interpretation,
- Transference analysis,
- Technical neutrality,
- Countertransference analysis.

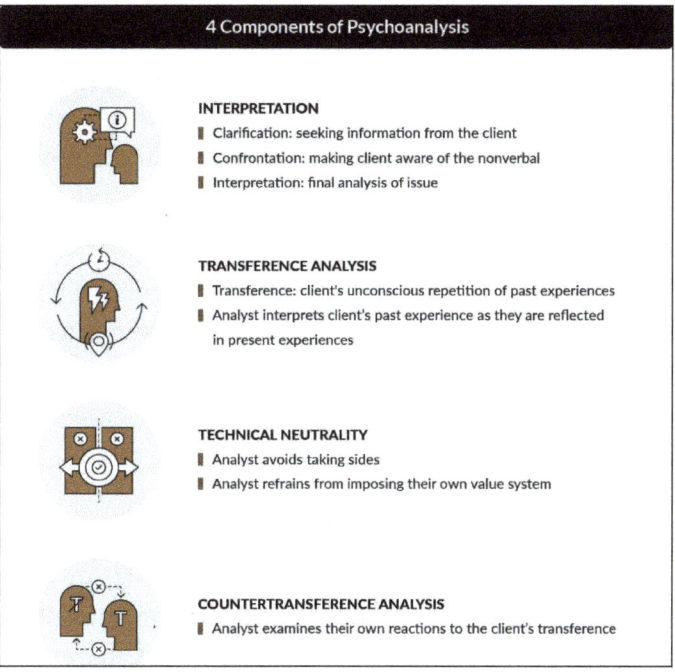

Interpretation

Interpretation is the verbal communication between analysts and clients in which analysts discuss their hypotheses of their clients' unconscious conflicts. Generally, analysts will help clients see the defensive mechanisms they are using and the context of the defensive mechanisms, or the impulsive relationship against which the mechanism was developed, and finally the client's motivation for this mechanism. There are three classifications of interpretation:

- Clarification, in which the analyst attempts to clarify what is going on in the patient's consciousness.

- Confrontation, which is bringing nonverbal aspects of the client's behavior into his or her awareness.

- Interpretation proper, which refers to the analyst's proposed hypothesis of the unconscious meaning that relates all the aspects of the client's communication with one another.

Transference Analysis

Transference is the term for the unconscious repetition in the "here and now" of conflicts from the client's past. Transference analysis refers to "the systematic analysis of the transference implications of the patient's total verbal and nonverbal manifestations in the hours as well as the c patient's direct and implicit communicative efforts to influence the analyst in a certain direction".

This analysis of the patient's transference is an essential component of psychoanalysis and is the main driver of change in treatment. In transference analysis, the analyst takes note of all communication, both verbal and nonverbal, the client engages in and puts together a theory on what led to the defensive mechanisms he or she displays. That theory forms the basis for any attempts to change the behavior or character of the client.

Technical Neutrality

Another vital piece of psychoanalysis is what is known as technical neutrality, or the commitment of the analyst to remain neutral and avoid taking sides in the client's internal conflicts; the analyst strives to remain at an equal distance from the client's id, ego, and superego, and from the client's external reality.

Additionally, technical neutrality demands that the analyst refrains from imposing his or her value systems upon the client. Technical neutrality is sometimes considered indifference or disinterest in the client, but that is not the goal; rather, analysts aim to serve as a mirror for their clients, reflecting clients' own characteristics, assumptions, and behaviors back at them to aid in their understanding of themselves.

Countertransference Analysis

This final key component of psychoanalysis is the analysis of countertransference, the analyst's reactions to clients and the material they present in sessions. "Contemporary view of counter-transference is that of a complex formation codetermined by the analyst's reaction to the patient's transference, to the reality of the patient's life, to the reality of the analyst's life, and to specific transference dispositions activated in the analyst as a reaction to the patient and his/her material".

Countertransference analysis can be generally understood as the analyst's attempts to analyze their own reactions to the client, whatever form they take. To engage in psychoanalytic treatment, the analyst must see the client objectively and understand the transference happening in the client and in their own experience.

Transference and other Forms of Resistance in Psychoanalysis

Speaking of transference, it is one of the many forms of resistance considered in psychoanalysis. In psychoanalytic theory, resistance has a specific meaning: the blocking of memories from consciousness by the client.

Resistance is the client's general unwillingness to change their behavior and engage in growth through therapy. This resistance can develop by myriad reasons, some conscious and some unconscious, and can even be present in those who want to change.

Transference occurs when clients redirect their emotions and feelings from one person to another, often unconsciously, and represents a resistance or obstacle between clients and their desired states (healing).

It frequently occurs in treatment in the form of transference onto the therapist, in which the client applies their feelings and expectations toward another person onto the therapist. There are many different types of transference, but the most common include:

- Paternal transference: In this type, the client looks to another person as a father or idealized father figure (e.g., wise, authoritative, powerful).

- Maternal transference: The client looks to another person as a mother or an idealized mother figure (e.g., comforting, loving, nurturing).

- Sibling transference: This type may occur when parental relationships break down or are lacking; instead of treating another person as a parent (in a leader/follower type relationship), the client transfers a more peer-based relationship onto the other person.

- Non-familial transference: This is a more general type of transference in which the client treats others as idealized versions of what the client expects them to be, rather than what they truly are; this type of transference can lead the client to form stereotypes.

Transference is not necessarily harmful but may be a form of client resistance to treatment. If the client is projecting inappropriate or unrealistic expectations onto the therapist, he or she may not be entirely open to the change that treatment can provoke.

Resistance to treatment can also be understood in a more general, non-psychoanalytic manner. After all, resistance to treatment is not an uncommon occurrence. Examples of ways in which a client may resist change in treatment include:

- Silence or minimal discussion with the therapist.

- Wordiness or verbosity.

- Preoccupation with symptoms.

- Irrelevant small talk.

- Preoccupation with the past or future.

- Focusing on the therapist or asking the therapist personal questions.

- Discounting or second-guessing the therapist.

- Seductiveness.

- False promises or forgetting to do what is agreed upon.

- Not keeping appointments.

- Failing to pay for appointments.

Freud's Perspective on Women

Freud believed that the psychosexual development of girls and boys is essentially the same up to the phallic phase when "the little girl is a little man". As they enter this phase they are both primarily still attached to their first love object, their mothers, and derive pleasurable sensations from their penis or penis-equivalent, the clitoris. Along with the intensified interest in their external genitalia that occurs in this phase, they become aware of the anatomical differences that exist between them. The girl is confronted with the fact that she does not have a penis and believes she has been castrated. He says' 'they notice the penis of a brother or playmate strikingly visible and of large proportions, at once recognize it as the superior counterpart of their own small and inconspicuous organ, and from that time forward fall a victim to envy for the penis. She makes her judgement and her decision in a flash. She has seen it and knows that she is without it and wants to have it'.

The resulting penis envy has profound psychological consequences. At first the girl perceives her damaged state to be a personal punishment, thus developing a sense of inferiority. Once she realizes that this is a characteristic common to all females she becomes contemptuous of her defective sex. There is now a loosening of the strong attachment to mother, her defective, who is held responsible for sending her into the world "so insufficiently equipped". Recognizing the boy's "superior equipment," the girl feels a narcissistic senses of humiliation and shame and subsequently abandons the pleasure of clitoral masturbation. Freud viewed this as a necessary precondition in the girl's shift from her previous active masculine interests to femininity. This process is continued in adolescence when the emergence of vaginal sexuality allows for the development of mature female heterosexual functioning.

The stage has now been set for the appearance of the Oedipus complex. Having turned away from mother, the girl focuses on her father as a love object. At first this attachment is in the hopes of getting a penis from him but once this wish is relinquished she replaces it with a wish for her father to give her a baby as a symbolic penis equivalent. A woman will eventually be most satisfied if she has a male child "who brings the longed for penis with him". Women will never, however, fully compensate for their penis envy and the task of analysis is, at best, to help them accept their deficient state.

Freud noted the important contrast between the sequence of the Oedipus and castration complexes between the two sexes. In the boy the Oedipus complex is destroyed by the fear that his rivalrous father will castrate him as punishment for his incestuous wishes for his mother. As he relinquishes his wishes for his mother, the boy will identify with his father, internalize his prohibitions and thereby develop a strong super-ego. Thus, the threat of castration leads to resolution of the Oedipus complex and a potent superego is its heir. In the girl the castration has already taken place and this recognition will usher in the Oedipus complex. The threat of castration, which is such a strong motivating factor in the boy's mental life, has no such power in the girl's. The, girl's Oedipus complex may be slowly abandoned, or dealt with by repression, or it may persist. As a result the girl will not have a strong super-ego emerge from the resolution of her oedipal situation. Freud says: "I cannot escape the notion (though I hesitate to give it expression) that for women the level of what is ethically normal is different from what it is in men. Their super-ego is never so inexorable, so impersonal, and so independent of its emotional origins as the route we require it to be in men".

Freud held that the discovery that she is castrated is a most significant turning point in a girl's growth, leading to three possible lines of development. The first is a neurotic solution resulting in a general revulsion to sexuality (i.e. frigidity). "The little girl is frightened by the comparison with boys, grows dissatisfied with her clitoris, and gives up her phallic activity and with it her sexuality in general as well as a good part of her masculinity in other fields". The second reaction leads to the "masculinity complex" in which the girl clings with defiant self-assertiveness to her threatened masculinity, including her clitoral masturbation, her hope of getting a penis, and identification with her phallic mother or father. He proposes that this outcome will occur if a girl has an excessive amount of "activity" as a predisposing constitutional factor. He suggests pursuing an intellectual profession may be a sublimated expression of the repressed wish to get a penis. In its extreme form the "masculinity complex" could result in female homosexuality.

Only the third, very circuitous, line of development will result in the achievement of a normal feminine attitude. This involves acceptance of anatomic inferiority, switching from active clitoral to passive vaginal sexuality, rejecting mother and turning to father for a baby to compensate for the absent penis. The penis envy motivating this results in permanent feelings of shame, jealousy, and inferiority. Freud saw the basic character triad of femininity as passivity, masochism and narcissism. When the girl relinquishes her active sexuality she gives up active strivings in all other areas. Her passive stance leads her to avoid aggressive behaviour causing her to turn her repressed aggression inward in the self-destructive attitudes and behaviour of masochism. He attributes a larger amount of narcissism to femininity so that "to be loved is a stronger need for them than to love," in order to lessen the huge narcissistic injury of sexual inferiority. Women also attempt to compensate for this inferiority by "overvaluing their charms" with the manifestation of physical vanity.

Sexism

In an attempt to understand more fully the nuances of gender-based prejudices, Peter Glick and Susan Fiske developed the idea of ambivalent sexism in the late 1990s. Although sexism has been the subject of academic interest for more than 100 years, Glick and Fiske sought to examine these attitudes in a more nuanced way, looking at the possibility of complex sexist attitudes that may entail both positive and negative attitudes toward women.

To understand ambivalent sexism, one must first understand its components: paternal and caring attitudes, or benevolent sexism, and aggressive and mistrusting attitudes, or hostile sexism. Together, these two attitudes are known as ambivalent sexism, as they imply attitudes that are seemingly both positive and negative.

Benevolent Sexism

Benevolent sexism is best thought of as a set of attitudes toward or beliefs about women that categorize them as fair, innocent, caring, pure, and fragile. Rather than being overtly misogynistic, these attitudes are often characterized by a desire to protect and preserve women. In many situations, these attitudes may be casually referred to as chivalry or traditional values. However, despite their seemingly positive characteristics, the attitudes that constitute benevolent sexism are often dangerous and damaging to women's rights and even their safety.

Hostile Sexism

Hostile sexism is much more openly misogynistic than benevolent sexism. A hostile sexist is likely to think of women as manipulative, angry, and seeking to control men through seduction. Hostile sexism often views gender equality as an attack on masculinity or traditional values and seeks to suppress movements such as feminism. Hostile sexism often represents a significant danger to women.

Ambivalent Sexism

At first, hostile and benevolent sexism seem to be incompatible. It may seem impossible for individuals to simultaneously believe that women are both pure and fragile and also manipulative and angry. However, ambivalent sexism may be understood in light of sexism more broadly. Particularly within Western societies, sexism is largely based on traditional gender norms, which place men in positions of authority in the home, the community, and government.

In the majority of cultures, women are expected to submit to male dominance. Until relatively recently (the late 19th century until the present), this system of male dominance was largely unchallenged in the Western world. However, women's liberation, universal suffrage, and the modern feminist movement have gained much power over the past century and a half, and traditional gender norms have progressively become less and less universal. In keeping with these changing societal norms, there have been increasing numbers of women who do not conform to traditional, male-dominated gender norms. Herein lies the basis for ambivalent sexism. Women who conform to gender norms by respecting and submitting to a largely patriarchal (male dominated) society are often the target of benevolent sexism. More simply, women who conform to expectations are viewed as pure, innocent, and gentle. By contrast, women who do not conform to patriarchal norms are viewed as deserving hostile sexism, in that they are perceived as manipulative, angry, and seeking to control men.

Impacts of Ambivalent Sexism

The impacts of ambivalent sexism are multifaceted. Individuals who endorse high levels of hostile sexism are more likely to tolerate and even engage in sexual harassment of women in a variety of settings. Individuals who endorse such attitudes are also more likely to accept and perpetrate violence toward their intimate partners. Finally, individuals who are high in hostile sexism are more likely to engage in or excuse sexual violence, such as rape, against women.

While benevolent sexism may not appear to be as overtly dangerous an attitude as hostile sexism, there are many consequences. At its core, benevolent sexism is still based on the assumption that women are somehow weaker than and inferior to men. Women may be seen as pure and caring, but they are also seen as fragile and needing protection. Although benevolent sexism is largely associated with positive emotions toward women, it still places men in a position of authority over the perceived weaker sex. Men who are high in benevolent sexism tend to express discomfort with women in leadership positions, to support male-dominated political systems, and to believe that a woman's place is in the home. Importantly, these associations often are above and beyond the associations between hostile sexism and the relevant outcome. Benevolent sexism predicts—perhaps even causes—inequalities between men and women in a way similar to hostile sexism.

Adding more concern is the notion that while hostile sexism predicts violence against women, benevolent sexism tends to predict victim blaming in the context of that violence. Although a benevolently sexist man may object to violence against women, he is also more likely to find the woman partially at fault for the violence she has experienced. Finally, benevolent sexism also affects how women view themselves. Women who are exposed to benevolently sexist statements are often less likely to disagree with such statements than they would with hostile sexist statements, less likely to organize against sexist inequalities, and less likely to challenge patriarchal norms. In short, benevolent sexism functions as a subtle, yet effective, means of perpetuating traditional gender norms.

Sexism in Women

Ambivalent sexism may extend beyond simple dichotomies between men and women. Although women are typically the target of sexist attitudes and behaviors, men are not the only perpetrators of such attitudes. Women can be prejudiced too, in both hostile and benevolent ways.

At first, the notion of women endorsing sexist values and behaviors seems absurd. After all, if sexism is inevitably damaging to women, then it makes little sense that women would endorse such attitudes. However, there is precedence for the notion that victims of discrimination and prejudice might internalize some of the views that have victimized them. As a by-product of living in a patriarchal society, both men and women are raised in an environment that subtly as well as openly enforces sexist ideals. In turn, women often internalize these ideals. In the face of rampant inequality, women are forced to either challenge the inequality by embracing more egalitarian and feminist values or accept the inequality by embracing sexist attitudes.

Women are less likely than men to endorse hostile sexism, but they are often just as likely as men to endorse benevolently sexist values. This is likely due to a variety of reasons. Given that conforming to traditional gender roles often acts as a buffer against hostile sexism, women may endorse benevolently sexist attitudes as a means of avoiding being the target of hostile sexism. In some sense then, women endorsing attitudes of benevolent sexism may be a means of self-preservation via choosing the lesser of the two evils. Finally, benevolent sexism may appeal to a sense of entitlement among some women. Taken at face value, benevolent sexism seems to be devoted to the well-being and protection of women, which may seem like good things. However, given the impact that benevolent sexism has in discouraging women from engaging in activism against gender-based inequalities, women's endorsement of benevolent sexism may be considered in some ways more subversive to gender equality than hostile sexism.

What is Benevolent Sexism?

Benevolent sexism is a type of sexism that includes seemingly positive views of women and is a component (along with hostile sexism) of ambivalent sexism. There are three subcomponents of benevolent sexism: (1) protective paternalism, which is the belief that because women are warm, caring, and maternal, they should be protected and provided for by men; (2) complementary gender differentiation, which is the belief that women (who are warm, other oriented, morally pure, and weak) and men (who are competent, independent, morally corruptible, and strong) have contrasting but complementary attributes; and (3) heterosexual intimacy, which is the belief that women and men are dependent on each other for both emotional closeness and reproduction.

Although benevolent sexism rewards women with pro-social treatment, it reinforces their subordinate position relative to men and has detrimental effects on women, both as individuals and as a collective. This entry briefly introduces benevolent sexism in relation to ambivalent sexism and then discusses the large-scale societal impacts as well as the smaller-scale individual impacts of benevolent sexism. The entry concludes with current research directions regarding benevolent sexism.

Connection to Ambivalent Sexism

Ambivalent sexism was conceptualized by Peter Glick and Susan Fiske to include both negative (hostile) and positive (benevolent) sexism and is measured with the self-report scale they created, the Ambivalent Sexism Inventory. The two types have been found to be moderately positively correlated in all the nations studied, with those men and women who score high on both scales being termed ambivalent sexist. Benevolent sexism has been identified in 19 different countries, with women typically endorsing benevolent sexism to a greater extent than hostile sexism. Benevolent sexism predicts positive evaluations of women who conform to traditional gender roles, whereas hostile sexism predicts negative evaluations of women who violate traditional gender roles. Thus, together they create ambivalent views of women as a whole.

Societal-Level Effects

Glick and Fiske, as well as other researchers, argue that the combination of hostile and benevolent sexism contributes to societal gender inequality. Benevolent sexism is pro-social treatment directed toward gender conforming or traditional women (e.g., mothers, wives), and thus rewards women for staying in lower-status roles relative to men. Indeed, national levels of benevolent sexism have been shown to be objective indicators of societal gender inequality. In cultures characterized by a high level of hostile sexism, women are more likely to endorse benevolent sexism, suggesting that they may enact gender conforming, lower-status behaviors to earn protection rather than risk overt hostility from men. Benevolent sexism therefore may weaken women's resistance to sexism and gender inequality. Priming women with complementary gender stereotypes as well as complementary (benevolent plus hostile) sexist items increased support for the societal status quo (i.e., reduced women's motivation to enact change in a sexist society). Thus, benevolent sexism is implicated in the maintenance of gender inequality at the societal level.

Individual-Level Effects

A great deal of research has also shown the negative effects of benevolent sexism on individual women. Benoit Dardenne and colleagues found that women exposed to benevolent sexist instructions prior to taking a test of job skills as part of an employment interview performed more poorly than women exposed to hostile sexist or non-sexist instructions. They argue that because benevolent sexism is not as easily recognized as sexist (i.e., it seems positive), exposure results in women doubting their competence and cognitive abilities in a workplace context that paternalistic/ benevolent sexist beliefs in employment settings can prevent women from being offered high-risk/ high-status opportunities, slowing their career advancement. Instead they are offered lower status, communal job roles that are more congruent with traditional gender norms.

Benevolent sexism has also been shown to limit women's opportunities in romantic relationship contexts and is associated with acquaintance rape victim blaming. Benevolent sexism is often unrecognized as sexist, yet research shows that it can have damaging consequences on individual women's lives.

Current and Future Directions

Benevolent sexism was first defined in the mid-1990s and is an active topic of research. Researchers who study benevolent sexism have begun investigating the social implications of confronting it, as well as interventions to reduce the endorsement of benevolent sexist attitudes and beliefs. Researchers have also begun studying the cardiovascular reactivity associated with experiences of benevolent sexism.

Much of the research conducted on benevolent sexism to date has used primarily White, middle-class participant samples; future research should consider whether the findings generalize to different racial and ethnic groups as well as people with differing levels of socioeconomic status. Intersectional research on benevolent sexism has been strongly encouraged. Because benevolent sexism is often subtly experienced and not actively resisted in the same way as hostile sexism, research investigating its antecedents, effects, and reduction is of paramount importance.

What is Hostile Sexism?

Hostile sexism is most often associated with negative prejudice against and hostile views of women that are rooted in the belief that women are inferior to men. People who harbour hostile sexist attitudes toward women tend to view women as intellectually inferior to men. In many cultures, men dominate high-status positions in areas including business, politics, religion, the military, law, and other professional careers related to societal power. To maintain male control in society, women are relegated to subservient roles. Hostile sexist ideologies serve to maintain men's dominant role in patriarchal societies; consequently, women who defy their prescribed gender role and behave in non-traditional ways are perceived in a negative light, derogated, and demeaned.

Hostile sexism comprises several philosophies. One is the notion that men need to control "their" women because women are less intelligent and less competent than men. Women are perceived as too emotional, as easily offended, and as having a proclivity to create major issues over trivial events. Because women are perceived as incapable of making important decisions, hostile sexists believe that it is men's responsibility to dictate to women what they should think and how they should behave. This dominant paternalistic view serves to keep women submissive and subservient to men.

Hostile sexism also comprises beliefs that women do not belong in the workplace and are too sensitive and emotional to be in high-status positions. A hostile sexist might believe that women who do enter the workforce will likely make excuses for their own incompetence by complaining that they are victims of discrimination. Hostile sexists also perceive women as weak and dependent and not able to independently handle life situations; therefore, men need to be the ones in control. As such, women should be grateful for everything men do for them, and they should submissively accept their prescribed female gender role. Such hostile sexist beliefs incorporate the idea that a woman's place is in the home and that women should be the ones to cook, clean, and take care of the children. Not too surprisingly, women oppose these hostile sexist attitudes more than men.

Another notion underlying hostile sexism is the idea that women use their feminine wiles to gain special favors from men. In this view, women use sex to tempt and manipulate men in order to achieve power over them. Women are perceived as "whiny teases" who want to control men by using their sexuality. For instance, hostile sexists believe that women enjoy leading men on but whenever men respond by showing interest, women delight in shutting them down and refusing their advances. Furthermore, hostile sexist views include the perception that once in relationship women will continue their attempts to control men by putting them on a "tight leash."

Hostile Sexism towards Men

Although hostile sexism is often associated with feelings and behaviors directed toward women, hostile sexism can also be directed toward men. As a response to being subordinated by men, some women hold negative views against men that include feelings of resentment and disgust. Women with this view tend to perceive men as inferior in several ways. For example, hostile sexists tend to have a negative perception of men as childlike and in need of someone to take care of them; for instance, they might believe that when men become sick they act like "babies."

Hostile sexism toward men also includes the idea that men are not capable of being successful without women to guide and care for them. Hostile sexists are likely to perceive men as arrogant individuals caring only about their own personal wants and desires and continually trying to gain the upper hand and to control women at every turn.

Women who harbor hostile sexist beliefs tend to view men's paternalistic attitudes and behaviors merely as selfish manipulation with the goal of asserting their superiority over women. Hostile sexists also hold the belief that men merely give lip service to the idea of gender equality. Although men might state that they are proponents of equality between the sexes, when it comes right down to it, men want "their" women to adhere to traditional gender roles.

Hostile sexism toward men also includes the idea that men use sexual aggressiveness as a means to control and dominate women. Hostile sexists perceive men as interested only in their own sexual satisfaction and conquests, and they believe that men will do whatever it takes to achieve their goal, regardless of how it affects women. Not surprisingly, this view leads to deep resentment and hostility toward men.

Sexism in STEM

The struggle for equal rights is a battle continuing ever since the two different sexes arrived on the planet. This legacy is a burden which mankind still carries in all walks of life and science is no exception. Science has been slow to open its doors to women. For a long time, science had been considered a masculine discipline and this gender discrimination is still being practised in science. Images of scientists are persistently masculine and women in science are referred to as "female scientists" and not merely as scientists. Science has no gender and the results and scientific solutions to problems come from research, technology and innovation and not from whether or not the originator was a woman or man. No theory or solution can be dismissed primarily on the basis of the sex or gender of the researcher.

It is established that institutions producing scientific knowledge have a long tradition of excluding women. Though scientists often consider themselves to be objective and unbiased, studies have shown that they are susceptible to the same biases and prejudices as the rest of the population. In fact, because male scientists believe they are objective and rational, their embedded subjectivities and stereotypical mind-sets are more difficult to address. History offers many examples of women scientists whose work and contributions were unfairly overlooked.

- In the 1950s, Rosalind Franklin's work on the structure of DNA was unfairly side-lined and later in 1962, based on Rosalind's discovery and contribution, the Nobel Prize for the discovery of the structure of DNA was awarded to Francis Crick, James Watson and Maurice Wilson.

- Nettie Stevens discovered XY sex chromosomes but she did not get credit because she had two X s.

Women's lives are governed by social norms and conventions that are patriarchal in nature and are not conducive to women taking on roles apart from the culturally assigned ones. These norms and conventions are difficult to break and often involve a heavy personal price. Despite increased access and participation of women in all disciplines of science, even in the 21st century the percentage of women at senior levels of research, innovation and technology is far from satisfactory even though women have as much potential to contribute to science as do the men.

Issues and Problems faced by Women in Science

Gender Bias and Inequality

Despite a wide range of initiatives and support being given to women in Science, Technology, Engineering and Mathematics (STEM) fields, there is still an underrepresentation of women in science around the globe particularly at senior levels of teaching, research and other professions of the scientific world. Inequities in promotion, grant awards, invitation to conferences, nomination for awards, professional collaborations still exist and continue to haunt women in the fields of science.

Constant efforts, policies and measures for gender equality and gender mainstreaming have gained recognition at the international level. They have changed the situation of women substantially in relation to their physical and financial autonomy but women even today face attitudinal biases and unsupportive work place environments preventing talented women from realizing their full potential in pursuit of productive and rewarding careers.

Several dimensions need to be considered with regard to the issues about women in science. First, being professional, their lives and work are affected by the overall environment of the institution and second by virtue of being women they face quite distinctive situations related to their role and status in the society.

Occupational Sexism

Sexism is discrimination, prejudice, or stereotyping on the basis of a person's sex or gender. Though it may affect both the sexes, it is most frequently expressed towards girls and women. It also includes the belief that one sex or gender is intrinsically superior to the other. The term sexism is not modern and was coined by Pauline M. Leet at a Student Faculty forum on November 18, 1965 at Franklin and Marshall College, Lancaster, Pennsylvania, USA.

Sexism is not limited to actions only though extreme sexism may foster sexual harassment, rape and other forms of sexual violence. Most institutions have formal complaint mechanism for women who have been subjected to illegal sex discrimination, sexual harassment, molestation and extremes of sexism-rape. The problems are discussed at several platforms and solved.

Subtle sexist remarks and sexist language at work place also constitute occupational sexism and second-generation gender bias which in most cases promotes superiority of men over women. This superiority becomes the standard and those who are not males are then relegated to the inferior.

Micro-Aggression

Though most studies now emphasize that gender differences in scientific careers are decreasing, the still prevailing subtle discrimination and sexism explains why women continue to remain in a minority in science. Even the subtle and un-intentional instances of gender insensitivity can result in lowered self- confidence, decreased job satisfaction and a sense of isolation for women. This negative or 'chilly' workplace climate with regard to overt and subtle sexism affects the success of women. Unconscious gender bias is well documented in academic science. Problems of sexual harassment are discussed at several platforms but less attention is paid to the subtle and often unintentional comments which women face every day.

This behaviour or micro-aggression, also referred to as micro-sexism poses a greater threat to women in science and has the potential to cause more widespread harm. The unintentional micro-aggression revolving around awkward questions and frequently offensive situations make it quickly and painfully clear that whereas women take situations at face value, men overlay sex or gender as a relevant consideration. Such comments are voiced by men without realizing their impact on women.

Since micro-aggression does not seem to be actionable, cases go unreported. However, the sting and shock of such subtle and unintentional acts and comments cannot be underestimated. To improve the climate in science, it is time to share stories of micro aggression.

Leaky Pipeline

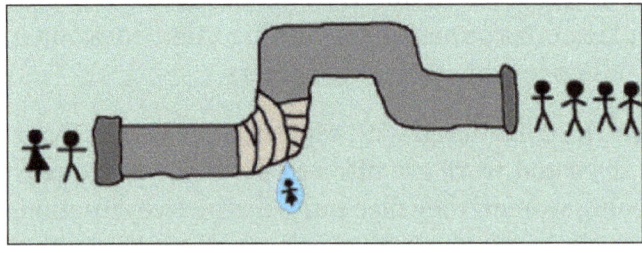

While it is important to keep attracting young women to science, gender based biases, sexist attitudes and gender discrimination at work placed together with the unequal and hierarchical power based relationship between man and woman within the family impact women's professional life. The problem lies not only in recruiting women or at the point of entry but in their retention in the profession. Across every scientific discipline, the proportion of women in the pipeline to become researchers falls significantly with every step of career progression. This is called the "leaky pipeline" syndrome. There is no single explanation for such a leaky pipeline. It is the result of perceptions and biases combined with the impracticality of combining career with family. Women scientists in the leaking pipeline themselves become a barrier to the commercialization of scientific knowledge.

Many women for one reason or another voluntarily renounce the opportunities to move upwards and demonstrate their potential. This is not merely because of their concern for the family and children or any doubt of their own capacity but due to patriarchal reasons. Any upward movement in her career may upset the stability and equilibrium and destroy the peace at home. Women exit from the pipeline by choosing other options.

Institutional Needs to Address Sex Related Issues in Science

Commitment and creativity in a profession are not merely functions of individual competence but a product of a social and institutional environment. Institutional support, opportunities and the ethos of the Institute are essential for professional identity, competency and greater productivity. Restriction of opportunities not only leads to frustration but reduces effectiveness.

Occupational Sexism – Gender Equality and Balance

"Fix the System, Not the Women".

Laws that enforce equality in the work place are important for any institution. The underrepresentation of women is a threat to equality and detrimental to excellence since gender based discrimination constitutes a violation of Human Rights. Gender equality in science improves scientific quality. It is not just a woman's career but a societal issue. Thoughtfulness, tolerance and nurturing are needed in institutions to realize the full potential of women in science and maintain gender equality and balance.

To improve the climate for women in science, it is high time and important to share incidents and stories of micro-aggression or micro-sexism openly and harassment should not be kept under wraps. All institutions must have proper complaint platforms to address such acts with senior women in the committees. Proper punitive procedures must be introduced to prevent future incidents which not only demoralize women but drive them to the extent of leaving their work .Formation of a Task Force at the Institute level comprising senior scientists including women, intellectuals and other eminent people of society must be essential for every institution to take stock of the situation on a regular basis, suggest action and follow up measures.

Fixing the Leaky Pipeline

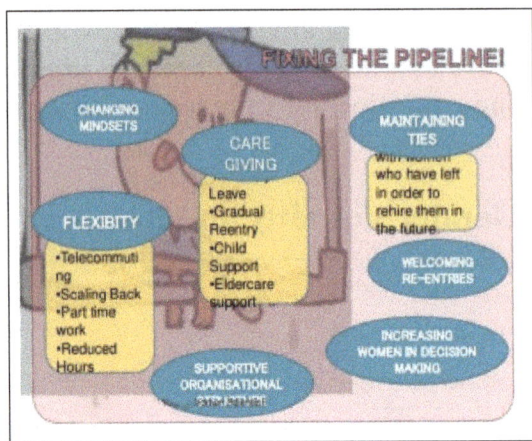

Women are entering the STEM pipeline in increasing numbers but exit more frequently than the men do leading to their under-representation. This under-representation of women in science often relates to shortage of women in the pipeline which flows from one stage to another in an upward direction. Institutions need to create women-friendly policies in order to retain women in the profession and plug the leaky pipeline. Women choose other options when the stress of the work place and family responsibilities clash. The full potential of women should be recognized and they must be given their due in promotions, grant of funds for research and innovations, opportunities for attending conferences, nomination for awards and other professional commitments as the men in their work place get.

Institutions also need to address some preconceptions and assumptions which lead to women quitting their work and also contribute to gender imbalance and leaky pipelines. An award system can be introduced for institutions creating plans and policies for changes that support women in science.

Safety Issues

Institutional Security

Institutional laws for women employees need to be protective. They should not assign night shifts for their women employees. Special security is required for women when working till late hours. Most women move around freely but mainly during daylight hours. It is the duty of the Institutions to provide safe transport and security to their women scientists.

Institutional Transport Facilities

Women generally should not drive or use public transport system such as taxi-cabs at night. It is sometimes difficult to attend conferences due to late hours and distant conference venues. Lack of proper transport facilities in scientific institution prevents the women from spending long hours at their work place or working during the week ends. Basic transport facilities during odd hours need to be provided to the women scientists in all Institution to realize their full potential.

Flexible Time Schedule

While the working hour concept is changing around the world, it is often perceived that long working hours are a testimony for hard work. This is detrimental for mothers of young children. Women tend to give better quality time to their work that compensates for their shorter working hours. Their time management in terms of output is believed to be better than men. Institutions need to have flexible time schedules for women to give them a better chance of attending to their work and family commitments. This is also a safety measure to ensure women do not work till late hours or during weekends when most of the people are away from work. By keeping timelines a little flexible, women can achieve quality outputs and juggle their roles more effectively.

Mobility of Women

Restriction in the mobility of women and behaviour act as serious barriers to the advancement of women as scientists. First women find it difficult to lobby with the higher authorities on matters related to their careers such as promotion. They express their inability to interact freely with the higher authorities because of social considerations and because society tends to mis-interprets their action.

Second, women feel they are not as effective as they cannot move around as freely or because they are not expected to behave the way the men do. Third, women are unable to develop and nurture contacts with officials of funding agencies which is necessary for obtaining research grants. Institutions need to encourage women scientists and establish them as professionals, in getting research grants and in their promotions.

Biological Issues

These are also issues which require immediate attention in Institutions to facilitate proper working conditions for women scientists. Certain modifications in rules need to be provided to women professionals to help to cope up with the dual responsibilities of home and profession. Sex, Biology and reproductive functions of women have been propounded as the bases of patriarchy. Instead of dealing with the unique capacity of women of being creative by bearing children or dealing with this function as a natural potential or as a positive contribution, women have been subjected to restrictions, societal taboos and patriarchy. Institutions need to identify the potential of women apart from their role as mothers, house wives and dependants and give them the opportunity to develop their skills and aspirations by creating women-friendly environments at their work place. The biology of women determines her gender and status in the society, the institution will determine her professional status.

Maternity and Child Rearing Issues

Child rearing and care is an acute problem worldwide for women in science. Childbearing and child rearing responsibilities affect women more than men. Lack of institutional child care centres

/crèches is a reflection of a systemic bias against employment and professional working of women. Younger women scientists in the present nuclear family system are harassed by the problems of child care. They cannot afford to take time off to look after their children as re-entry to profession is difficult because of age restrictions. This is a comment on our society that only women are expected to prioritize their domestic responsibilities over their professional ones.

All Scientific Institutions need to address this and provide facilities for maternity and child rearing to women professionals. These facilities would be a boon to men as well since child care responsibilities, in nuclear families are becoming more and more the task of both parents. Institutional support in terms of leave, care and medical facilities to the women scientist are required. Institutions must encourage more women to choose tenure track jobs and modify the tenure –clock.

Extended tenure, sanctioning of leave up to one year or more as required, flexible working hours, crèche facilities, leave to the husband whether in the same institute or another science institute and medical facilities to the mother and the child are required for the institution to retain and promote women scientists. These facilities, relevant to both child bearing and child rearing, will not only retain women in science but also give them the opportunity to write and publish research papers and get the best of both the worlds , her personal and professional lives.

Role of Media

Institutions must involve both print and electronic media to provide coverage to women achievers who can become role models and encourage more women participation. Mass awareness programs/campaigns should be launched by the institutions and made public through the media, advertisements and other sources to encourage girls to pursue science and choose science as a career option. Voluntary organizations and NGOs can also collaborate to take up the campaigns. Incentives to girls taking up science should be given in terms of scholarship, certificates and prizes to create a drive in them to choose science as their profession.

Sexual Identity Models

Heterosexual," "homosexual" and "bisexual" are examples of specific sexual orientations. Sexual orientation refers to feelings and identity, not just behavior. Individuals do not always express their sexual orientation through their sexual behaviors.

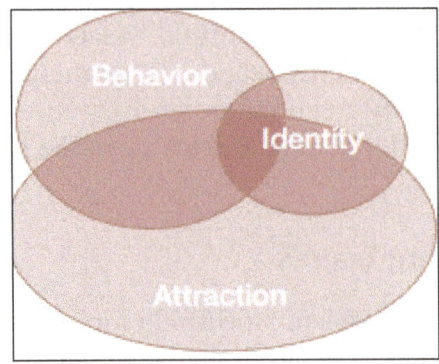

The purpose of this guide is to help congregations welcome a range of people who are attracted in varying degrees to people of more than one sex or gender. We can define bisexuality as "an enduring romantic, emotional and/or sexual attraction toward people of more than one sex or gender."

A bisexual person may be attracted to one sex or gender more than another, equally attracted to all sexes and genders, or may consider sex and gender unimportant in terms of their sexual and romantic attractions. The intensity of a bisexual person's attractions toward one sex or gender or another may vary over time.

Some bisexuals have not had sexual behaviors with another person. Others have had only same-sex experiences or have been only with partners of a different sex or gender from their own. Many people who identify as lesbian, heterosexual, gay, or another label have had sex with partners of more than one sex or gender.

Some people have been identified in the professional literature as "mostly heterosexual." These are people who identify as heterosexual but who also have "a small degree of same-sex sexuality in at least one indicator of sexual orientation (sexual/romantic attraction, arousal, fantasy, infatuation, and identity).

For some people, gender expression and gender identity are also factors in sexual attraction. For some bisexuals, gender is an important part of attraction. For other bisexuals, it is totally irrelevant. And to make things even more complex, some people are bisexual throughout their life while others find that their sexual and romantic attractions change during different periods of their lives.

Those who are attracted to people of more than one sex or gender may use a variety of words to describe their sexual orientation, including bisexual, "bi," same and other gender loving, pansexual, ambisexual, omnisexual, fluid, and queer. There is no one word that everyone agrees captures the complexity of the range of sexual orientations.

Models to help Understand the Range of Sexual Orientations

In order to have a greater understanding about bisexuality, it is important to understand the complexity of sexual orientation. Many models of sexual orientation have been developed by researchers, social scientists and advocates over the past fifty years.

The Kinsey Scale

In 1948, the sexuality researcher Alfred Kinsey and his colleagues proposed a seven-point scale for sexual orientation based on an individual's overt sexual experience and/or psychosexual reactions, although Kinsey's research focused on behaviors.4 The Kinsey Institute now describes the scale this way: "The scale ranges from 0, for those who would identify themselves as exclusively heterosexual with no experience with or desire for sexual activity with their same sex, to 6, for those who would identify themselves as exclusively homosexual with no experience with or desire for sexual activity with those of the opposite sex, and 1–5 for those who would identify themselves with varying levels of desire or sexual activity with either sex."5 Kinsey's 1948 report on American men estimated that 46% were in the range of 1–5 at some point in their lives.

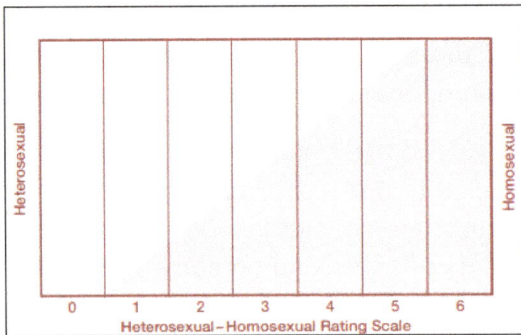

Kinsey described each point on the scale as follows:

- 0–Exclusively heterosexual with no homosexual.

- 1–Predominantly heterosexual, only incidentally homosexual.

- 2–Predominantly heterosexual, but more than incidentally homosexual.

- 3–Equally heterosexual and homosexual.

- 4–Predominantly homosexual, but more than incidentally heterosexual.

- 5–Predominantly homosexual, only incidentally heterosexual.

- 6–Exclusively homosexual.

Limitations of the Kinsey Scale

While the Kinsey scale was revolutionary at its publication in advancing the understanding of sexual orientation as a spectrum, it has significant limitations, especially in its conception of bisexuality. The Kinsey scale could imply (and has been used to assert) that the only "true bisexuals" are those who have sexual behaviors equally with men and women. Instead of expressly using the term "bisexual," the Kinsey scale uses the terms "heterosexual" and "homosexual," even for people with behaviors in the 1 to 5 range. The Kinsey scale is also a linear scale that does not account for the possibility of changes over time, or the interaction of one's own gender expression and identity with sexual attraction. It conflates the many dimensions of sexual orientation into a single number, whereas people may differ in the erotic, romantic, and affectional components of their sexual orientation.

The Klein Sexual Orientation Grid

Several decades later, building on the work of Dr. Kinsey and his colleagues, Dr. Fritz Klein developed a more nuanced two-dimensional model of sexual orientation, now known as the Klein Sexual Orientation Grid. It was first published in his book, The Bisexual Option, in 1978. The Klein Grid is designed to expand on Kinsey's work in several ways. First, it accounts for the fact that a person's sexual orientation may change over time, and asks people to rate their past, present, and ideal orientation on each factor. The Klein Grid includes seven variables that use 1 to 7 rating criteria similar to the Kinsey scale, ranging from exclusive "opposite" sex attraction to exclusive same sex attraction. The 21 boxes are rated, and then can be viewed as a complex individual picture that cannot be reduced to a single number on a one-dimensional scale. The variables are:

- Sexual Attraction: To whom an individual is sexually attracted.

- Sexual Behavior: With whom an individual engages in sexual behaviors.

- Sexual Fantasies: About whom one has fantasies.

- Emotional Preference: With whom one falls in love.

- Social Preference: The sex of the people with whom one socializes.

- Lifestyle Preference: Sexual identity of the people with whom one socializes.

- Sexual Identity: How an individual self-identifies.

Klein Sexual Orientation Grid

Sexual Attraction	Past	Present	Ideal Future
Sexual Behavior			
Sexual Fantasies			
Emotional Preference			
Social Preference			
Heterosexual-Homosexual Lifestyle			
Self-Identification			

Although some of the terms that Klein uses (such as "lifestyle" or "preference") are out-dated today, his insights that sexual orientation is composed of many variables that may fall at different places in Kinsey's continuum and that sexual orientation is "an on-going dynamic process" help explain the complexity of sexual orientation in a way that Kinsey's model did not.

AER (Affectional/Erotic/Romantic) Model

Wayne Pawlowski, an AASECT-certified sexuality educator, created the AER model to address the complex interplay between affectional feelings, erotic feelings, and romantic feelings. He labeled these as affectional orientation, erotic orientation, and romantic orientation. The model is based on the following open-ended questions:

- A: Affectional orientation: "With whom do you prefer to socialize? With which sex(es) do you feel most comfortable and relaxed?"

- E: Erotic orientation: "Which sex(es) turn(s) you on erotically? To whom are you attracted as real, potential, or fantasy sexual partners?"

- R: Romantic orientation: "With whom do you fall in love? With whom do you fall in love most easily?"

It is common to assume that these three areas are the same or at least closely related, but Pawlowski cautions that they can be three separate and distinct aspects of sexual orientation. In fact, he suggests that what we call "sexual orientation" is actually a complex interplay of an individual's affectional, erotic and romantic orientations working in concert with one another, not simply to whom one is attracted erotically. Consider, for example, a man married to a woman--and the man periodically has sexual encounters with other men. Although some might assume he is gay, he indeed could be romantically in love with his wife and socially much more comfortable being in a relationship with a woman. His erotic attractions could fall anywhere from a Kinsey 1 to a 6, but his affectional and romantic attractions could indicate a bisexual orientation.

The AER model is completely different from the Kinsey Scale and the Klein Grid in that it doesn't depend on a two-dimensional continuum of orientation. Instead, it asks open-ended questions. It allows for the possibility that a person may actually answer "no one" to the questions pertaining to one or more of the three orientations. Further, it allows for gender diversity in a way that previous models did not. Pawlowski suggests that of the three orientations, affectional is the most influenced by environment/upbringing/life experience. The other two orientations (erotic and romantic) tend to be far less influenced by environment.

Cass Model

This model can be used to understand aspects of identity development, but are not generalizable to every experience. Individuals can move through these stages of identity in different orders and may return to stages or skip stages through their lives. Bisexual individuals may have additional stages after identifying as straight or lesbian/gay. Gender is societally considered much less fluid, and has its own complicated steps of identity development. Cross-culturally, gender and sexual identities have different significance and meanings. There may be additional steps of identity development, coming of age traditions, and/or more/less cultural significance attached to certain identities. Socioeconomic status, religion/spirituality, age, abilities, race/ethnicity, and other factors also effect identity development and cohesion. The first stages of identity development are often experienced through a denial of homosexuality because of heteronormativity, heterosexism, and/or homophobia. Identity Development Stages:

Identity Confusion

Generally, but not in every case, individuals have assumed an identity with the heterosexual or gender conforming (cisgender) majority. This identity comes into question, through thoughts, emotions, physical reactions, and other experiences may bring the individual to question their identity as heterosexual (cisgendered). There may also be a search for information in this part of identity formation. This stage may continue if the individual can avoid identityquestioning situations, can continue in denial, or continue on with ideas of asexuality, heterosexuality and/or cisgender identity.

Identity Comparison

If stage one does not end with denial or avoidance, the individual may move on to identity comparison. This stage involves social alienation, a feeling of being out of place, or difference. There are many different routes examined in this stage, the individual can create strategies in order to deal with difference. This is a stage where:

- Acceptance of an identity and further exploration of the identity in question may emerge.

- Creative denial of the identity may continue despite evidence to the contrary.

- Acceptance of the personal application of identity may emerge alongside coping mechanisms for passing, with no intention of revealing the identity in the future.

- The identity is accepted as the individual's identity, but is seen as totally unacceptable, and inhibition of behavior is attempted. In route if strategies to inhibit behavior routinely fail, the individual may attempt suicide.

Identity Tolerance

This stage exemplifies a greater level of commitment to an LGBTQ+ identity. This stage is where an individual may begin to think "I am probably gay/lesbian/bisexual/transgendered/etc." This is a stage where individuals sometimes seek out LGBTQ+ subculture, as they begin to ask if they fit within the culture and feel more alienated from their heterosexual or cisgender identity. Contacting people within the subculture is seen as an option to lessen overall alienation or loneliness. The new identity is seen as something to tolerate at this stage, it is not treated with total acceptance. Though alienation is less prevalent, the individual may not have a sense of belonging with heterosexual others.

Identity Acceptance

This stage involves more interaction or connection with the LGBTQ+ community. They start to validate their identity and may begin to have a preference to be around others who are LGBTQ+. There are two general ways that the legitimacy of their identity can be interpreted at this stage:

- Identifying oneself as LGBTQ+ is legitimate in private, but should not be displayed in public.

- Identifying oneself as LGBTQ+ is legitimate in public and in private, and expression of LGBTQ+ subcultures are desirable.

The second way generally leads to Identity Pride. The first way can lead to attempts at:

- Passing for heterosexual/cisgendered.

- Limiting contact with LGBTQ+ community.

- Disclosing sexuality/gender identity only to select individuals who will keep it confidential.

Identity Pride

This is a stage where the individual clearly identifies within the LGBTQ+ community and chooses it over the heterosexual/cisgendered community. In this stage, because of societal rejection of homosexuality/gender nonconformity, the individual may devalue heterosexual/cisgendered individuals and institutional values in order to revalue LGBTQ+ individuals. Frustration and anger may occur in everyday life when feelings of alienation and having to adhere to heterosexual/cisgendered norms do not disappear. The total acceptance and public activism associated with this stage can:

- Make more legitimate the individual's identity in their own eyes as they begin to become 'out' to many others and/or in public.

- Align public and private identities and allow the individual to recognize themselves as having intersectional identities.

External reactions to this stage may either lead the individual to stage 6, or keep them in the previous five stages.

Identity Synthesis

The dichotomy created in stage five, where LGBTQ+ individuals and institutions are always good, and heterosexual/cisgender individuals and institutions are always bad, is no longer true to the individual. Rejecting heterosexual/cisgender individuals are still devalued, often further than in stage five, but accepting, supportive heterosexual/cisgender individuals are now valued. Pride is still felt, but no longer emphasized as there is no clear dichotomy between heterosexual/cisgender and LGBTQ+ worlds. The developed LGBTQ+ identity is considered a part of many identities, no longer the singular defining identity of the individual. The awareness that comes with this realization brings the development process full circle, and the individual integrates the identity. These stages of identity are not the same for everyone, as everyone's identity development has unique components to it. Not everyone visits these steps in the same order, if at all.

Hagan's Power Control Theory

Hagan and associates used both macro-level and micro-level concepts to explain the link between gender and delinquency, integrating traditional theories of class (power) and family function (control). In his initial version of power-control theory, Hagan centered the theory on Marxist ideas of class relations and positions of authority held by the head of the household in families. He argued that class affects the gender difference in delinquency. Specifically, higher classes with greater occupational authority held by the head of the household (i.e. owners, managers) present a greater difference in delinquency between genders. In families of lower classes (i.e. workers, unemployed-surplus population) the gender disparity in delinquency narrows. According to Hagan, males are freer to deviate from social norms than females and they are freest to deviate in the higher classes. However, Hagan's initial version of power-control theory did not directly address gender relations in the workplace and at home; instead, the gender-power imbalance was assumed by virtue of the class position of the male "head of household." In response to counterarguments on this point, Hagan further elaborated on the power-control model in 1987. By looking at the relative difference in authority in the workplace between the wife and the husband, instead of simply the absolute authority of the male head of the household, the gender power relations within the family unit could be observed.

In this elaborated model, Hagan and his colleagues introduced the basic elements of power-control theory as it is commonly known today. The main idea of the theory is that the amount of authority parents have in the workplace, relative to one another, is reproduced within the two-parent household. The difference in power between parents is then believed to differentially influence the social control of daughters and sons, in turn, having an effect on gender differences in the child's preference for risky behavior, as well as assessments of risk. At last, it is these differences in control and access to risk that explain the gender difference in delinquency.

In particular, the aim of power-control theory is not to predict the probability of females being involved in delinquent behavior; instead, it seeks to clarify the differences between males and females in delinquency and how these differences may be greater in certain types of households compared with others. Distinguish households as being "more patriarchal" or "less patriarchal" on the basis of whether individuals have positions of authority in the workplace relative to their spouse. For example, a household would typically be described as "more patriarchal" if the father holds an authority position, while the mother does not have authority in her job or is unemployed. Additionally, even if the father has no authority in his job outside the home, but the mother is unemployed, the household is considered more patriarchal. On the other hand, a "less patriarchal" family would exist when both parents hold jobs of equal authority, creating a more even balance of power between the two spouses.

Basically, the theory looks at the relational rather than absolute measures of authority of the father and mother. Alternatively, less patriarchal families, where mothers and fathers have similar levels of occupational authority and power in the family, do not exhibit such pronounced differences between sons and daughters since they are controlled more similarly than in unbalanced families. It is the similarity in the controls and ideation of risk that narrows the gender gap in delinquency within less patriarchal families in comparison to more patriarchal families.

"Power-control theory is not merely a theory of the gender pattern of delinquency; rather, it is a theory of the gender patterning of risk preferences more generally, which could potentially lead to a wide variety of risk-taking behaviors".

Hagan's first attempt to advance power-control theory reveals his awareness of the impact of private patriarchy on the gender difference in crime. In homes where wives do not work outside the home but husbands are fully employed, private patriarchy prevails. It is in these "more patriarchal" households that Hagan hypothesizes a larger gender difference in delinquency. Alternatively, in families where both husband and wife are employed and enjoy equal levels of authority in their employment, private patriarchy is diminished; likewise, the gender gap in delinquency in these "less patriarchal" households is expected to be reduced. Although Hagan makes no explicit distinction between private and public patriarchy in his development of power-control theory, it is clear that the theoretical statement singles out the influence of private patriarchy specifically on the gender gap in delinquency. This emphasis on private patriarchy is further evident in empirical tests of power-control theory.

References

- Psychoanalysis: positivepsychology.com, Retrieved 30, August 2020

- Ambivalent-Sexism-Sage17, sex-and-gender: nyu.edu, Retrieved 08, January 2020

- Definitions-and-Models-of-Sexual-Orientation: religiousinstitute.org, Retrieved 19, April 2020

- Identity-Development-Stages, gender-equity: uwsuper.edu, Retrieved 21, June 2020

Masculinity: An Integrated Study

The set of behaviors, characteristics and roles which are associated with boys and men is termed ass masculinity. The study of masculinity within the field of gender studies focuses on men's movement, toxic masculinity, hegemonic masculinity and machismo. This chapter discusses in detail these aspects of masculinity in gender studies.

In nature there is almost a universal distinction between male and female types in most animal species. We, as human beings, too share this difference with them. We have males who are biologically distinct from females of the species. The male-female difference is based on the type of sex organs we possess, the type of sex-chromosomes we have and other anatomical and physiological features. This difference is designed, as biologists argue, to help the species in procreation. Being female and male is biologically given and almost impossible to alter unless one goes for surgery and other hormonal replacement therapy. But being masculine and feminine is not exactly the same as being male or female respectively.

Masculine means "having the qualities or appearance considered to be typical of men, connected with or like men". This definition points to the qualities or appearance which are typical of men and this may further refer to those qualities and appearance which the majority agree about. Likewise, feminine means "having qualities or appearance traditionally associated with women, especially delicacy and prettiness". This definition points to those qualities and appearance which women traditionally show, for example, being delicate and pretty. Thus we can see being masculine or feminine has to do with having specific types of qualities and appearances which society agrees upon. Being male does not necessarily mean being masculine and being female too does not necessarily mean being feminine. One may be male but not masculine and likewise one may be female but not feminine.

The notions of masculinity and femininity are associated with how the society expects one to behave appropriately according to one's gender. Gender, as you have studied in previous modules, is different from what you mean by sex. Gender is the socio-cultural definition given to girls and boys, men and women. It is a social construct and refers to norms, values, customs and practices by which biological differences are transformed and exaggerated into a much wider social system. While biologically we are male or female, socially we are feminine or masculine gender. The figure below shows the masculine and feminine traits our societies usually refer to.

Gender and Sex

Our understanding of the notions of masculinity and femininity will not be complete without reference to gender and sex. Gender, as you might have come across in previous schedules, is different from what we mean by sex. The concept of gender was introduced in the 1970s to indicate the social roles, characteristics, and values assigned to men and women in a given society. Sex is considered natural or biological unlike gender. The relationship between sex and gender is described as below:

"With a few exceptions, there are two sexes, male and female. To determine the sex one must assay the following physical conditions: external genetalia, internal genetalia, gonads, hormonal states and secondary sex characteristics one's sex then is determined by an algebraic sum of all these qualities and, as is obvious, most people fall under one of two separate bell curves, the one of which is called 'male' and the other 'female'".

Gender is a term that has psychological and cultural rather than biological connotations; if the proper terms for sex are 'male' and 'female', the corresponding terms for gender are masculine and feminine; these latter may be quite independent of sex. Gender denotes the degree of masculinity or femininity found in a person, and obviously, while there is a mix of both in many humans, the normal male is a preponderance of masculinity and the normal female a preponderance of femininity.

Thus masculinity and femininity are terms used to mean socio-cultural expectations, traits, actions and objects associated with men and women. Masculinity and femininity do not mean the same thing everywhere. There are also not valued the same way everywhere. Now we shall discuss how these notions are built in our society? Are they biologically determined or socially constructed?

Femininity and Masculinity: Biology or Culture?

Gender roles and what is feminine and masculine varies according to culture. In our society we associate various behaviours and qualities with masculinity and femininity. The following list shows various male or female qualities:

Masculine	Feminine
Independent	Dependent
Rational	Emotional
Dominating	Tolerant
Smart	Beautiful
Aggressive	Nurturing
Competitive	Submissive
Strong	Weak
Sexually aggressive	Sexually Submissive

Clearly these qualities are mere constructions in our society which reflect only the ideal standards of being men and women and may not reflect real life situations. Every individual possesses a combination of both masculine and feminine qualities, as has been argued by anthropologists and it is the preponderance of a particular type which differentiates masculine and feminine. Further the masculine and feminine qualities are expressed in each individual at different situations and times. Explaining the role of power in masculinity and femininity Researchers have described how individuals show both types in different situations. Men who may be aggressive and dominating husbands at home may act like timid creatures in front of their bosses. This means men take on masculine (aggressive, dominating) traits in situations where they are in power, and behave in a feminine way (follow orders, be submissive) when they are in a subordinate position. Thus femininity and masculinity have more to do with power than with biology.

The notions of masculinity and femininity are socially constructed and the criteria on which they are based are fluid. Being masculine or feminine is not given and changes according to culture, race and historical factors.

Masculinity and femininity is dependent on historical, cultural factors too. For example, among the Etoro of Papua New Guinea masculinity is a form of institutionalised homosexuality. Heterosexuality is discouraged and is practised only for the sake of procreation. The adolescent boys need to acquire the characteristics of masculinity from the older men. This includes the acquisition of semen from older men. Beginning around age ten and continuing into adulthood, males are inseminated orally by older men, usually their maternal uncles.

Anthropologists have supported the view that masculinity and femininity are shaped by socio-cultural factors. Researchers have studied the relation between sex and temperament" and concluded that there are no necessary differences in traits or temperaments between the sexes. Observed difference between temperaments are a result of difference in socialisation and cultural expectations held for each sex. Thus development of masculinity and femininity in cultures is a function of socio-cultural features in a society. Citing examples from three societies researchers explained that among the Arapesh both males and females displayed feminine temperaments like being passive, cooperative and expressive. Among the Mundugamor, both males and females displayed masculine temperamenst like being active, competitive and instrumental. Among the Tchambuli, males and females showed opposite temperament but not according to the usual conceptions of masculinity and femininity. Here, the males displayed emotions and they were more expressive whereas the females were active and instrumental. Thus the study discarded the biological reductionist approach to masculinity and femininity and argued that masculinity and femininity were a function of cultural constructions.

Masculinity and femininity are constantly reconstructed in response to changing economy, natural and man-made disasters, war or migration. Norms, values, practices, and customs signifying masculinity and femininity keep on changing. Thus femininity and masculinity are not out there but are created or constructed differently in different cultures. Further, these notions are not attached to our biological identity. Anyone, biologically male or female, who has masculine or feminine qualities, is called masculine or feminine. Males with so-called feminine characters are called feminine (often derisively) and females who are strong and are in control are called masculine. Transvestites are biologically male but have feminine characters/behaviours. Thus biology is not a determining factor in masculinity and femininity which are rather socially constructed and culturally signified.

There are many ways in which a culture identifies certain norms, values, practices and customs with femininity and masculinity. Those are called signifiers which are created at institutional, ideological and symbolic levels.

How Different Cultures Create Signifiers for Masculinity and Femininity?

Let us begin with a discussion of the recent move by Ferrero Company for introducing a separate candy called kinder joy for girls. The company used to manufacture gender neutral kinder joy that contained toys that any child could play with. But now the company finds it more appropriate to manufacture toys "suitable" for girls only. Marketing of this product attests to and encourages the symbols which stand for femininity. The type of toys for girls manufactured by the company includes among others, dolls resembling Barbie and accessories and ornaments featuring Barbie and other similar female characters. These products exemplify the cultural tools which create conditions for young girls to imbibe femininity expressed by beauty, prettiness, fashion-consciousness, fairness or whiteness, slimness etc. Like this we have various ways of creating and using signifiers for masculinity and femininity in our society.

The processes which help in creating and using various signifiers of masculinity and femininity are socialisation and gendering. Gendering, the way individuals learn gender specific behaviour as a process of upbringing, starts at a very early stage of our lives. There are various processes at different levels of the society which help in gender socialisation.

Role of Parental and Familial Reactions

Let's consider a boy about four years old, the family decided to send him to a nearby dance school. He hated the idea of learning dance. The reason? He already had firm ideas about what boys did. He had already imbibed the idea that dancing with girls was not an activity suitable for boys. At the age of four he not only had a clear idea that he was a boy but also he knew that he would remain a boy for life. Further, he had also good idea about what a boy should or should not do. This happens as a result of continuous feedback by the immediate members of a family regarding the identity and role of a child. The type of reactions or feedback enables us to learn what it means to be a man or woman in a particular society. The parental and familial reactions are mostly motivated by cultural factors. Studies of motherinfant interactions show differences in treatment of boys and girls even when parents believe their reactions to both are same. When asked to assess the personality of a baby the parents answered according to their belief about the sex of the child.

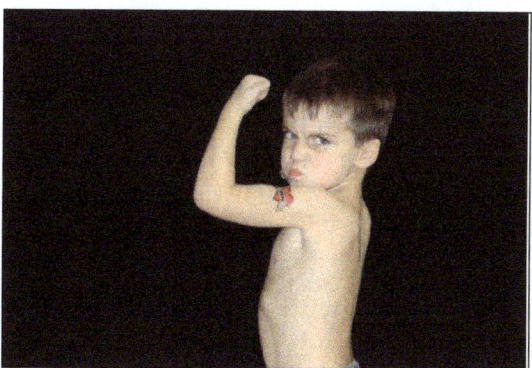

From various behaviours, customs, symbols and gender roles a child comes to know what it means to be a man or woman. Subjective gender identity and the stakes involved are learnt from the family at a very early stage. The learning continues till one becomes adult. The behaviour and roles parents play as father and mother are the basis for various signifiers at this stage.

Role of Rituals and Customs

We have many signifiers of femininity and masculinity created by our culture which help us building our subjective gender identity. The moment a child hears the proclaim "it's a boy" or "it's a girl" by a nurse or physician at the time of his or her sibling's birth, a particular social image of boy or girl is built in a child's mind. The subjective gender identity is built on these signifiers. You might have observed the birth rituals performed in your own society when a difference in the ritual is observed depending upon the sex of the child. Among the Hindus the birth ritual of a baby boy is elaborate and is almost compulsory whereas the birth ritual for a baby girl is neither elaborate nor mandatory. The kind of arrangement and seriousness observed in the birth ritual for the baby boy signifies the importance of boy or man in the society. These act as crucial signifiers for masculinity and femininity. Birth rituals, naming ceremonies, and other related rituals signify what it means to be a man or woman in the society and the differential social status between them. Children learn gender specific roles, rights and obligations and start to identify with masculinity or femininity.

Crucial signifiers for masculinity and femininity exist in the family itself. We have distinct male and female behaviour and institutional practices right in the family which symbolize masculinity and femininity. Differential treatment of boys and girls in various familial customs create strong signifiers of masculinity and femininity. Researchers analysed various cultural practices among the Alor and has shown how food distribution and consumption is linked to gendering in the society. They concluded that:

Although a girl has more regular access to food she does not have the guest privileges of the small boy. She gets no presents during butchering unless an unusually indulgent and thoughtful male kin happens to remember her and give her a bit of meat. The meat at feasts is always distributed to the women but only in terms of the males in their household. That is, women get meat for their husbands and sons but not for themselves or their daughters. This is consistent with the theory that flesh food is the property of men. Since feasts are primarily occasions for food distribution and actual consumption is at home, women do get a share, but only as dependents of the men. Also, since meat is eaten primarily in connection with feasts or sacrifices and is definitely a treat, the way is open for it to become set in children's minds as a symbol of masculine prerogative. The system of meat distribution helps to reinforce early in life, and on a very basic level, the role of masculine prestige in the culture. Men are not the providers; in fact, they are quite the contrary. They are the ones provided for, but they are also the purveyors of a delicacy.

The girl, then, is set during early childhood in the essential and intimate relationship to the food cycle that she will follow all her life. Yet no girl who is unmarried may make a contribution in her own name to food displays, even though she may have grown and prepared some of the food that is brought in her mother's name. This means that she may be assuming adult responsibilities without receiving adult recognition. It is worth noting in this connection that public food contributions are the symbol of female adulthood.

Other institutional practices in various cultures which signify masculinity and femininity are mode of inheritance and post-marital residential pattern. Girls at a very younger stage witness these norms and come to build a particular image about what it means to be a man or woman.

It is a common sight in Indian households that parents of a girl child or children are pitied. Bringing up a daughter is like 'pouring water in sand'. The future of parents bringing up daughters is considered bleak for they will have no support or succour in old age. An expression conveys this effectively: 'Bringing up a daughter is like watering a plant in another's courtyard'. Spontaneous response to the birth of a female child is often made explicit by outsiders. Remarks by relatives, outsiders, and hospital staff upon birth of a second daughter often create an image among little girls that women are only the temporary residents in their maternal home. Accordingly an image of passiveness, softness, and dependence is created among the girls at a very early stage.

Role of Media

The contemporary television shows and cinemas, barring some notable exceptions, mostly show programmes where the main character is a male around whom the entire story revolves. Analysis of children's programmes also confirms the above findings. Studies of the most popular cartoon serials in the television show that virtually all the leading figures are male and males occupy the centrality of the stories depicted. Thus media creates signifiers of masculinity as dominance, success, achievement and intelligence.

The role of the media in creating symbols of masculinity is evident worldwide. One of the wide spread symbols of masculinity is martial arts which have spread across the world through films and media. Wide portrayal of martial arts though Hollywood and Hingking Film industries is the cause of its spreading worldwide. This is a rich illustration of the ways in which long-standing martial arts traditions, reformulated to meet the fantasies of contemporary (sometimes lumpen) youth populations, create new cultures of masculinity and violence, which are in turn the fuel for increased violence in national and international politics.

The depiction of a central male figure in most films, barring a few, with increasing use of electronic and communication gadgets, arms like AK-47 is creating a type of masculinity marked with violence and insensitivity. Such violence is in turn the spur to an increasingly rapid and amoral arms trade that penetrates the entire world. Cultural creation of signifiers of masculinity such as the above are linked to images of violence and terror. The contemporary mass media is creating images of femininity which feeds to the existing gender stereotypes. Barring some exceptions most of the films, songs and commercials create symbols of femininity marked by weakness, dependence and passivity. A look at the Bollywood songs and American music albums can give an idea how women are depicted. These songs are about men using women and having control over them. Barring very few, most music albums and commercials portray women as property, object of desire and sex objects and show no respect for women as human beings. Thus media creates and uses signifiers of femininity contributing to the continuity of gender stereotypes.

Creation and Use of Symbols of Sexuality

Like femininity and masculinity, sexuality too is conditioned by socio-cultural factors. The fact that human beings reproduce sexually leads us to accept that sexuality is part of our nature. But no society leaves sexuality to nature: almost every society has built rules on the 'proper' way to behave sexually. The need to have sex is natural or instinctual but it is not 'natural' when we decide what sex can be, where, when and with whom. Sexuality is all about this. Sexuality is about the sexual feelings, attractions and preferences we have towards other people. Everyone's sexuality is different. Some people are attracted to opposite sex, some towards the same sex and others may be attracted towards both. Some people may be attracted towards only one sex, others are attracted towards a variety of people regardless of sex or gender with a lot of different preferences in between. Some people feel attracted to the same sex right from the adolescence and some people realise their orientation quite late in their life. Bruce Jenner, ex-Olympic athlete, realised at the age of sixty five that she was a female trapped in the body of a male.

Whether sexuality is biologically driven or socio-culturally conditioned has long been debated. The biological essentialism has been criticised by many scholars. Of central importance to critical analysis of sexuality is the work of Michel Foucault. He analysed sexuality in a historical perspective and explained it as a socio-political and historical construction. He adopted an anti-essentialist notion of sexual drives and identity in favour of a constructionist view. He argued that sexuality with all its regulative aspects is a result of the society's need to control human beings. According to Foucault, 'sexuality is a name that can be given to a historical construct'.

Cultures create and use symbols of sexuality in various ways. The symbols of sexuality vary across cultures in time and space. Among the Sambia of Papua New Guenea sexuality is symbolised as a form of cultural category where both homosexuality and heterosexuality find their place. The dominant sexuality is a form of ritualised male homosexuality where masculinity is learned institutionally by practising oral sex with senior male members of the society. Heterosexuality is practised only for procreation and is generally considered to be debilitating as it drains one's energy if practised for the sake of pleasure.

Misandry

The term has been around since 1898, according to Merriam Webster dictionary. Some believe misandry has, for a very long time, had an impact on society, in which men have been attributed as the inferior and morally deficient members of society by misandrists.

Philosopher and writer Helene von Druskowitz wrote a radically feminist response in 1905 to an male, anti-feminist writer's work. Titled, "Pessimistic Cardinal Propositions — Man as a Logical and Moral Impossibility," she wrote a futuristic depiction in which men destroyed the world. And she outlined how the same world would prosper if led and inhabited only by women. More than 60 years later, the SCUM Manifesto by Valerie Jean Solanas was written and expressed similar ideas — which hadn't been done since Helene von Druskowitz.

Modern Misandry

Misandry has been a topic of conversation in more recent years with the increasing intensity of the feminist movement. Men have begun associating feminism with misandry and citing more radical versions of feminism that discuss a hatred for men in addition to an all-encompassing support of women.

Certain examples of what are being dubbed misandrist speak may include any overgeneralization of the male, involving their likes, dislikes, their interests, their motivations, their sex lives, etc. Examples of other labeled misandrist speak:

- "All men care about is sex."

- "Men don't respect the female opinion."

- "Man up."

- "He doesn't care about me because I am a woman."

Modern feminism has done a great job addressing the discrepancies in societal structure and the discrimination that has kept women subject to patriarchal ideologies for centuries, but no one has addressed the backlash it has generated against men.

Misandry, defined as the hatred of men, is the counterpart to the more well-known term misogyny, though both have proven to be equally damaging. Yet, while misogyny is generally condemned, misandry is much less admonished, despite both behaviors impeding the goal of equality. Like misogyny, misandry can manifest in several forms, including acts of denigration, vilification, discrimination, gender violence and sexual reification.

It's one thing to generalize and hate men after a bad breakup, an event that entitles one to briefly exaggerate in order to cope with the feeling of indignation. It's another thing entirely to hate men for being men, feeling contempt toward them and disregarding their opinions simply because they are not women.

Some women believe that condemning all men for the acts committed by a few is their right; however, they are not conscious of the fact that they are imitating the very behavior of men discriminating against women.

It appears that some feminists don't intend to negotiate with egalitarian ideologies, and would rather institutionally displace men and presume women as supreme. A large part of the feminist rhetoric used today has gone beyond the limits that differentiate criticism in regards to sexist beliefs. It has come to criticize men themselves by focusing on individual behaviors, such as the way men speak, the way men interact socially, and even the way men sit in public spaces.

Certain characteristics of masculinity are often arbitrarily seen as absolute defects, and men are condemned for such traits, along with any woman who dares to object to the idea that masculinity is detrimental to society.

If such accusations were made toward women, the accuser would be seen as a misogynist, without hesitation. Still, while misogyny is seen as a problem in today's society, misandry is a term few are familiar with, despite the conflicting nature of both behaviors. By supporting ideas that are prejudiced against men, women seeking equality will suffer since men will think feminism is hateful and vindictive against them.

The antagonism between sexes does not contribute to the promoting of social equality. Obsessing over the misconduct of individuals from either sex diverts the attention that should be focused on bigger issues, such as implementing institutional changes that create equitability toward women's needs, or accommodations for men raising a family as a single parent.

Since the publishing of the Declaration of Sentiments in 1848, in which women listed their complaints in regards to misrepresentation, feminism has challenged the ideology of masculinity and patriarchy alike. These complaints however, were directed toward institutions and governments, not individuals.

The evolution of these feminist complaints occurred in the '70s, with the ascent of radical feminism promoting the idea that "the personal is political." During this time, it seems that many feminists portrayed men as barbaric soldiers defending the patriarchal structure of society, yet few understood, or even considered, that the patriarchal ideologies after which society was structured harmed countless men as well.

Patriarchy upholds a standard regarded as absolute when it comes to appearances and behavior and when men do not resemble that standard, they are judged discriminately, often condemned by both sexes under the pretense that they need to "man-up."

A man who disregards the societal criteria of masculinity or fails to assimilate to the alpha role exposes himself to the rejection of men and women alike. Not all men are evil, and while men are not always considerate of those who are discriminated against, not all men discriminate. It is important to remember that men, too, are the victims of social pressures and have expectations put on them by society. It's time to stop accusing one another and come together to fight for equal pay, equity as guardians and recognition of intellect and strength.

Men's Movement

Men's movements are a collection of social, political, and philosophical organizations that seek to redefine men's relationship to their prescribed gender roles. Although male-centered organizations have existed throughout history, the organizations usually referred to as men's movements begin in the 1970s. They generally formed after second-wave feminist movements and sought to reform (or reassert) men's position in a society with new values.

The earliest men's movements (those of the 1970s and 1980s) were largely pro-feminist, followed by a period of backlash agendas aimed at reclaiming rights that were thought to have been lost to women. From the 1990s onward, men's movements became highly formalized and aimed at niche groups with various interests, which make it difficult to claim that man's movements as a whole share any particular ideology other than their general focus on men in society. The early pro-feminist movement was fairly small and had more female than male supporters, but as the focus turned away from supporting women toward male-focused agendas, overall participation has grown. Women are active in some organizations, although usually in small numbers, but many organizations either do not allow women as members or only allow them limited access to activities and trainings.

Mythopoetic Movement

The most famous of the men's movements is the Mythopoetic Movement. It is based on the ideas of the U.S. poet Robert Bly, particularly those expressed in an interview he gave in 1982 published under the title "What Do Men Really Want? A New Age Interview with Robert Bly," and on Bly's 1990 publication Iron John: A Book about Men. In this book Bly relies heavily on mythology and religion scholar Joseph Campbell's teachings about the archetypal nature of fairy tales, which he derived from Jungian analytical psychology. Bly used a fairy tale by the German linguists and folklorists brothers Jakob L.K. Grimm and Wilhelm K. Grimm called "Iron John" as a model for contemporary men and as a way of guiding men on a spiritual journey to reconnect with the deep masculine parts of themselves that modern society has hidden from them. It strives to reassert a primitive masculinity to allow men to deal with the pain of their lives and is thus a combination of essentialist and relativist gender constructions.

The movement's basis in psychology shaped the application of its teachings: It kept away from overtly political issues related to men (which other movements focused on), and was concerned with the emotional, spiritual, and psychological well-being of men. The Iron John movement has several organizations, some more formal than others, associated with it, each with their own objectives. The general subjects of interest to the movement, however, are those traditionally associated with men: war, violence, the ability (or inability) to live up to ideals of masculinity, and how to be fathers to sons. Although members of the movement claim to be at least somewhat pro-feminist, the concept of the feminine and issues relating to women are usually excised from discussion or consideration. The Mythopoetic Movement has often been ridiculed by people who claim that it prioritizes the emotional over the physical, thereby overturning masculine gender stereotypes. The movement does emphasize the emotional, but a devotee of the movement might claim that it seeks to reshape masculine gender roles rather than to overturn them. In fact, the physical is sometimes emphasized as a means of access to the emotional. Workshops and retreats often take place outdoors, and the stereotypical images of men beating drums and passing talking sticks are derived from this movement. The Mankind Project is an organization founded in 1984 based on ideas found in the Mythopoetic Movement.

One of its programs is the New Warrior Training Adventure, a weekend retreat where men take part in the mythical hero's journey, described by Campbell, which resembles a tribal initiation rite. The retreats take place in wooded areas, and participants are required to leave behind cell phones, radios, and any other items that connect them with the outside world or provide comfort. The specific activities of these weekends remain secret, given that all participants are required to sign a confidentiality agreement, but sleep deprivation and physical exertion are highly rumored to be components. The financial structure of the organization, the secrecy of the weekend retreats, along with the setting, which critics claim is ideal for mind control activities, has caused many to label the organization a cult. Other activities of the Mankind Project include leadership training, mentoring of young men, veterans' assistance, and prison outreach. These programs stress the movement's ideas, but have come under much less scrutiny than the New Warrior Training Adventure.

Promise Keepers

The Promise Keepers is a Christian men's group founded by Bill McCartney in 1990. Like the concept of Muscular Christianity promoted by the evangelist and one-time professional baseball player Billy Sunday in response to first-wave feminism, Promise Keepers seeks to reassert the male as the head of the family, to whom women should willingly submit. In return for his wife's submission, the husband will lead the family in a gentle and loving way based on the model of Jesus Christ. They actively seek to overturn what they call the sissified status of men in the late twentieth century, including reimagining Jesus as a warrior figure.

It is an antifeminist movement that seeks to reassert essentialist views of gender and to promote a conservative Christian agenda. As with most men's movements, it has a primarily white, middle-class membership. It has actively engaged in outreach to other racial groups, however, and attempts to overcome racial barriers between men as one of its goals. Promise Keepers functions through a series of events held in stadiums and sports arenas, at times attracting more than 100,000 men to a single event. The organization's membership peaked in October 1997 with a nationally televised event on the National Mall in Washington, DC, that attracted more than a million participants. Financial difficulties following the rally caused the organization to become volunteer run instead of having a paid staff, and admission costs to Promise Keepers events increased sharply in an effort to raise money. The change in organizational model and the increased expense are credited with the decline in popularity of the organization.

Million Man March

The Million Man March is unusual among men's movements in that it has a primarily nonwhite membership. The organization is devoted to a broad slate of social and economic justice goals centering on the African-American community. Since its inception the organization has been divided between those who wish to use the Million Man March events as a platform to demand redress of past racial injustice, and those who look to the African-American man as a catalyst for future change within their community. The second formulation is the more popularly promoted one and the one that most members claim to be in favor of. As with many of the other movement groups, the Million Man March encourages members to look to themselves, and specifically their role as men, to promote change and prosperity in the African-American community.

One particularly large focus has been on the issue of fatherhood, as the African-American community has a higher percentage of out-of-wedlock births and children raised by single mothers than the national average. The Million Man March tries to work through black men to help other black men be responsible members of their families and their communities. The movement began as an event, with the hope of drawing 1 million African-American men to the National Mall in Washington, DC, on October 16, 1995 in an act of dedication to their communities. More than 800,000 men did participate that day, making it one of the largest rallies of its kind in history. Because it was originally an event, not an organization, the Million Man March suffered from a lack of direction following the march itself and has also been subject to its internal factional tensions. Although no other march of the size of the original has been held, regional marches are held periodically across the United States.

Toxic Masculinity

This claim of a singular, real masculinity has been roundly rejected since the late 1980s by a new sociology of masculinity. Led by the sociologist Raewyn Connell, this school of thought presents gender as the product of relations and behaviors, rather than as a fixed set of identities and attributes.

Connell's work describes multiple masculinities shaped by class, race, culture, sexuality, and other factors, often in competition with one another as to which can claim to be more authentic. In this view, which is now the prevailing social-scientific understanding of masculinity, the standards by which a "real man" is defined can vary dramatically across time and place.

Connell and others theorized that common masculine ideals such as social respect, physical strength, and sexual potency become problematic when they set unattainable standards. Falling short can make boys and men insecure and anxious, which might prompt them to use force in order to feel, and be seen as, dominant and in control. Male violence in this scenario doesn't emanate from something bad or toxic that has crept into the nature of masculinity itself. Rather, it comes from these men's social and political settings, the particularities of which set them up for inner conflicts over social expectations and male entitlement.

"The popular discussion of masculinity has often presumed there are fixed character types among men". It's more important to understand the situations in which groups of men act, the patterns in their actions, and the consequences of what they do.

As this research was popularized, however, it was increasingly mischaracterized. By the mid-2000s, despite Connell's objections, her complex theories were being portrayed in ways that echoed mythopoetic archetypes of healthy and destructive masculinity. In a 2005 study of men in prison researchers defined toxic masculinity as the constellation of socially regressive male traits that serve to foster domination, the devaluation of women, homophobia, and wanton violence. Referencing Connell's work, they argued that prison brings out the "toxic" aspects of masculinity in prisoners, but that this toxicity is already present in the wider cultural context. Kupers believes critics of his study incorrectly assumed that he claimed masculinity itself is toxic, though he acknowledged that the article could have explained his position in greater detail.

Since then, the return to toxic masculinity has leaked from academic literature to wide cultural circulation. Today the concept offers an appealingly simple diagnosis for gendered violence and masculine failure: Those are the "toxic" parts of masculinity, distinct from the "good" parts. New proponents of the concept, sometimes unaware of its origins, tend to agree that men and boys are affected by a social "sickness" and that the cure is cultural renewal—that is, men and boys need to change their values and attitudes. Former President Barack Obama is championing mentoring programs as the solution to a "self-defeating model for being a man" in which respect is gained through violence. A range of classes and programs encourage boys and men to get in touch with their feelings and to develop a healthy, "progressive" masculinity. In some educational settings, these programs are becoming mandatory.

Certainly, these programs can have a positive impact. Research consistently shows that boys and men who hold sexist attitudes are more likely to perpetrate gendered violence. Connell herself notes that when the term toxic masculinity refers to the assertion of masculine privilege or men's power, it is making a worthwhile point. There are well-known gender patterns in violent and abusive behavior.

The question is: Where do these sexist attitudes come from? Are men and boys just the victims of cultural brainwashing into misogyny and aggression, requiring re-education into the "right" beliefs? Or are these problems more deep-seated, and created by the myriad insecurities and contradictions of men's lives under gender inequality? The problem with a crusade against toxic masculinity is that in targeting culture as the enemy, it risks overlooking the real-life conditions and forces that sustain culture.

There's genuine danger in this misperception. By focusing on culture, people who oppose toxic masculinity can inadvertently collude with institutions that perpetuate it. For example, the alcohol industry has funded research to deny the relationship between alcohol and violence, instead blaming "masculinity" and "cultures of drinking." In this regard, the industry is repeating liberal feminist arguments about toxic masculinity. However, there is strong evidence that the density of liquor shops in a given geographic area increases the local rate of domestic violence. Any serious framework for preventing violence against women will address alcohol availability as well as masculine norms and sexism.

Machismo

Machismo is defined as a strong sense of masculine pride. In Latino culture machismo is more than just a word as it is so embedded in the culture that it is not only accepted, but often even expected. In any study on Latino groups, machismo is a subject that should be considered, but it is often forgotten. Some use the word "Hispanic" and others use "Latino," they are used interchangeably in the literature review because the groups mentioned in all are articles fall under both terms.

In Latin American culture, machismo is a social behavior pattern in which the Latino male exhibits an overbearing attitude to anyone in a position he perceives as inferior to his, demanding complete subservience. Machismo is usually used and defined with a negative connotation; however within the traditional Latino culture, "macho" also has good aspects that are usually neglected. Latin men are expected to be a "varoon," who is caring, responsible, decisive, strong of character, and the protector of the extended family. Some of the more commonly known negative aspects of machismo are aggressiveness, physical strength, emotional insensitivity, and womanizing.

Another concept that is rarely mentioned is "marianismo," which is the female counterpart of machismo. It is a behavior pattern in which the traditional Latin female perceives herself as morally and spiritually superior to the man in direct proportion to his sexual behavior. This social behavior comes from the expectation to be virgin like. "Marianismo, a popular term that implies an idealized view of femininity based on the image of Mary, the Virgin Mother, connotes passivity and submissiveness and the appetence of a virgin like model for women.

Impact of Machismo on Hispanic Women

Through the analysis of the impact of machismo in Hispanic women the definition of machismo in Latin American culture is discussed and the social behavior called "marianismo" is also mentioned. In Latin American countries, where Latin American culture is obviously more prevalent, the extent to which machismo and marianismo are expected and accepted is great. The Roman Catholic religion enforces these expectations of social behavior for both men and women. The social behaviors were stated to be learned behaviors through the generations.

Women are told they have to learn to cook well for their future husband as well as do household chores well in order not to displease their future husbands. "Latin American women are equalized by the dictates of male superiority and are reared and trained to respond to the needs and expectations of their future husbands".

Acculturation becomes a factor when it comes to Latino women in the United States, "these women tend to be more verbal and assertive than their Latin American counterparts". They may be less submissive but these women still remain attached to this social behavior; they are caught between the old culture of their countries of origin and the new culture of the United States. "Their hesitance to pander how to bring about changes that would merge the two social cultural systems often makes them seems complacent, unmotivated, and accepting of the status quo". Although the extremes of both machismo and marianismo are challenged in the United States the self-concept of Latin women in the Unites States is still attached to the social behavior of the older culture.

Hispanic Househusbands and Machismo

A study of Hispanic "househusbands" in southern California shed more light on machismo in the United States. A Hispanic "househusband" is a man who challenges "the norms of the larger American culture as well as the traditions of the Hispanic subculture, and opt for a role which focuses upon household maintenance and emotional family support". The issues of machismo came up because is an accepted social behavior in Latin American culture and a Hispanic "househusband" defies the norms because of the economic situation and the women have to go out of the home and make some if not all the economic stability of the household. "Machismo is being challenged by the present situation affecting the Hispanic adult male's role, social status, and martial obligations".

Hegemonic Masculinity

The concept of hegemonic masculinity allows us to understand how the presence of plural masculinities generates hierarchical domination not only between men and women, but also between men themselves. Initially formulated in the 1980s to shed light on a series of practices that promoted the favourable social condition of men over women, the concept of hegemonic masculinity is premised on the existence of a dominant form of masculinity. All men position themselves in relation to it, and therefore internalise personal codes of behaviour that contribute to its reproduction. The pressure to conform and relate to this ideal dominant masculinity perpetuates this structure of gender-biased hierarchy in society.

Obviously, the type of hegemonic masculinity that dominates social hierarchies has different characteristics depending on the community in which it is embedded. Nevertheless, it displays common features throughout different geographical and historical communities. A popular definition of the concept has been 'an idealised, dominant, heterosexual masculinity, constructed in relation to women and to subordinated masculinities, and closely connected to the institution of marriage' Any man that aspires to embody this masculinity must display aggressive and violent behaviour whilst restraining the flow of vulnerable emotions. He should also exhibit strength and toughness, and be competitive and successful. Finally, and most notably, the dominant man should be heterosexual.

An exemplar of such perfect dominant masculinity seems not to exist; however, as men strive to achieve it, they create different forms of masculinities that generate a social hierarchical structure that exerts profound effects on society. All men are subject to a social pressure to conform to the dominant ideas of being a man; those who do not, are typically subordinated and socially marginalised. This happens, for instance, to those that identify as LGBTQ+, or those that are labelled as 'effeminate'. As a consequence, a range of gender forms and sexualities that are not 'dominant' are subordinated.

There are also many other, more subtle consequences. For the individual, the necessity to hide one's emotions may lead to psychological distress during life. LGBTQ+ individuals, for instance, experience difficulties in coming to terms with their nature since they fear rejection of their personal gender identity. Being oneself thus becomes a conviction to inferiority and to everlasting social exclusion. Moreover, the marginalisation of those that diverge from the dominant gender stereotype gives rise to social conflicts, from bullying in schools to anti-gay rights movements. This reduces the quality of life and impedes human development since it disempowers people by relegating them to the margins of the social group.

The effects of the presence of hegemonic masculinity are then translated to the institutional, legal, political and economic spheres of society which perpetuate the inequality between and within genders. In many countries, for instance, gender pay gaps and glass ceilings between women, minorities and men are still present; or rights for LGBTQ+ people have not yet been introduced. Furthermore, expectations regarding the social role of a man can lead to the perpetuation of gender-biased social roles that impede innovation, since men and women have to fit the roles that are socially assigned to them. For example, up to a few decades ago, being a man in Ireland meant to either become a priest, or a hardworking family man. The lack of life options and choices drastically reduces the degree of individual freedom in deciding the life one has reason to value. Hegemonic masculinity, therefore, produces far-reaching effects on society, harming social equality and human development.

How to tackle the oppressive effects of inter and intra gender hierarchies? There is no easy answer. Hegemonic masculinity is arguably a global phenomenon that takes place across various social levels in different societies. Hegemonic masculinity affects international relations, domestic politics, military practices; education and sport; corporate governance and the emergence of transnational business masculinities, just to give a few examples. It operates on three levels: the local (family, community, and local culture); the regional (the nation state and the culture embedded in it) and the global (influencing the transnational areas of politics, business and media). Efforts to promote gender equality and a de-hierarchisation of the gender system need to take this into account, and operate on these three levels.

Numerous institutions and organisations throughout the world are seeking to empower women and the LGBTQ community, therefore encouraging gender equality. Women's organisations such as UN Women, The Girl Effect, Girls not Brides and Half the Sky all aim at ending women's economic, cultural and social oppression. LGBTQ organisations such as ILGA and Global Action for Trans Equality seek to promote LGBT and intersex rights, with the ultimate aim of demolishing those hierarchies that see the heterosexual man as superior to all other forms of masculinities.

Tackling hegemonic masculinity entails putting a stop to the development of stereotypical, socially constructed differences between male and female. This form of gender socialisation perpetuates dominance and subordination between and within gender roles. The first step is to recognise the effects that hegemonic masculinity produces on society. By understanding them, we can change our society, favouring the emergence of a true, full equality between and within genders.

The cogency of the theory of hegemonic masculinity resides in its conception of man. The domination takes place not only between genders, but even within them. The problem is, therefore, not man per se, but certain types of behaviour associated with dominance and power. Men face gender-related problems, just like women. This creates a bond of mutual understanding and solidarity between men and women, which could generate a renewed awareness on gender perceptions. A solution could be the promotion of public reasoning processes and debates regarding the effects of marginalisation and disempowerment generated by hegemonic masculinities. In this way, men will play an active role in theories of gender and development along with women, contributing to making society fairer.

Masculism

Masculism (also referred to as Masculinism) is an ideology associated with the men's movement. It consists of social theories, political movements, and moral philosophies primarily based on the experiences of men. Although masculism provides a general critique of social relations, many of its proponents also seek to analyze gender inequality and promote men's rights, interests, and issues. Masculism is viewed by its proponents as having an egalitarian view of gender issues, even though it focuses on men's experience.

The first secular response to feminism came from Ernest Belfort Bax, a socialist theoretician in the height of socialism at the beginning of the 20th century, and an associate of Karl Marx. Bax wrote The Fraud of Feminism in 1913, which was in essence the first masculinist text, with chapter titles such as The Anti-Man Crusade, Always The 'Injured Innocent', and The 'Chivalry' Fake. Another possible early text, which covers many topics still in current circulation, was H.L. Mencken's post-WWI book In Defense of Women.

In its modern form, masculism has evolved as a response to changing women's roles. The feminist advocacy for professional women led to a similar advocacy for fathers. For example, following the "working woman" TV programs of the 1970s (such as The Mary Tyler Moore Show) came numerous "single father" shows (such as Diff'rent Strokes and Silver Spoons), as well as the child-custody themed motion picture Kramer vs. Kramer.

However, masculism is not merely a response to feminism. Although many masculinist ideas serve as a rejoinder to feminist views, there are many issues, such as military conscription and fatherhood that have been identified as concerns for men in their own right. Warren Farrell is probably the most prominent author using the term "masculinist" today.

Masculinist Concerns

Masculinists cite one-sided legislation, selective enforcement, and neglected civil rights as examples of discrimination against men and boys. Examples may include.

Violence

Masculinist concerns focus on societal acceptance of violence harming men paired with the stigma against violence harming women, as well as males being taught or expected to take on violent roles.

- Men forced to risk their lives in male-only conscripted military service.

- Portrayal of "violence against women" as more important than other forms of violence, including "violence against men" (e.g. "never hit a woman/girl, but it is acceptable for a woman to beat a man").

- Parents conditioning boys into violent roles and girls into nurturing ones (e.g., boys receive toy soldiers as gifts, when girls receive dolls).

- Depiction of violence against men as humorous, in the media (e.g., the movie I Love You to Death) and elsewhere, when women are equally violent.

- Specifying in news articles about violence whether or not women and children were harmed, implying that the life of a woman or child is worth more than the life of a man.

- Assumption of female innocence or sympathy for women, which may result in problems such as disproportionate penalties for similar crimes, male victims charged in domestic violence cases, more boys killed by parents than girls and male rape victims by women.

- Societal failure to address prison rape issues such as prevention (e.g., reducing prison crowding that requires sharing of cells), enforcement, and even correctional staff punishing prisoners by confining them with known rapists. Attention has been drawn to portrayals of male rape by women, or implied rape, as humorous (as seen in the Virgin Mobile adverts featuring Wyclef Jean) where portrayals of female rape could not acceptably be used in this fashion.

Parenting

- Equality in child custody, such as shared parenting.

- Pregnancies carried to term despite agreements ahead of time that they would not be, subjecting men to unwanted parental responsibilities and/or child support expectations.

- The opposite of the above, where a man who may want to have a child also has no right to decide if his wife/girlfriend/etc. decides to abort.

- Equality in adoption rights (several states allow single women to adopt children but not single men).

Discrimination

- Legislation that addresses women's needs without considering the corresponding need in men (e.g., Women, Infants, and Children Act; Violence Against Women Act).

- Biases in the justice system against men, such as higher incarceration rates and longer sentences for men (compared to women) for the same crimes.

- Statutory rape laws enforced more vehemently in instances where the victim is female and/or the perpetrator is male (e.g. the cases of Mary Kay Letourneau and Vili Fualaau, Pamela Rogers, and Debra Lafave Double Standard: The Bias Against Male Victims of Sexual Abuse).

- Rape shield laws, which prevent men from having a fair trial.

- Cathy Young argues that in rape cases, "the dogma that "women never lie" means that there is, for all intents and purposes, no presumption of innocence for the defendant".

- Women may marry at younger ages than men in some U.S. states.

- Men pay higher premiums for auto, health, life and disability insurance, though other forms of discrimination are prohibited.

- Men not being 'believed' when being raped by their Wife, Girlfriend or Fiancee; lesser or no penalty for women that rape men

Social Concerns

- Increasing suicide rate amongst young men, four times higher than amongst young women.

- Lack of advocacy for men's rights; more social programs for women than for men.

- Special government agencies for women's affairs with no corresponding agencies for men's affairs.

- Men being incarcerated for the inability to pay child support payments.

- Lack of legal ramifications or enforcement for paternity fraud.

Health

- Relative lack of funding for men's health; far more money funded for female causes than for male causes (e.g., prostate cancer vs. breast cancer research).

- Limited choices regarding male contraception.

- Cosmetic circumcision (in contrast to the treatment of phimosis for example) is widespread and acceptable in infant males, despite risks of tissue damage and other complications during the procedure.

Education

- Lack of educational aid for boys and men, given that their performance/enrollment at most levels lags behind that of girls and women; some states declaring (de jure or de facto) all-male schools illegal and all-female schools legal.

There is concern that some university Women's studies departments are more concerned with teaching feminist ideology than equality of gender. The content and emphasis of these courses vary, and some even discuss "masculinities"; but masculinists fear that many such courses contribute to animosity towards men.

Some universities also carry "men's studies" courses. Some feminists argue that these are redundant, stating that academia throughout history was predominantly focused on men; supporters of these courses note that most subjects do not deal with or study gender directly.

Employment

- Harder physical entrance criteria for men in many occupations - such as the army, police and fire service. Requiring men to be physically stronger than women in these occupations leaves men responsible for a greater share of the physical work, for no more pay.

- Legal inequality and protections of paternal vs. maternal leave.

Differences in Masculinist Ideology

As with most social movements, there is no consensus as to what exactly constitutes "masculism." Some feel the word describes a belief that the male and female genders should be considered complementary and interdependent by necessity. Such expressions of masculism are built around the belief that differentiated gender roles are natural and should be exempt from government interference. Others masculinists, such as Warren Farrell, support an ideology of equivalence between the sexes, rather than a belief in unchangeable gender differences. A more encompassing definition might be "a movement to empower males in society, and to redress discrimination against men."

Because it is the name of a political and social movement, masculism is sometimes considered synonymous with the men's rights or fathers' rights movements. However, many of the fathers' rights movement make a clear distinction between masculism and their own often quite varied approaches to gender relations.

Some masculinists state that there is a covert matriarchy and that one of their goals is to overturn it, and elect masculinist politicians, whom they would consider more altruistically motivated. Theorists such as David Constantine envision structural changes in taxation or other areas to compensate for what they see as natural differences and expectations between genders.

Gender roles in religion are a source of disagreement among masculinists: some support a general leadership role for men, while others argue for relative equality between the genders. Liberal masculinists such as Warren Farrell tend to favour a secular, gender-neutral stance, whereas conservatives tend to prefer a religious approach, such as represented in The Inevitability of Patriarchy by Steven Goldberg. Conservatives may promote a "New Patriarchy" by countering feminist ideology with their own. Such liberal-conservative dynamics illustrate the diversity of a movement that nonetheless has a unified purpose of promoting men's welfare.

Conservative Views

Conservative masculinists tend to believe that profound gender differences are inherent in human nature. They believe that feminists who have denounced differentiated gender roles as an oppressive artificial construct are conducting a fallacious experiment by attempting to negate these differences via legislation and other means. Many conservatives believe that feminism has played a role in the high rates of divorce , alienation of the genders, female chauvinism, love-shyness, disintegrating communities, fatherless children, high school dropout, drug addiction, consumerism, teenage pregnancy, male suicide, violent crime (especially murder), road rage, and over-filled prisons.

Critics of gender equality laws (beginning with the U.S. Civil Rights Act of 1964) believe they have helped to make feminist ideology mainstream - that such laws serve primarily women and have created significant unconstitutional discrimination against men. While some feminists fight against an "all-powerful patriarchy," conservative masculinists tend to consider patriarchy an inevitable result of the biological differences between the sexes. Some disagree that women are powerless victims of patriarchal oppression; they suggest that feminists use this idea to curtail men's rights and to justify their negative views of men. They claim this has achieved a covert matriarchy, aided by chivalry towards women that itself undermines the theory of female oppression. Some men honestly urge a return to responsible patriarchy, often by appealing to traditional religious views of male power being ordained by God.

Liberal Views

Liberals tend to view masculism as a complementary movement to feminism, the so-called "New Masculinity." Both feminism and masculism are seen as attempts to correct disadvantages induced by gender roles. Whereas feminists address areas they believe women to be disadvantaged, such as equal pay and promotion, masculinists address areas they believe men to be disadvantaged, such as divorce and custody, health and education, criminal prosecution and sentencing. These masculinists may object to specific aspects of feminism or to the expressed views of specific feminist groups, but do not reject feminism as a concept, or believe that the feminist movement as a whole is hostile to masculism. Some sociologists regard masculism with suspicion, seeing it as a reactionary, even misogynistic movement at odds with feminism. Others accept that feminists and masculinists are natural allies against a common enemy, sexism, which is or can be as damaging to men as it is to women.

For example, Warren Farrell states in The Myth of Male Power that both genders are hampered by the "bisexist" roles of the past: sexism that oppresses both genders. He emphasises the compatibility of both movements: "I use two podiums: Dr. Farrell, masculinist; and Dr. Farrell, Feminist." Fred Hayward, in his speech to the National Congress for Men in 1981, states: "We must not reverse the women's movement; we must accelerate it... [Men's liberation] is not a backlash, for there is nothing about traditional sex roles that I want to go back to."

This suggests that masculism in some form can assist and aid the women's movement. Feminists have responded to this with both encouragement and trepidation. Some feminists believe that space for women to have a voice would be threatened by the presence of men, or that a growing presence of men in the women's movement would displace the voices of the women. Others greet masculinist interests in the women's movement as important for the eradication of sexism in society.

Likewise, gender egalitarians call for both masculinists and feminists who are truly interested in equality to unite under the banner of gender egalitarianism. This philosophy is sympathetic to legitimate grievances of both males and females.

Criticisms of Masculism

While agreeing they are legitimate concerns, and are in some ways underrepresented in society, some critics of masculism disagree with the approach being taken. They argue that too much criticism is being directed at other philosophies, namely feminism. What masculinists often contend is censorship of points-of-view that don't fall in line with what they perceive as "feminist" and/or "pro-feminist," critics assert is merely widespread disagreement with masculinist views and that nothing protects anybody from criticism no matter what their beliefs. Some critics question the validity of masculinist claims and the use of individual anecdotes to assert prevalence of anti-male discrimination. To masculinists who bemoan a tendency to treat alleged rapists as "guilty until proven innocent," critics contend that such views are not specific to alleged rapists and suggest a failure to differentiate between the legal view ("innocent until proven guilty") and what is true among citizens.

Critics suggest that the ability to eradicate many disadvantages lies within men. These critics believe only men can take the reins in their own masculinity, as for example women unhappy with their own situation have taken with femininity over the years, or ethnic-minority groups have. For these critics, men themselves should be the focus of change: they should fundamentally re-evaluate how male gender roles are defined and conserved in society and pursue meaningful change through means over which they only, being males, have control. The idea is that in essence, the problems identified by masculinists often originate in a lack of accountability and initiative on the part of men themselves and/or a desire of males who identify the problems to want it what is perceived as "both ways".

Role of Looks

While suffragettes and feminists had been struggling for their rights, society watched avidly as women won over the right to vote and work where they wanted. But no one ever stopped to wonder how men were doing. Turns out, this struggle resulted in a loss of a "piece" of their rights and their opportunities became infringed upon in some aspects.

What Masculism is All about and why we should Care about it?

According to societal rules, men aren't supposed to feel this way, but representatives of this "stronger half" have slowly started to show dissatisfaction with the one-sidedness of feminism. Thus, a men's movement called masculism appeared in 1960 in the US. Its representatives are fighting for the equal rights of men and women. They also claim that boys and men are often humiliated because of stereotypes associated with gender.

Masculinists are not people who try to offend women. They don't confront feminists, they simply don't want society to demand that they match the idea of a "prince on a white horse". Here are the biggest problems that bother modern masculinists.

Lookism Applied to Men

Lookism is a prejudiced attitude toward the appearance of a person. Ordinary men also suffer from stereotypes because in their private lives and at work, attractive and courageous guys have advantages. Scientists have confirmed masculinists' claims:

- The average woman dreams about being with a tall man whose height starts at 6 feet. However, men's average height doesn't match this ideal. In reality, men on average are 5.74-5.76 feet tall.

- Brunette men usually win over redhead or bald men. All because most women dream about a brunette man with brown eyes. Why is this? Girls say that men with this hair color give off the impression of having a stronger spirit as well as being more energetic and self-confident.

- A beard is a good bonus. Men with facial hair are perceived as brave, decisive, and strong. Moreover, they're hired more often.

- Women like men with broad shoulders which has been confirmed with research.

Advertising and entertainment have formed the image of an ideal man which is infinitely far from reality. Nevertheless, big manufacturers use this image widely and women are more likely to buy certain goods if they're advertised by a cool, macho guy.

However, men's lookism has very sad consequences such as dysmorphophobia. Modern men start to feel ashamed of their bodies because it's not fit, tan, or brawny enough. Dysmorphophobia leads to the abuse of steroids and depression due to the inability to achieve the ideal look.

Men also Suffer from Domestic Violence

In our society, home violence is closely associated with women playing the role of the victim and the husband, the abusive tyrant. But men can suffer from domestic violence as well.

- 30% of domestic violence victims are men that are abused by women (girlfriends, wives, mothers, etc.) Unfortunately, these victims don't have a place to seek help — there are almost no special centers for supporting men in difficult life situations.

- Women are more inventive when it comes to abuse. Of course, there are ladies who simply beat men and injure them of varying severity. However, the abuse they dish out is most often not physical. This can consist of emotional torture, stalking, financial blackmail, and sexual abuse.

- Men feel ashamed to ask for help because society doesn't take this issue seriously. It's assumed that real men don't complain about that stuff and that women can't hurt them.

However, times are changing and nowadays one can go to prison for coercive behavior in the UK. For example, Valerie Sanders from North Yorks spent several hours behind bars and was sued for nagging her husband to vacuum their house.

Fathers have Fewer Rights when it Comes to Raising Kids

It's the mother who receives custody of the children in cases of divorce in most countries of the world. No matter how good the father is, he has to fight for the right to raise his kids:

- Men have no rights at all when it comes to reproduction. The right to decide whether or not to have a child, when to do it, and who the father will be, almost always belongs to a woman.

- Moreover, as a rule, fathers are depicted as zany in modern television, cinematography, and modern literature. They don't seem to know what to feed their kids with, they put their little girls' tights on their heads instead of hats, and faint at the smell of a diaper.

References

- Misandry: fairygodboss.com, Retrieved 18, February 2020

- Misandry-is-as-socially-dangerous-as-misogyny: dailytitan.com, Retrieved 25, July 2020

- Toxic-masculinity-history, health-583411: theatlantic.com, Retrieved 12, March 2020

- Hegemonic-masculinity-how-dominant-man-subjugates-other-men-women-and-society: globalpolicyjournal. com, Retrieved 29, June 2020

- What-masculism-is-all-about-and-why-men-no-longer-want-to-appear-cool-and-macho-780610: brightside. me, Retrieved 09, August 2020

Feminism and Feminist Theory

Feminism covers a range of political and social movements as well ideologies which are aimed at defining and establishing all sexes as equal in a political, economic, personal and social manner. The topics elaborated in this chapter will help in gaining a better perspective about the branches of feminism as well as feminist theory.

Women's studies is an interdisciplinary field of academic study that examines gender as a social and cultural construct, the social status and contributions of women, and the relationships between power and gender.

Popular methodologies within the field of women's studies include standpoint theory, intersectionality, multiculturalism, transnational feminism, autoethnography, and reading practices associated with critical theory, post-structuralism, and queer theory. The field researches and critiques societal norms of gender, race, class, sexuality, and other social inequalities. It is closely related to the broader field of gender studies. Women's studies preceded gender studies as an established field: in the United States the first PhD in women's studies was created in 1990 and the first PhD in gender studies was created in 2005.

History

The first accredited women's studies course was held in 1969 at Cornell University. After a year of intense organizing of women's consciousness raising groups, rallies, petition circulating, and operating unofficial or experimental classes and presentations before seven committees and assemblies, the first women's studies program in the United States was established in 1970 at San Diego State College (now San Diego State University). In conjunction with National Women's Liberation Movement, students and community members created the AD HOC Committee for women's studies. By 1974 SDSU faculty members began a nationwide campaign for the integration of the department. At the time, these actions and the field was extremely political. Due to the sensitive political nature of the movement and harsh backlash to the feminist movement, there are still a lot of unknowns about the creation of women's studies.

The first scholarly journal in interdisciplinary women's studies, *Feminist Studies*, began publishing in 1972. The National Women's Studies Association (of the United States) was established in 1977.

The first Ph.D. program in Women's Studies was established at Emory University in 1990. In 2015 at Kabul University the first master's degree course in gender and women's studies in Afghanistan began. As of 2012, there are 16 institutions offering a Ph.D. in Women's Studies in the United States. Since then, UC Santa Cruz (2013), the University of Kentucky-Lexington (2013), Stony Brook University (2014), and Oregon State University (2016) also introduced a Ph.D. in the field. Courses in Women's Studies in the United Kingdom can be found through the Universities and Colleges Admissions Service.

Methodology

Women's studies faculty practice a diverse array of pedagogies. However, there are common themes to the ways that many women's studies courses are taught; teaching and learning practices may draw on feminist pedagogy. Women's studies curricula often encourage students to participate in service-learning activities in addition to discussion and reflection upon course materials. The development of critical reading, writing, and oral expression are often key to these courses, which can be listed across curricula in the humanities, social sciences, and sciences. The decentralization of the professor as the source of knowledge is often fundamental to women's studies classroom culture. Courses are often more egalitarian than those in traditional disciplines, stressing the critical analysis of texts and the development of critical writing. Not dissimilar to gender studies, women's studies employs feminist, queer, and critical theories. Since the 1970s, scholars of women's studies have taken post-modern approaches to understanding gender as it intersects with race, class, ethnicity, sexuality, religion, age, and (dis)ability to produce and maintain power structures within society. With this turn, there has been a focus on language, subjectivity, and social hegemony, and how the lives of subjects, however they identify, are constituted. At the core of these theories is the notion that however one identifies, gender, sex, and sexuality are not intrinsic, but are socially constructed.

Women studies programs are involved in social justice and design curricula that are embedded with theory and also activism outside of the classroom. Some women studies programs offer internships that are community-based allowing students the opportunity to gain a better understanding of how oppression directly affects women's lives. This experience, informed by theory from feminist studies, queer theory, black feminist theory, African studies, and many other theoretical frameworks, allows students the opportunity to critically analyze experience as well as create creative solutions for issues on a local level. However, Daphne Patai, from the University of Massachusetts Amherst, has criticized this aspect of women's studies programs, arguing that they place politics over education, arguing that "the strategies of faculty members in these programs have included policing insensitive language, championing research methods deemed congenial to women (such as qualitative over quantitative methods), and conducting classes as if they were therapy sessions".

Education

In most institutions, Women's Studies bases its teachings off of a Triad Model. This means it has equal components of research, theory and praxis. Faculty incorporate these components into classes across a variety of topics including: Popular Culture, Women in the Economy, Reproductive and Environmental Justice, classes centered on Women of Color, Globalization, Feminist Principles, and Queer Studies. Women's Studies programs and courses are designed to explore the intersectionality of gender, race, sexuality, class and other topics that are involved in identity politics and societal norms through a feminist lens. Many of these programs involve classes around media literacy, sexuality, race, history involving women, queer theory, multiculturalism and many other closely related courses.

Throughout these classes students and faculty take an intersectional framework approach to analyze and critique various institutional structures such as: education, media, industry, language, family, medicine, research, and prisons. This means they think about the effects on people of differing genders, races, sexualities, cultures, religions, social classes, and economic statuses within the institution as well as how those identities intersect.

A common theme Women's Studies students engage with is Power and Power Imbalance. Because Women's Studies students analyze gender, race, class, sexuality, etc. it often results in dissecting an institutionalized power relationship. Learning through analysis, working in the community, and research Women's Studies students leave university with a toolset to make social change and do something about the power inequalities they study.

Some of the most prominent undergraduate women's studies programs include the University Of California system, Emory University, and the University of Michigan, Wisconsin, New Jersey, Connecticut, Pennsylvania, and New York.

Notable scholars in the Women's Studies field include authors Gloria Anzaldúa, bell hooks, Sandra Cisneros, Angela Davis, Cherríe Moraga, and Audre Lorde.

Criticisms within Women's and Gender Studies (WGS)

Religion and Spirituality

According to Karlyn Crowley, a contributing author for *Rethinking Women's and Gender Studies,* rarely are issues related to spirituality and religion seriously addressed, which she argues can lead to multiple consequences that impact the field. In her chapter titled *Secularity,* she observes that the resulting dynamic is one of "bifurcation" where secularity is privileged as being more progressive. Crowley claims, "By not interrogating these categories of the good and the bad religions, the secular and the religious, and the racial, cultural, and colonialist impulses at work, WGS often succumbs to two main secular narratives: (1) spirituality/religion is seemingly absent or neglected while signifying certain normative assumptions; (2) spirituality/religion is placed into easy binarisms and dismissed" (2012, 248). The dismissals and unexamined presuppositions that Crowley describes also reveals what she notes as leading to barriers. She suggests these barriers prevent one from at least engaging with ideas that could potentially inspire different ways of approaching issues connected to social change and to social justice.

Considering these critiques, Crowley discusses the work of AnaLouise Keating for the purpose of examining how the exploration of spirituality and religion in dialogues, debates, and other forms of exchanges within Women's Studies, can encourage more constructive, productive, and meaningful engagement. Cited by Crowley, Keating states:

Unlike "New Age" versions of spirituality, which focus almost exclusively on the personal (so that the goals become increased wealth, a "good life," or other solipsistic materialistic terms), spiritual activism begins with the personal yet moves outward, acknowledging our radical interconnectedness. This is spirituality for social change, spirituality that recognizes the many difference among us yet insists on our commonalities and uses these commonalities as catalysts for transformation. What a contrast: while identity politics requires holding onto specific categories of identity, spiritual activism demands that we let them go (qtd. in Crowley 252).

Keating reveals that current discourses in Women's Studies appear to remain within the boundaries of one's identity, such as that of one's racial, political, social, religious, and/or economic backgrounds. She considers the approaches espoused by different spiritual and religious ideologies that promote the interconnectedness of humanity as concepts that can provide solutions that enable the flourishing of the ecosystem and of humanity. However, as Keating and Crowley suggest without seriously considering issues related to spirituality and religion within Women's Studies, one is limited to unexamined presuppositions that lead to the dismissal of the unknown and of making limited progress in social change and in social justice.

Feminism

International Women's Day rally in Dhaka, Bangladesh, on 8 March 2005, organized by the National Women Workers Trade Union Centre.

Feminism is a range of political movements, ideologies, and social movements that share a common goal: to define, establish, and achieve political, economic, personal, and social rights for women. This includes seeking to establish educational and professional opportunities for women that are equal to such opportunities for men.

Feminist movements have campaigned and continue to campaign for women's rights, including the right to vote, to hold public office, to work, to earn fair wages or equal pay, to own property, to receive education, to enter contracts, to have equal rights within marriage, and to have maternity leave. Feminists have also worked to promote bodily autonomy and integrity, and to protect women and girls from rape, sexual harassment, and domestic violence.

Feminist campaigns are generally considered to be a main force behind major historical societal changes for women's rights, particularly in the West, where they are near-universally credited with achieving women's suffrage, gender neutrality in English, reproductive rights for women (including access to contraceptives and abortion), and the right to enter into contracts and own property. Although feminist advocacy is, and has been, mainly focused on women's rights, some feminists, including bell hooks, argue for the inclusion of men's liberation within its aims because men are also harmed by traditional gender roles. Feminist theory, which emerged from feminist movements, aims to understand the nature of gender inequality by examining women's social roles and lived experience; it has developed theories in a variety of disciplines in order to respond to issues concerning gender.

Numerous feminist movements and ideologies have developed over the years and represent different viewpoints and aims. Some forms of feminism have been criticized for taking into account only white, middle class, and college-educated perspectives. This criticism led to the creation of ethnically specific or multicultural forms of feminism, including black feminism and intersectional feminism.

History

Feminist Suffrage Parade in New York City, 6 May 1912.

Charles Fourier, a Utopian Socialist and French philosopher, is credited with having coined the word "féminisme" in 1837. The words "féminisme" ("feminism") and "féministe" ("feminist") first appeared in France and the Netherlands in 1872, Great Britain in the 1890s, and the United States in 1910, and the *Oxford English Dictionary* lists 1852 as the year of the first appearance of "feminist" and 1895 for "feminism". Depending on the historical moment, culture and country, feminists around the world have had different causes and goals. Most western feminist historians contend that all movements working to obtain women's rights should be considered feminist movements, even when they did not (or do not) apply the term to themselves. Other historians assert that the term should be limited to the modern feminist movement and its descendants. Those historians use the label "protofeminist" to describe earlier movements.

The history of the modern western feminist movements is divided into three "waves". Each wave dealt with different aspects of the same feminist issues. The first wave comprised women's suffrage movements of the nineteenth and early twentieth centuries, promoting women's right to vote. The second wave was associated with the ideas and actions of the women's liberation movement beginning in the 1960s. The second wave campaigned for legal and social equality for women. The third wave is a continuation of, and a reaction to, the perceived failures of second-wave feminism, which began in the 1990s.

Nineteenth and Early Twentieth Centuries

After selling her home, Emmeline Pankhurst, pictured in New York City in 1913, travelled constantly, giving speeches throughout Britain and the United States.

In the Netherlands, Wilhelmina Drucker (1847–1925) fought successfully for the vote and equal rights for women through political and feminist organizations she founded.

Simone Veil (1939–), former French Minister of Health (1974–79). She made easier access to contraceptive pills and legalized abortion (1974–75) – which was her greatest and hardest achievement.

Louise Weiss along with other Parisian suffragettes in 1935. The newspaper headline reads "The Frenchwoman Must Vote."

First-wave feminism was a period of activity during the 19th century and early twentieth century. In the UK and US, it focused on the promotion of equal contract, marriage, parenting, and property rights for women. By the end of the 19th century, a number of important steps had been made with the passing of legislation such as the UK Custody of Infants Act 1839 which introduced the Tender years doctrine for child custody arrangement and gave woman the right of custody of their children for the first time. Other legislation such as the Married Women's Property Act 1870 in the UK and extended in the 1882 Act, these became models for similar legislation in other British territories. For example, Victoria passed legislation in 1884, New South Wales in 1889, and the remaining Australian colonies passed similar legislation between 1890 and 1897. Therefore, with the turn of the 19th century activism had focused primarily on gaining political power, particularly the right of women's suffrage, though some feminists were active in campaigning for women's sexual, reproductive, and economic rights as well.

Women's suffrage began in Britain's Australasian colonies at the close of the 19th century, with the self-governing colonies of New Zealand granting women the right to vote in 1893 and South Australia granting female suffrage (the right to vote and stand for parliamentary office) in 1895. This was followed by Australia granting female suffrage in 1902.

In Britain the Suffragettes and the Suffragists campaigned for the women's vote, and in 1918 the Representation of the People Act was passed granting the vote to women over the age of 30 who owned property. In 1928 this was extended to all women over 21. Emmeline Pankhurst was the most notable activist in England, with *Time* naming her one of the 100 Most Important People of the 20th Century stating: "she shaped an idea of women for our time; she shook society into a new pattern from which there could be no going back." In the U.S., notable leaders of this movement included Lucretia Mott, Elizabeth Cady Stanton, and Susan B. Anthony, who each campaigned for the abolition of slavery prior to championing women's right to vote. These women were influenced by the Quaker theology of spiritual equality, which asserts that men and women are equal under God. In the United States, first-wave feminism is considered to have ended with the passage of the Nineteenth Amendment to the United States Constitution (1919), granting women the right to vote in all states. The term *first wave* was coined retroactively to categorize these western movements after the term *second-wave feminism* began to be used to describe a newer feminist movement that focused on fighting social and cultural inequalities, as well political inequalities.

During the late Qing period and reform movements such as the Hundred Days' Reform, Chinese feminists called for women's liberation from traditional roles and Neo-Confucian gender segregation. Later, the Chinese Communist Party created projects aimed at integrating women into the workforce, and claimed that the revolution had successfully achieved women's liberation.

According to Nawar al-Hassan Golley, Arab feminism was closely connected with Arab nationalism. In 1899, Qasim Amin, considered the "father" of Arab feminism, wrote *The Liberation of Women*, which argued for legal and social reforms for women. He drew links between women's position in Egyptian society and nationalism, leading to the development of Cairo University and the National Movement. In 1923 Hoda Shaarawi founded the Egyptian Feminist Union, became its president and a symbol of the Arab women's rights movement.

The Iranian Constitutional Revolution in 1905 triggered the Iranian women's movement, which aimed to achieve women's equality in education, marriage, careers, and legal rights. However, during the Iranian revolution of 1979, many of the rights that women had gained from the women's movement were systematically abolished, such as the Family Protection Law.

In France, women obtained the right to vote only with the Provisional Government of the French Republic of 21 April 1944. The Consultative Assembly of Algiers of 1944 proposed on 24 March 1944 to grant eligibility to women but following an amendment by Fernand Grenier, they were given full citizenship, including the right to vote. Grenier's proposition was adopted 51 to 16. In May 1947, following the November 1946 elections, the sociologist Robert Verdier minimized the "gender gap", stating in *Le Populaire* that women had not voted in a consistent way, dividing themselves, as men, according to social classes. During the baby boom period, feminism waned in importance. Wars (both World War I and World War II) had seen the provisional emancipation of some women, but post-war periods signalled the return to conservative roles.

Mid-Twentieth Century

By the mid 20th century, in some European countries, women still lacked some significant rights. Feminists in these countries continued to fight for voting rights. In Switzerland, women gained the right to vote in federal elections in 1971; but in the canton of Appenzell Innerrhoden women obtained the right to vote on local issues only in 1991, when the canton was forced to do so by the Federal Supreme Court of Switzerland. In Liechtenstein, women were given the right to vote by the women's suffrage referendum of 1984. Three prior referendums held in 1968, 1971 and 1973 had failed to secure women's right to vote.

Photograph of American women replacing men fighting in Europe, 1945.

Feminists continued to campaign for the reform of family laws which gave husbands control over their wives. Although by the 20th century coverture had been abolished in the UK and the US, in many continental European countries married women still had very few rights. For instance, in France married women did not receive the right to work without their husband's permission until 1965. Feminists have also worked to abolish the "marital exemption" in rape laws which precluded the prosecution of husbands for the rape of their wives. Earlier efforts by first-wave feminists such as Voltairine de Cleyre, Victoria Woodhull and Elizabeth Clarke Wolstenholme Elmy to criminalize marital rape in the late 19th century had failed; this was only achieved a century later in most Western countries, but is still not achieved in many other parts of the world.

French philosopher Simone de Beauvoir provided a Marxist solution and an existentialist view on many of the questions of feminism with the publication of *Le Deuxième Sexe* (*The Second Sex*) in 1949. The book expressed feminists' sense of injustice. Second-wave feminism is a feminist movement beginning in the early 1960s and continuing to the present; as such, it coexists with third-wave feminism. Second-wave feminism is largely concerned with issues of equality beyond suffrage, such as ending gender discrimination.

Second-wave feminists see women's cultural and political inequalities as inextricably linked and encourage women to understand aspects of their personal lives as deeply politicized and as reflecting sexist power structures. The feminist activist and author Carol Hanisch coined the slogan "The Personal is Political", which became synonymous with the second wave.

Second- and third-wave feminism in China has been characterized by a reexamination of women's roles during the communist revolution and other reform movements, and new discussions about whether women's equality has actually been fully achieved.

In 1956, President Gamal Abdel Nasser of Egypt initiated "state feminism", which outlawed discrimination based on gender and granted women's suffrage, but also blocked political activism by feminist leaders. During Sadat's presidency, his wife, Jehan Sadat, publicly advocated further women's rights, though Egyptian policy and society began to move away from women's equality with the new Islamist movement and growing conservatism. However, some activists proposed a new feminist movement, Islamic feminism, which argues for women's equality within an Islamic framework.

In Latin America, revolutions brought changes in women's status in countries such as Nicaragua, where feminist ideology during the Sandinista Revolution aided women's quality of life but fell short of achieving a social and ideological change.

In 1969, Betty Friedan's book The Feminine Mystique was published and helped voice the discontent that American women felt. The book proved highly successful, almost becoming a bible for feminists and a spur for political activists. The book's success also meant that Friedan could lecture her views while she was on tour in 1970. Within ten years, after Friedan's successful publishing, women made up more than half of the total percentage in the First World workforce.

Late Twentieth and Early Twenty-first Centuries

Third-wave

Feminist, author and social activist bell hooks (b. 1952).

In the early 1990s in the USA, third-wave feminism began as a response to perceived failures of the second wave and to the backlash against initiatives and movements created by the second wave. Third-wave feminism distinguished itself from the second wave around issues of sexuality, challenging female heterosexuality and celebrating sexuality as a means of female empowerment. Third-wave feminism also seeks to challenge or avoid what it deems the second wave's essentialist definitions of femininity, which, they argue, over-emphasize the experiences of upper middle-class white women. Third-wave feminists often focus on "micro-politics" and challenge the second wave's paradigm as to what is, or is not, good for women, and tend to use a post-structuralist interpretation of gender and sexuality. Feminist leaders rooted in the second wave, such as Gloria Anzaldúa, bell hooks, Chela Sandoval, Cherríe Moraga, Audre Lorde, Maxine Hong Kingston, and many other non-white feminists, sought to negotiate a space within feminist thought for consideration of race-related subjectivities. Third-wave feminism also contains internal debates between difference feminists, who believe that there are important differences between the sexes, and those who believe that there are no inherent differences between the sexes and contend that gender roles are due to social conditioning.

Standpoint

Standpoint theory is a feminist theoretical point of view that believes a persons' social position influences their knowledge. This perspective argues that research and theory treats women and the feminist movement as insignificant and refuses to see traditional science as unbiased. Since the 1980s, standpoint feminists have argued that the feminist movement should address global issues (such as rape, incest, and prostitution) and culturally specific issues (such as female genital mutilation in some parts of Africa and the Middle East, as well as glass ceiling practices that impede women's advancement in developed economies) in order to understand how gender inequality interacts with racism, homophobia, classism and colonization in a "matrix of domination".

Post-feminism

The term post-feminism is used to describe a range of viewpoints reacting to feminism since the 1980s. While not being "anti-feminist", post-feminists believe that women have achieved second wave goals while being critical of third wave feminist goals. The term was first used to describe a backlash against second-wave feminism, but it is now a label for a wide range of theories that take critical approaches to previous feminist discourses and includes challenges to the second wave's ideas. Other post-feminists say that feminism is no longer relevant to today's society. Amelia Jones has written that the post-feminist texts which emerged in the 1980s and 1990s portrayed second-wave feminism as a monolithic entity. Dorothy Chunn notes a "blaming narrative" under the post-feminist moniker, where feminists are undermined for continuing to make demands for gender equality in a "post-feminist" society, where "gender equality has (already) been achieved." According to Chunn, "many feminists have voiced disquiet about the ways in which rights and equality discourses are now used against them."

Theory

Feminist theory is the extension of feminism into theoretical or philosophical fields. It encompasses work in a variety of disciplines, including anthropology, sociology, economics, women's studies, literary criticism, art history, psychoanalysis and philosophy. Feminist theory aims to understand gender inequality and focuses on gender politics, power relations, and sexuality. While providing a critique of these social and political relations, much of feminist theory also focuses on the promotion of women's rights and interests. Themes explored in feminist theory include discrimination, stereotyping, objectification (especially sexual objectification), oppression, and patriarchy. In the field of literary criticism, Elaine Showalter describes the development of feminist theory as having three phases. The first she calls "feminist critique", in which the feminist reader examines the ideologies behind literary phenomena. The second Showalter calls "gynocriticism", in which the "woman is producer of textual meaning". The last phase she calls "gender theory", in which the "ideological inscription and the literary effects of the sex/gender system are explored".

This was paralleled in the 1970s by French feminists, who developed the concept of *écriture féminine* (which translates as 'female or feminine writing'). Helene Cixous argues that writing and philosophy are *phallocentric* and along with other French feminists such as Luce Irigaray emphasize "writing from the body" as a subversive exercise. The work of Julia Kristeva, a feminist psychoanalyst and philosopher, and Bracha Ettinger, artist and psychoanalyst, has influenced feminist theory in general and feminist literary criticism in particular. However, as the scholar Elizabeth Wright points out, "none of these French feminists align themselves with the feminist movement as it appeared in the Anglophone world". More recent feminist theory, such as that of Lisa Lucile Owens, has concentrated on characterizing feminism as a universal emancipatory movement.

Movements and Ideologies

A symbol of feminism based on the Venus symbol.

Many overlapping feminist movements and ideologies have developed over the years.

Political Movements

Some branches of feminism closely track the political leanings of the larger society, such as liberalism and conservatism, or focus on the environment. Liberal feminism seeks individualistic equality of men and women through political and legal reform without altering the structure of society. Catherine Rottenberg has argued that the neoliberal shirt in Liberal feminism has led to that form of feminism being individualized rather than collectivized and becoming detached from social inequality. Due to this she argues that Liberal Feminism cannot offer any sustained analysis of the structures of male dominance, power, or privilege.

Radical feminism considers the male-controlled capitalist hierarchy as the defining feature of women's oppression and the total uprooting and reconstruction of society as necessary. Conservative feminism is conservative relative to the society in which it resides. Libertarian feminism conceives of people as self-owners and therefore as entitled to freedom from coercive interference. Separatist feminism does not support heterosexual relationships. Lesbian feminism is thus closely related. Other feminists criticize separatist feminism as sexist. Ecofeminists see men's control of land as responsible for the oppression of women and destruction of the natural environment; ecofeminism has been criticized for focusing too much on a mystical connection between women and nature.

Materialist Ideologies

Rosemary Hennessy and Chrys Ingraham say that materialist forms of feminism grew out of Western Marxist thought and have inspired a number of different (but overlapping) movements, all of which are involved in a critique of capitalism and are focused on ideology's relationship to women. Marxist feminism argues that capitalism is the root cause of women's oppression, and that discrimination against women in domestic life and employment is an effect of capitalist ideologies. Socialist feminism distinguishes itself from Marxist feminism by arguing that women's liberation can only be achieved by working to end both the economic and cultural sources of women's oppression. Anarcha-feminists believe that class struggle and anarchy against the state require struggling against patriarchy, which comes from involuntary hierarchy.

Black and Postcolonial Ideologies

Sara Ahmed argues that Black and Postcolonial feminisms pose a challenge "to some of the organizing premises of Western feminist thought." During much of its history, feminist movements and theoretical developments were led predominantly by middle-class white women from Western Europe and North America. However women of other races have proposed alternative feminisms. This trend accelerated in the 1960s with the civil rights movement in the United States and the collapse of European colonialism in Africa, the Caribbean, parts of Latin America, and Southeast Asia. Since that time, women in developing nations and former colonies and who are of colour or various ethnicities or living in poverty have proposed additional feminisms. Womanism emerged after early feminist movements were largely white and middle-class. Postcolonial feminists argue that colonial oppression and Western feminism marginalized postcolonial women but did not turn them passive or voiceless. Third-world feminism and Indigenous feminism are closely related to postcolonial feminism. These ideas also correspond with ideas in African feminism, motherism, Stiwanism, negofeminism, femalism, transnational feminism, and Africana womanism.

Social Constructionist Ideologies

In the late twentieth century various feminists began to argue that gender roles are socially constructed, and that it is impossible to generalize women's experiences across cultures and histories. Post-structural feminism draws on the philosophies of post-structuralism and deconstruction in order to argue that the concept of gender is created socially and culturally through discourse. Postmodern feminists also emphasize the social construction of gender and the discursive nature of reality; however, as Pamela Abbott et al. note, a postmodern approach to feminism highlights "the existence of multiple truths (rather than simply men and women's standpoints)".

Cultural Movements

Riot grrrls took an anti-corporate stance of self-sufficiency and self-reliance. Riot grrrl's emphasis on universal female identity and separatism often appears more closely allied with second-wave feminism than with the third wave. The movement encouraged and made "adolescent girls' standpoints central", allowing them to express themselves fully. Lipstick feminism is a cultural feminist movement that attempts to respond to the backlash of second-wave radical feminism of the 1960s and 1970s by reclaiming symbols of "feminine" identity such as make-up, suggestive clothing and having a sexual allure as valid and empowering personal choices.

Demographics

According to 2015 poll, 18 percent of Americans consider themselves feminists, while 85 percent reported they believe in "equality for women". Despite the popular belief in equal rights, 52 percent did not identify as feminist, 26 percent were unsure, and four percent provided no response.

According to 2014 Ipsos poll covering 15 developed countries, 53 percent of respondents identified as feminists, and 87% agreed that "women should be treated equally to men in all areas based on their competency, not their gender". However, only 55% of women agreed that they have "full equality with men and the freedom to reach their full dreams and aspirations".

Among women, some of the strongest support for feminism was found in Sweden, where one in three (36%) agreed very much that they defined themselves as feminists. They were followed by women in Italy (31%) and Argentina (29%). Those in the middle of the ranking were from Great Britain (22%), Spain (22%), United States (20%), Australia (18%), Belgium (18%), France (18%), Canada (17%), Poland (17%), and Hungary (15%). Women least likely to agree very much were from Japan (8%), Germany (7%) and South Korea (7%).

One quarter of men in Italy (25%) and Argentina (25%), and two in ten of those in Poland (21%) and France (19%), agreed very much they defined themselves as feminist. They were followed by those from Sweden (17%), Spain (16%), the United States (16%), Canada (15%), Great Britain (14%), Hungary (12%), Belgium (11%) and Australia (10%). Men least likely to identify this way were from South Korea (7%), Germany (3%) and Japan (3%).

Women were more likely to self-identify as being feminists than men in every country except Poland, where men (21%) were four points more likely than women (17%) to agree very much with the statement. In South Korea, there was no difference between men and women (7%) on this measure.

Sexuality

Feminist views on sexuality vary, and have differed by historical period and by cultural context. Feminist attitudes to female sexuality have taken a few different directions. Matters such as the sex industry, sexual representation in the media, and issues regarding consent to sex under conditions of male dominance have been particularly controversial among feminists. This debate has culminated in the late 1970s and the 1980s, in what came to be known as the feminist sex wars, which pitted anti-pornography feminism against sex-positive feminism, and parts of the feminist movement were deeply divided by these debates. Feminists have taken a variety of positions on different aspects of the sexual revolution from the 1960s and 70s. Over the course of the 1970s, a large number of influential women accepted lesbian and bisexual women as part of feminism.

Sex Industry

Opinions on the sex industry are diverse. Feminists critical of the sex industry generally see it as the exploitative result of patriarchal social structures which reinforce sexual and cultural attitudes complicit in rape and sexual harassment. Alternately, feminists who support at least part of the sex industry argue that it can be a medium of feminist expression and a means for women to take control of their sexuality.

Feminist views of pornography range from condemnation of pornography as a form of violence against women, to an embracing of some forms of pornography as a medium of feminist expression. Feminists' views on prostitution vary, but many of these perspectives can be loosely arranged into an overarching standpoint that is generally either critical or supportive of prostitution and sex work.

Affirming Female Sexual Autonomy

For feminists, a woman's right to control her own sexuality is a key issue. Feminists such as Catharine MacKinnon argue that women have very little control over their own bodies, with female sexuality being largely controlled and defined by men in patriarchal societies. Feminists argue that sexual violence committed by men is often rooted in ideologies of male sexual entitlement, and that these systems grant women very few legitimate options to refuse sexual advances. In many cultures, men do not believe that a woman has the right to reject a man's sexual advances or to make an autonomous decision about participating in sex. Feminists argue that all cultures are, in one way or another, dominated by ideologies that largely deny women the right to decide how to express their sexuality, because men under patriarchy feel entitled to define sex on their own terms. This entitlement can take different forms, depending on the culture. In many parts of the world, especially in conservative and religious cultures, marriage is regarded as an institution which requires a wife to be sexually available at all times, virtually without limit; thus, forcing or coercing sex on a wife is not considered a crime or even an abusive behaviour. In more liberal cultures, this entitlement takes the form of a general sexualization of the whole culture. This is played out in the sexual objectification of women, with pornography and other forms of sexual entertainment creating the fantasy that all women exist solely for men's sexual pleasure, and that women are readily available and desiring to engage in sex at any time, with any man, on a man's terms.

Science

Sandra Harding says that the "moral and political insights of the women's movement have inspired social scientists and biologists to raise critical questions about the ways traditional researchers have explained gender, sex and relations within and between the social and natural worlds." Some feminists, such as Ruth Hubbard and Evelyn Fox Keller, criticize traditional scientific discourse as being historically biased towards a male perspective. A part of the feminist research agenda is the examination of the ways in which power inequities are created or reinforced in scientific and academic institutions. Physicist Lisa Randall, appointed to a task force at Harvard by then-president Lawrence Summers after his controversial discussion of why women may be underrepresented in science and engineering, said, "I just want to see a whole bunch more women enter the field so these issues don't have to come up anymore."

Lynn Hankinson Nelson notes that feminist empiricists find fundamental differences between the experiences of men and women. Thus, they seek to obtain knowledge through the examination of the experiences of women, and to "uncover the consequences of omitting, misdescribing, or devaluing them" to account for a range of human experience. Another part of the feminist research agenda is the uncovering of ways in which power inequities are created or reinforced in society and in scientific and academic institutions. Furthermore, despite calls for greater attention to be paid to structures of gender inequity in the academic literature, structural analyses of gender bias rarely appear in highly cited psychological journals, especially in the commonly studied areas of psychology and personality.

One criticism of feminist epistemology is that it allows social and political values to influence its findings. Susan Haack also points out that feminist epistemology reinforces traditional stereotypes about women's thinking (as intuitive and emotional, etc.), Meera Nanda further cautions that this may in fact trap women within "traditional gender roles and help justify patriarchy".

Biology and Gender

Modern feminism challenges the essentialist view of gender as biologically intrinsic. For example, Anne Fausto-Sterling's book, *Myths of Gender*, explores the assumptions embodied in scientific research that support a biologically essentialist view of gender. In *Delusions of Gender,* Cordelia Fine disputes scientific evidence that suggests that there is an innate biological difference between men's and women's minds, asserting instead that cultural and societal beliefs are the reason for differences between individuals that are commonly perceived as sex differences.

Feminist Psychology

Feminism in psychology emerged as a critique of the dominant male outlook on psychological research where only male perspectives were studied with all male subjects. As women earned doctorates in psychology, females and their issues were introduced as legitimate topics of study. Feminist psychology emphasizes social context, lived experience, and qualitative analysis. Projects such as Psychology's Feminist Voices have emerged to catalogue the influence of feminist psychologists on the discipline.

Culture

Architecture

Gender-based inquiries into and conceptualization of architecture have also come about, leading to feminism in modern architecture. Piyush Mathur coined the term "archigenderic". Claiming that "architectural planning has an inextricable link with the defining and regulation of gender roles, responsibilities, rights, and limitations", Mathur came up with that term "to explore ... the meaning of 'architecture' in terms of gender" and "to explore the meaning of 'gender' in terms of architecture".

Businesses

Feminist activists have established a range of feminist businesses, including women's bookstores, feminist credit unions, feminist presses, feminist mail-order catalogs, and feminist restaurants. These businesses flourished as part of the second and third-waves of feminism in the 1970s, 1980s, and 1990s.

Visual Arts

Corresponding with general developments within feminism, and often including such self-organizing tactics as the consciousness-raising group, the movement began in the 1960s and flourished throughout the 1970s. Jeremy Strick, director of the Museum of Contemporary Art in Los Angeles, described the feminist art movement as "the most influential international movement of any during the postwar period", and Peggy Phelan says that it "brought about the most far-reaching transformations in both artmaking and art writing over the past four decades". Feminist artist Judy Chicago, who created *The Dinner Party*, a set of vulva-themed ceramic plates in the 1970s, said in 2009 to *ARTnews*, "There is still an institutional lag and an insistence on a male Eurocentric narrative. We are trying to change the future: to get girls and boys to realize that women's art is not an exception—it's a normal part of art history." A feminist approach to the visual arts has most recently developed through Cyberfeminism and the posthuman turn, giving voice to the ways "contemporary female artists are dealing with gender, social media and the notion of embodiment".

Literature

Octavia Butler, award-winning feminist science fiction author.

The feminist movement produced both feminist fiction and non-fiction, and created new interest in women's writing. It also prompted a general reevaluation of women's historical and academic contributions in response to the belief that women's lives and contributions have been underrepresented as areas of scholarly interest. Much of the early period of feminist literary scholarship was given over to the rediscovery and reclamation of texts written by women. Studies like Dale Spender's *Mothers of the Novel* (1986) and Jane Spencer's *The Rise of the Woman Novelist* (1986) were ground-breaking in their insistence that women have always been writing. Commensurate with this growth in scholarly interest, various presses began the task of reissuing long-out-of-print texts. Virago Press began to publish its large list of 19th and early-20th-century novels in 1975 and became one of the first commercial presses to join in the project of reclamation. In the 1980s Pandora Press, responsible for publishing Spender's study, issued a companion line of 18th-century novels written by women. More recently, Broadview Press continues to issue 18th- and 19th-century novels, many hitherto out of print, and the University of Kentucky has a series of republications of early women's novels. *A Vindication of the Rights of Woman* (1792) by Mary Wollstonecraft, is one of the earliest works of feminist philosophy. *A Room of One's Own* (1929) by Virginia Woolf, is noted in its argument for both a literal and figural space for women writers within a literary tradition dominated by patriarchy.

The widespread interest in women's writing is related to a general reassessment and expansion of the literary canon. Interest in post-colonial literatures, gay and lesbian literature, writing by people of colour, working people's writing, and the cultural productions of other historically marginalized groups has resulted in a whole scale expansion of what is considered "literature", and genres hitherto not regarded as "literary", such as children's writing, journals, letters, travel writing, and many others are now the subjects of scholarly interest. Most genres and subgenres have undergone a similar analysis, so that one now sees work on the "female gothic" or women's science fiction.

According to Elyce Rae Helford, "Science fiction and fantasy serve as important vehicles for feminist thought, particularly as bridges between theory and practice." Feminist science fiction is sometimes taught at the university level to explore the role of social constructs in understanding gender. Notable texts of this kind are Ursula K. Le Guin's *The Left Hand of Darkness* (1969), Joanna Russ' *The Female Man* (1970), Octavia Butler's *Kindred* (1979) and Margaret Atwood's *Handmaid's Tale* (1985).

Music

Women's music (or womyn's music or wimmin's music) is the music by women, for women, and about women. The genre emerged as a musical expression of the second-wave feminist movement as well as the labour, civil rights, and peace movements. The movement was started by lesbians such as Cris Williamson, Meg Christian, and Margie Adam, African-American women activists such as Bernice Johnson Reagon and her group Sweet Honey in the Rock, and peace activist Holly Near. Women's music also refers to the wider industry of women's music that goes beyond the performing artists to include studio musicians, producers, sound engineers, technicians, cover artists, distributors, promoters, and festival organizers who are also women. Riot grrrl is an underground feminist hardcore punk movement.

Feminism became a principal concern of musicologists in the 1980s as part of the New Musicology. Prior to this, in the 1970s, musicologists were beginning to discover women composers and performers, and had begun to review concepts of canon, genius, genre and periodization from a feminist perspective. In other words, the question of how women musicians fit into traditional music history was now being asked. Through the 1980s and 1990s, this trend continued as musicologists like Susan McClary, Marcia Citron and Ruth Solie began to consider the cultural reasons for the marginalizing of women from the received body of work. Concepts such as music as gendered discourse; professionalism; reception of women's music; examination of the sites of music production; relative wealth and education of women; popular music studies in relation to women's identity; patriarchal ideas in music analysis; and notions of gender and difference are among the themes examined during this time.

While the music industry has long been open to having women in performance or entertainment roles, women are much less likely to have positions of authority, such as being the leader of an orchestra. In popular music, while there are many women singers recording songs, there are very few women behind the audio console acting as music producers, the individuals who direct and manage the recording process.

Cinema

Feminist cinema, advocating or illustrating feminist perspectives, arose largely with the development of feminist film theory in the late '60s and early '70s. Women who were radicalized during the 1960s by political debate and sexual liberation; but the failure of radicalism to produce substantive change for women galvanized them to form consciousness-raising groups and set about analysing, from different perspectives, dominant cinema's construction of women. Differences were particularly marked between feminists on either side of the Atlantic. 1972 saw the first feminist film festivals in the U.S. and U.K. as well as the first feminist film journal, *Women and Film*. Trailblazers from this period included Claire Johnston and Laura Mulvey, who also organized the Women's Event at the Edinburgh Film Festival. Other theorists making a powerful impact on feminist film include Teresa de Lauretis, Anneke Smelik and Kaja Silverman. Approaches in philosophy and psychoanalysis fuelled feminist film criticism, feminist independent film and feminist distribution.

It has been argued that there are two distinct approaches to independent, theoretically inspired feminist filmmaking. 'Deconstruction' concerns itself with analysing and breaking down codes of mainstream cinema, aiming to create a different relationship between the spectator and dominant cinema. The second approach, a feminist counterculture, embodies feminine writing to investigate a specifically feminine cinematic language. Some recent criticism of "feminist film" approaches has centred around a Swedish rating system called the Bechdel test.

During the 1930s–1950s heyday of the big Hollywood studios, the status of women in the industry was abysmal and, while much has improved, many would argue that there is still much to be done. From art films by Sally Potter, Catherine Breillat, Claire Denis and Jane Campion to action movies by Kathryn Bigelow, women now have a stronger voice, but are only too aware of the still lingering gender gap.

Politics

British-born suffragist Rose Cohen became victim of Stalin's great terror, executed in November 1937, two months after the execution of her Soviet husband.

Feminism had complex interactions with the major political movements of the twentieth century.

Socialism

Since the late nineteenth century some feminists have allied with socialism, whereas others have criticized socialist ideology for being insufficiently concerned about women's rights. August Bebel, an early activist of the German Social Democratic Party (SPD), published his work *Die Frau und der Sozialismus*, juxtaposing the struggle for equal rights between sexes with social equality in general. In 1907 there was an International Conference of Socialist Women in Stuttgart where suffrage was described as a tool of class struggle. Clara Zetkin of the SPD called for women's suffrage to build a *"socialist order, the only one that allows for a radical solution to the women's question"*.

In Britain, the women's movement was allied with the Labour party. In the U.S., Betty Friedan emerged from a radical background to take leadership. Radical Women is the oldest socialist feminist organization in the U.S. and is still active. During the Spanish Civil War, Dolores Ibárruri (*La Pasionaria*) led the Communist Party of Spain. Although she supported equal rights for women, she opposed women fighting on the front and clashed with the anarcha-feminist Mujeres Libres.

Fascism

Chilean feminists protest against the regime of Augusto Pinochet.

Fascism has been prescribed dubious stances on feminism by its practitioners and by women's groups. Amongst other demands concerning social reform presented in the Fascist manifesto in 1919 was expanding the suffrage to all Italian citizens of age 18 and above, including women (accomplished only in 1946, after the defeat of fascism) and eligibility for all to stand for office from age 25. This demand was particularly championed by special Fascist women's auxiliary groups such as the *fasci femminilli* and only partly realized in 1925, under pressure from Prime Minister Benito Mussolini's more conservative coalition partners.

Cyprian Blamires states that although feminists were among those who opposed the rise of Adolf Hitler, feminism has a complicated relationship with the Nazi movement as well. While Nazis glorified traditional notions of patriarchal society and its role for women, they claimed to recognize women's equality in employment. However, Hitler and Mussolini declared themselves as opposed to feminism, and after the rise of Nazism in Germany in 1933, there was a rapid dissolution of the political rights and economic opportunities that feminists had fought for during the pre-war period and to some extent during the 1920s. Georges Duby et al. note that in practice fascist society was hierarchical and emphasized male virility, with women maintaining a largely subordinate position. Blamires also notes that Neofascism has since the 1960s been hostile towards feminism and advocates that women accept "their traditional roles".

Civil Rights Movement and Anti-racism

The civil rights movement has influenced and informed the feminist movement and vice versa. Many Western feminists adapted the language and theories of black equality activism and drew parallels between women's rights and the rights of non-white people. Despite the connections between the women's and civil rights movements, some tension arose during the late 1960s and early 1970s as non-white women argued that feminism was predominantly white and middle class, and did not understand and was not concerned with race issues. Similarly, some women argued that the civil rights movement had sexist elements and did not adequately address minority women's concerns. These criticisms created new feminist social theories about the intersections of racism, classism, and sexism, and new feminisms, such as black feminism and Chicana feminism.

Neoliberalism

Neoliberalism has been criticized by feminist theory for having a negative effect on the female workforce population across the globe, especially in the global south. Masculinist assumptions and objectives continue to dominate economic and geopolitical thinking. Women's experiences in non-industrialized countries reveal often deleterious effects of modernization policies and undercut orthodox claims that development benefits everyone.

Proponents of neoliberalism have theorized that by increasing women's participation in the workforce, there will be heightened economic progress, but feminist critics have noted that this participation alone does not further equality in gender relations. Neoliberalism has failed to address significant problems such as the devaluation of feminized labour, the structural privileging of men and masculinity, and the politicization of women's subordination in the family and the workplace. The "feminization of employment" refers to a conceptual characterization of deteriorated and devalorized labour conditions that are less desirable, meaningful, safe and secure. Employers in the global south have perceptions about feminine labour and seek workers who are perceived to be undemanding, docile and willing to accept low wages. Social constructs about feminized labour have played a big part in this, for instance, employers often perpetuate ideas about women as 'secondary income earners to justify their lower rates of pay and not deserving of training or promotion.

Societal Impact

The feminist movement has effected change in Western society, including women's suffrage; greater access to education; more nearly equitable pay with men; the right to initiate divorce proceedings; the right of women to make individual decisions regarding pregnancy (including access to contraceptives and abortion); and the right to own property.

Civil Rights

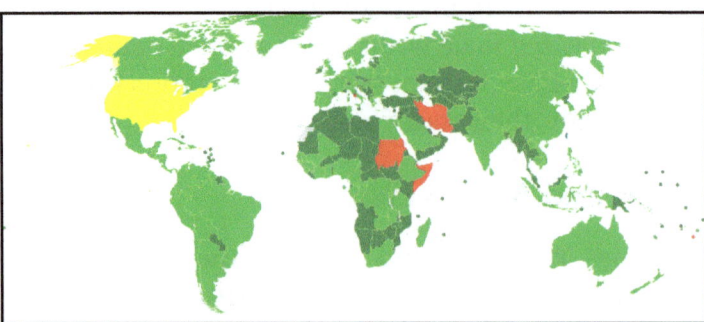

Participation in the Convention on the Elimination of All Forms of Discrimination Against Women.

<table>
<tr><td>🟩 Signed and ratified</td><td>🟨 Only signed</td></tr>
<tr><td>🟩 Acceded or succeeded</td><td>🟧 Non-signatory</td></tr>
<tr><td>🟦 Unrecognized state, abiding by treaty</td><td></td></tr>
</table>

From the 1960s on, the campaign for women's rights was met with mixed results in the U.S. and the U.K. Other countries of the EEC agreed to ensure that discriminatory laws would be phased out across the European Community.

Some feminist campaigning also helped reform attitudes to child sexual abuse. The view that young girls cause men to have sexual intercourse with them was replaced by that of men's responsibility for their own conduct, the men being adults.

In the U.S., the National Organization for Women (NOW) began in 1966 to seek women's equality, including through the Equal Rights Amendment (ERA), which did not pass, although some states enacted their own. Reproductive rights in the U.S. centred on the court decision in *Roe* v. *Wade* enunciating a woman's right to choose whether to carry a pregnancy to term. Western women gained more reliable birth control, allowing family planning and careers. The movement started in the 1910s in the U.S. under Margaret Sanger and elsewhere under Marie Stopes. In the final three decades of the 20th century, Western women knew a new freedom through birth control, which enabled women to plan their adult lives, often making way for both career and family.

The division of labour within households was affected by the increased entry of women into workplaces in the 20th century. Sociologist Arlie Russell Hochschild found that, in two-career couples, men and women, on average, spend about equal amounts of time working, but women still spend more time on housework, although Cathy Young responded by arguing that women may prevent equal participation by men in housework and parenting. Judith K. Brown writes, "Women are most likely to make a substantial contribution when subsistence activities have the following characteristics: the participant is not obliged to be far from home; the tasks are relatively monotonous and do not require rapt concentration; and the work is not dangerous, can be performed in spite of interruptions, and is easily resumed once interrupted."

In international law, the *Convention on the Elimination of All Forms of Discrimination Against Women* (CEDAW) is an international convention adopted by the United Nations General Assembly and described as an international bill of rights for women. It came into force in those nations ratifying it.

Jurisprudence

Feminist jurisprudence is a branch of jurisprudence that examines the relationship between women and law. It addresses questions about the history of legal and social biases against women and about the enhancement of their legal rights.

Feminist jurisprudence signifies a reaction to the philosophical approach of modern legal scholars, who typically see law as a process for interpreting and perpetuating a society's universal, gender-neutral ideals. Feminist legal scholars claim that this fails to acknowledge women's values or legal interests or the harms that they may anticipate or experience.

Language

Proponents of gender-neutral language argue that the use of gender-specific language often implies male superiority or reflects an unequal state of society. According to *The Handbook of English Linguistics*, generic masculine pronouns and gender-specific job titles are instances "where English linguistic convention has historically treated men as prototypical of the human species."

Theology

Feminist theology is a movement that reconsiders the traditions, practices, scriptures, and theologies of religions from a feminist perspective. Some of the goals of feminist theology include increasing the role of women among the clergy and religious authorities, reinterpreting male-dominated imagery and language about God, determining women's place in relation to career and motherhood, and studying images of women in the religion's sacred texts.

Christian feminism is a branch of feminist theology which seeks to interpret and understand Christianity in light of the equality of women and men, and that this interpretation is necessary for a complete understanding of Christianity. While there is no standard set of beliefs among Christian feminists, most agree that God does not discriminate on the basis of sex, and are involved in issues such as the ordination of women, male dominance and the balance of parenting in Christian marriage, claims of moral deficiency and inferiority of women compared to men, and the overall treatment of women in the church. The Christian Bible refers to women in positions of authority in Judges 4:4 and Kings 22:14.

Islamic feminists advocate women's rights, gender equality, and social justice grounded within an Islamic framework. Advocates seek to highlight the deeply rooted teachings of equality in the Quran and encourage a questioning of the patriarchal interpretation of Islamic teaching through the Quran, *hadith* (sayings of Muhammad), and *sharia* (law) towards the creation of a more equal and just society. Although rooted in Islam, the movement's pioneers have also utilized secular and Western feminist discourses and recognize the role of Islamic feminism as part of an integrated global feminist movement.

Buddhist feminism is a movement that seeks to improve the religious, legal, and social status of women within Buddhism. It is an aspect of feminist theology which seeks to advance and understand the equality of men and women morally, socially, spiritually, and in leadership from a Buddhist perspective. The Buddhist feminist Rita Gross describes Buddhist feminism as "the radical practice of the co-humanity of women and men."

Jewish feminism is a movement that seeks to improve the religious, legal, and social status of women within Judaism and to open up new opportunities for religious experience and leadership for Jewish women. The main issues for early Jewish feminists in these movements were the exclusion from the all-male prayer group or *minyan*, the exemption from positive time-bound *mitzvot*, and women's inability to function as witnesses and to initiate divorce. Many Jewish women have become leaders of feminist movements throughout their history.

Dianic Wicca is a feminist-centred thealogy.

Secular or atheist feminists have engaged in feminist criticism of religion, arguing that many religions have oppressive rules towards women and misogynistic themes and elements in religious texts.

Patriarchy

Patriarchy is a social system in which society is organized around male authority figures. In this system fathers have authority over women, children, and property. It implies the institutions of male rule and privilege, and is dependent on female subordination. Most forms of feminism characterize patriarchy as an unjust social system that is oppressive to women. Carole Pateman argues that the patriarchal distinction "between masculinity and femininity is the political difference between freedom and subjection." In feminist theory the concept of patriarchy often includes all the social mechanisms that reproduce and exert male dominance over women. Feminist theory typically characterizes patriarchy as a social construction, which can be overcome by revealing and critically analyzing its manifestations. Some radical feminists have proposed that because patriarchy is too deeply rooted in society, separatism is the only viable solution. Other feminists have criticized these views as being anti-men.

Men and Masculinity

Feminist theory has explored the social construction of masculinity and its implications for the goal of gender equality. The social construct of masculinity is seen by feminism as problematic because it associates males with aggression and competition, and reinforces patriarchal and unequal gender relations. Patriarchal cultures are criticized for "limiting forms of masculinity" available to men and thus narrowing their life choices. Some feminists are engaged with men's issues activism, such as bringing attention to male rape and spousal battery and addressing negative social expectations for men.

Male participation in feminism is encouraged by feminists and is seen as an important strategy for achieving full societal commitment to gender equality. Many male feminists and pro-feminists are active in both women's rights activism, feminist theory, and masculinity studies. However, some argue that while male engagement with feminism is necessary, it is problematic because of the ingrained social influences of patriarchy in gender relations. The consensus today in feminist and masculinity theories is that both genders can and should cooperate to achieve the larger goals of feminism. It has been proposed that, in large part, this can be achieved through considerations of women's agency.

Reactions

Different groups of people have responded to feminism, and both men and women have been among its supporters and critics. Among American university students, for both men and women, support for feminist ideas is more common than self-identification as a feminist. The US media tends to portray feminism negatively and feminists "are less often associated with day-to-day work/leisure activities of regular women." However, as recent research has demonstrated, as people are exposed to self-identified feminists and to discussions relating to various forms of feminism, their own self-identification with feminism increases. Roy Baumeister has criticized feminists who "look only at the top of society and draw conclusions about society as a whole. Yes, there are mostly men at the top. But if you look at the bottom, really at the bottom, you'll find mostly men there, too."

Pro-feminism

Pro-feminism is the support of feminism without implying that the supporter is a member of the feminist movement. The term is most often used in reference to men who are actively supportive of feminism. The activities of pro-feminist men's groups include anti-violence work with boys and young men in schools, offering sexual harassment workshops in workplaces, running community education campaigns, and counselling male perpetrators of violence. Pro-feminist men also may be involved in men's health, activism against pornography including anti-pornography legislation, men's studies, and the development of gender equity curricula in schools. This work is sometimes in collaboration with feminists and women's services, such as domestic violence and rape crisis centres.

Anti-feminism and Criticism of Feminism

Anti-feminism is opposition to feminism in some or all of its forms.

In the nineteenth century, anti-feminism was mainly focused on opposition to women's suffrage. Later, opponents of women's entry into institutions of higher learning argued that education was too great a physical burden on women. Other anti-feminists opposed women's entry into the labour force, or their right to join unions, to sit on juries, or to obtain birth control and control of their sexuality.

Some people have opposed feminism on the grounds that they believe it is contrary to traditional values or religious beliefs. These anti-feminists argue, for example, that social acceptance of divorce and non-married women is wrong and harmful, and that men and women are fundamentally different and thus their different traditional roles in society should be maintained. Other anti-feminists oppose women's entry into the workforce, political office, and the voting process, as well as the lessening of male authority in families.

Writers such as Camille Paglia, Christina Hoff Sommers, Jean Bethke Elshtain, Elizabeth

Fox-Genovese, Lisa Lucile Owens and Daphne Patai oppose some forms of feminism, though they identify as feminists. They argue, for example, that feminism often promotes misandry and the elevation of women's interests above men's, and criticize radical feminist positions as harmful to both men and women. Daphne Patai and Noretta Koertge argue that the term "anti-feminist" is used to silence academic debate about feminism. Lisa Lucile Owens argues that certain rights extended exclusively to women are patriarchal because they relieve women from exercising a crucial aspect of their moral agency.

First-wave Feminism

First-wave feminism was a period of feminist activity and thought, that occurred within the time period of the 19th and early 20th century throughout the world. It focused on legal issues, primarily on gaining women's suffrage (the right to vote).

Feminism has its source in the 18th century, specifically in the Enlightenment. In this cultural and philosophical movement there was a controversy over equality and gender differences. At the time appeared a new critical discourse that used the universal categories of this political philosophy. Enlightenment movement therefore was not feminist at its roots.

The political origins of feminism came from The French Revolution (1789). This event raised legal equality, freedoms and political rights as its central objectives but soon came the great contradiction that marked the struggle of early feminism: freedoms, rights and legal equality that had been the great conquests of the liberal revolutions didn't affect women. Rousseau's political theory designed the exclusion of women from the field of property and rights. So in the French Revolution the voice of women began to express themselves collectively.

The term *first-wave* was coined in March 1968 by Martha Lear writing in *The New York Times Magazine*, who at the same time also used the term "second-wave feminism". At that time, the women's movement was focused on *de facto* (unofficial) inequalities, which it wished to distinguish from the objectives of the earlier feminists.

According to Miriam Schneir, Simone de Beauvoir wrote that the first woman to "take up her pen in defense of her sex" was Christine de Pizan in the 15th century. Heinrich Cornelius Agrippa and Modesta di Pozzo di Forzi worked in the 16th century. Marie Le Jars de Gournay, Anne Bradstreet and François Poullain de la Barre wrote in the 17th.

Mary Wollstonecraft's most famous work, which is called Vindication, was created in 1792. Its previous feminist work was Poullain de la Barre's Equality of sexes (1673). This period was affected by Rousseau's philosophy, the Illustration. The father of the Illustration defined an ideal democratic society that was based on the equality of men, where women were totally discriminated. Mary Wollstonecraft based her work on the ideas of Rousseau. Although at first it seems to be contradictory, Wollstonecraft's idea was to expand Rousseau's democratic society but based on gender equality.

Mary Wollstonecraft published one of the first feminist treatises, *A Vindication of the Rights of Woman* (1792), in which she advocated the social and moral equality of the sexes, extending the work of her 1790 pamphlet, *A Vindication of the Rights of Men*. Her later unfinished novel, *Maria, or the Wrongs of Woman*, earned her considerable criticism as she discussed women's sexual desires. She died young, and her widower, the philosopher William Godwin, quickly wrote a memoir of her that, contrary to his intentions, destroyed her reputation for generations.

Early Feminism was directly correlated with the abolitionist movements and as a result many famous feminists and activists began to have their voices heard. Some of these early activists include, Sojourner Truth, Dr. Elizabeth Blackwell, Jane Addams, and Dorothy Day. The first wave of feminism was primarily led by white women in the middle class, and it was not until the second wave of feminism that women of color began developing a voice. The term Feminism was created like a political illustrated ideology at that period. Feminism emerged by the speech about the reform and correction of democracy based on equalitarian conditions. With Wollstonecraft's work, the illustrated feminist polemic was displayed, and as a result, suffragist movements were stood up. Wollstonecraft is regarded as the grandmother of British feminism and her ideas shaped the thinking of the suffragettes, who campaigned for the women's vote. After generations of work, this was eventually achieved.

A 1932 Soviet poster for International Women's Day.

Louise Weiss along with other Parisian suffragettes in 1935. The newspaper headline reads,
in translation, "THE FRENCHWOMAN MUST VOTE".

Australia

The first wave of Australian feminism, which dates back to the late 19th century, was chiefly concerned with suffrage (women's right to vote) and consequently with women's access to parliaments and other political activities.

In 1882, Rose Scott, a women's rights activist, began to hold a weekly salon meetings in her Sydney home, left to her by her late mother. Through these meetings, she became well known amongst politicians, judges, philanthropists, writers and poets. In 1889, she helped to found the Women's Literary Society, which later grew into the Womanhood Suffrage League in 1891. Leading politicians hosted by Scott included Bernhard Ringrose Wise, William Holman, William Morris Hughes and Thomas Bavin, who met and discussed the drafting of the bill that eventually became the Early Closing Act of 1899.

Tribute to the Suffragettes memorial in Christchurch, New Zealand. The figures shown from left to right are Amey Daldy, Kate Sheppard, Ada Wells and Harriet Morison.

Denmark

The first women's movement was led by the *Dansk Kvindesamfund* ("Danish Women's Society"), founded in 1871. Line Luplau was one of the most notable woman in this era. Tagea Brandt was also part of this movement, and in her honor was established the Tagea Brandt Rejselegat or Travel Scholarship for women. The Dansk Kvindesamfund's efforts as a leading group of women for women led to the existence of the revised Danish constitution of 1915, giving women the right to vote and the provision of equal opportunity laws during the 1920s, which influenced the present-day legislative measures to grant women access to education, work, marital rights and other obligations.

New Zealand

Early New Zealand feminists and suffragettes included Maud Pember Reeves (Australian-born; later lived in London), Kate Sheppard and Mary Ann Müller. In 1893, Elizabeth Yates became Mayor of Onehunga, the first time such a post had been held by a female anywhere in the British Empire. Early university graduates were Emily Siedeberg (doctor, graduated 1895) and Ethel Benjamin (lawyer, graduated 1897). The Female Law Practitioners Act was passed in 1896 and Benjamin was admitted as a barrister and solicitor of the Supreme Court of New Zealand in 1897.

149

Netherlands

Although in the Netherlands during the Age of Enlightenment the idea of the equality of women and men made progress, no practical institutional measures or legislation resulted. In the second half of the nineteenth century many initiatives by feminists sprung up in The Netherlands. Aletta Jacobs (1854–1929) requested and obtained as the first woman in the Netherlands the right to study at university in 1871, becoming the first female medical doctor and academic. She became a lifelong campaigner for women's suffrage, equal rights, birth control, and international peace, travelling worldwide for, e.g., the International Alliance of Women. Wilhelmina Drucker (1847–1925) was a politician, a prolific writer and a peace activist, who fought for the vote and equal rights through political and feminist organisations she founded. In 1917–1919 her goal of women's suffrage was reached.

Persia

While in some distance in culture and language, the events of the Conference of Badasht (1848) presented progress on the concerns of first wave feminism. There is a synchronicity in time and a likeness in theme and events between Persia (later named Iran) and the United States between the conference at Badasht and the Seneca Falls Convention. First the conference happened over three weeks from late June to mid-July 1848 and the Seneca Falls Convention happened in mid-July 1848. Both conferences had women (Tahirih and Elizabeth Cady Stanton) take strong stances on the role of women in the public arena that some attending reacted to harshly. And lastly leading men present (Quddús and Frederick Douglass) supported these calls during the meetings healing the breach. Some even see a parallel in the background discussions that are partially documented to arrange how things would be brought up and settled.

The conference of Badasht is considered by Bahá'ís as a signal moment that demonstrated that Islamic Sharia law had been abrogated as well as a key demonstration of the thrust of raising the social position of women. Although the unveiling led to accusations of immorality the Báb responded by supporting her position and naming her *the Pure* (Táhirih). Modern women scholars review this kind of accusation as part of a pattern faced by women leaders and writers then and since in a way that Azar Nafisi says "...the Islamic regime today... fears them and feels vulnerable in the face of a resistance that is not just political but existential."

Sweden

Feminist issues and gender roles were discussed in media and literature during the 18th century by people such as Margareta Momma, Catharina Ahlgren, Anna Maria Rückerschöld and Hedvig Charlotta Nordenflycht, but it created no movement of any kind. The first person to hold public speeches and agitate in favor of feminism was Sophie Sager in 1848, and the first organization created to deal with a women's issue was *Svenska lärarinnors pensionsförening* (Society for Retired Female Teachers) by Josefina Deland in 1855.

In 1856, Fredrika Bremer published her famous *Hertha*, which aroused great controversy and created a debate referred to as the *Hertha Debate*. The two foremost questions was to abolish coverture for unmarried women, and for the state to provide women an equivalent to a university. Both questions were met: in 1858, a reform granted unmarried women the right to apply for legal majority by a simple procedure, and in 1861, Högre lärarinneseminariet was founded as a "Women's University". In 1859, the first women's magazine in Sweden and the Nordic countries, the *Tidskrift för hemmet*, was founded by Sophie Adlersparre and Rosalie Olivecrona. This has been referred to as the starting point of a women's movement in Sweden.

The organized women's movement begun in 1873, when Married Woman's Property Rights Association was co-founded by Anna Hierta-Retzius and Ellen Anckarsvärd. The prime task of the organization was to abolish coverture. In 1884, Fredrika Bremer Association was founded by Sophie Adlersparre to work for the improvement in women's rights. The second half of the 19th century saw the creation of several women's rights organisations and a considerable activity within both active organization as well as intellectual debate. The 1880s saw the so-called *Sedlighetsdebatten*, were gender roles were discussed in literary debate in regards to sexual double standards in opposed to sexual equality. In 1902, finally, the National Association for Women's Suffrage was founded.

In 1921, women's suffrage was finally introduced. The women suffrage reform was followed by the *Behörighetslagen* of 1923 (Act of Access of 1923), in which males and females were formally given equal access to all professions and positions in society, the only exceptions being military and priesthood positions. The last two restrictions were removed in 1958, when women were allowed to become priests, and in a series of reforms between 1980 and 1989, when all military professions were opened to women.

United Kingdom

The early feminist reformers were unorganized, and including prominent individuals who had suffered as victim of injustice. This included individuals such as Caroline Norton whose personal tragedy where she was unable to obtain a divorce and was denied access to her three sons by her husband, led her to a life of intense campaigning which successful led to the passing of the Custody of Infants Act 1839 and the introduced the Tender years doctrine for child custody arrangement. The Act gave married women, for the first time, a right to their children. However, because women needed to petition in the Court of Chancery, in practice few women had the financial means to petition for their rights.

The first organized movement for English feminism was the Langham Place Circle of the 1850s, which included among others Barbara Bodichon (née Leigh-Smith) and Bessie Rayner Parkes. The group campaigned for many women's causes, including improved female rights in employment, and education. It also pursued women's property rights through its Married Women's Property Committee. In 1854, Bodichon published her *Brief Summary of the Laws of England concerning Women*, which was used by the Social Science Association after it was formed in 1857 to push for the passage of the Married Women's Property Act 1882. In 1858, Barbara Bodichon, Matilda Mary Hays and Bessie Rayner Parkes established the first feminist British periodical, the *English Woman's Journal*, with Bessie Parkes the chief editor. The journal continued publication until 1864 and was succeeded in 1866 by the *Englishwoman's Review* edited until 1880 by Jessie Boucherett which continued publication until 1910. Jessie Boucherett and Adelaide Anne Proctor joined the Langham Place Circle in 1859. The group was active until 1866. Also in 1859, Jessie Boucherett, Barbara Bodichon and Adelaide Proctor formed the Society for Promoting the Employment of Women to promote the training and employment of women. The society is one of the earliest British women's organisations, and continues to operate as the registered charity *Futures for Women*. Helen Blackburn and Boucherett established the Women's Employment Defence League in 1891, to defend women's working rights against restrictive employment legislation. They also together edited the *Condition of Working Women and the Factory Acts* in 1896. In the beginning of the 20th century, women's employment was still predominantly limited to factory labor and domestic work. During World War I, more women found work outside the home. As a result of the wartime experience of women in the workforce, the *Sex Disqualification (Removal) Act 1919* opened professions and the civil service to women, and marriage was no longer a legal barrier to women working outside the home.

In 1918 Marie Stopes published the very influential *Married Love*, in which she advocated gender equality in marriage and the importance of women's sexual desire. Importation of the book into the United States was banned as obscene until 1931.

The *Representation of the People Act 1918* extended the franchise to women who were at least 30 years old and they or their husbands were property holders, while the *Parliament (Qualification of Women) Act 1918* gave women the right to sit in Parliament, although it was only slowly that women were actually elected. In 1928, the franchise was extended to all women over 21 by the *Representation of the People (Equal Franchise) Act 1928*, on an equal basis to men. Women started serving on school boards and local bodies, and numbers kept increasing. This period also saw more women gaining access to higher education. In 1910, "women were attending many leading medical schools, and in 1915 the American Medical Association began to admit women members." A *Matrimonial Causes Act 1923* gave women the right to the same grounds for divorce as men.

The rise in unemployment during the Great Depression which started in the 1920s hit women first, and when the men also lost their jobs there was further strain on families. Many women served in the armed forces during World War II, when around 300,000 American women served in the navy and army, performing jobs such as secretaries, typists and nurses.

Many feminist writers and women's rights activists argued that it was not equality to men which they needed but a recognition of what women need to fulfill their potential of their own natures, not only within the aspect of work but society and home life too. Virginia Woolf produced her essay *A Room of One's Own* based on the ideas of women as writers and characters in fiction. Woolf said that a woman must have money and a room of her own to be able to write. New Zealand was the first country to grant women the right to vote at a national level, while Finland, as well as some American states gave women voting rights at a state level before Australian women obtained that right across the nation.

United States

Woman in the Nineteenth Century by Margaret Fuller has been considered the first major feminist work in the United States and is often compared to Wollstonecraft's *A Vindication of the Rights of Woman*. Prominent leaders of the feminist movement in the United States include Lucretia Coffin Mott, Elizabeth Cady Stanton, Lucy Stone, and Susan B. Anthony; Anthony and other activists such as Victoria Woodhull and Matilda Joslyn Gage made attempts to cast votes prior to their legal entitlement to do so, for which many of them faced charges. Other important leaders included several women who dissented against the law in order to have their voices heard,(Sarah and Angelina Grimké), in addition to other activists such as Carrie Chapman Catt, Alice Paul, Sojourner Truth, Ida B. Wells, Margaret Sanger and Lucy Burns.

Suffragist with banner, Washington DC, 1918.

First-wave feminism involved a wide range of women, some belonging to conservative Christian groups (such as Frances Willard and the Woman's Christian Temperance Union), others such as Matilda Joslyn Gage of the National Woman Suffrage Association (NWSA) resembling the radicalism of much of second-wave feminism. The majority of first-wave feminists were more moderate and conservative than radical or revolutionary—like the members of the American Woman Suffrage Association (AWSA) they were willing to work within the political system and they understood the clout of joining with sympathetic men in power to promote the cause of suffrage. The limited membership of the NWSA was narrowly focused on gaining a federal amendment for women's suffrage, whereas the AWSA, with ten times as many members, worked to gain suffrage on a state-by-state level as a necessary precursor to federal suffrage. The NWSA had broad goals, hoping to achieve a more equal social role for women, but the AWSA was aware of the divisive nature of many of those goals and instead chose to focus solely on suffrage. The NWSA was known for having more publicly aggressive tactics (such as picketing and hunger strikes) whereas the AWSA used more traditional strategies like lobbying, delivering speeches, applying political pressure and gathering signatures for petitions.

The first wave of feminists, in contrast to the second wave, focused very little on the subjects of abortion, birth control, and overall reproductive rights of women. Though she never married, Anthony published her views about marriage, holding that a woman should be allowed to refuse sex with her husband; the American woman had no legal recourse at that time against rape by her husband.

In 1860, New York passed a revised Married Women's Property Act which gave women shared ownership of their children, allowing them to have a say in their children's wills, wages, and granting them the right to inherit property. Further advances and setbacks were experienced in New York and other states, but with each new win the feminists were able to use it as an example to apply more leverage on unyielding legislative bodies. The end of the first wave is often linked with the passage of the Nineteenth Amendment to the United States Constitution (1920), granting women the right to vote. This was the major victory of the movement, which also included reforms in higher education, in the workplace and professions, and in health care.

During the First Wave, there was a notable connection between the slavery abolition movement and the women's rights movement. Frederick Douglass was heavily involved in both movements and believed that it was essential for both to work together in order to attain true equality in regards to race and sex. Different accounts of the involvement of African-American women in the Women's Suffrage Movement are given. In a 1974 interview, Alice Paul notes that a compromise was made between southern groups to have white women march first, then men, then African-American women. In another account by the National Association for the Advancement of Colored People (NAACP), difficulties in segregating women resulted in African-American women marching with their respective States without hindrance. Among them was Ida B. Wells-Barnett, who marched with the Illinois delegation.

Timeline

1809

- US, Connecticut: Married women were allowed to execute wills.

1810

- Sweden: The informal right of an unmarried woman to be declared of legal majority by royal dispensation was officially confirmed by parliament.

1811

- Austria: Married women were granted separate economy and the right to choose their professions.

- Sweden: Married businesswomen were granted the right to make decisions about their own affairs without their husband's consent.

1821

- US, Maine: Married women were allowed to own and manage property in their own name during the incapacity of their spouse.

1827

- Brazil: The first elementary schools for girls and the profession of school teacher were opened.

1829

- India: Sati was banned.

- Sweden: Midwives were allowed to use surgical instruments, which were unique in Europe at the time and gave them surgical status.

1832

- Brazil: Dionísia Gonçalves Pinto, under the pseudonym Nísia Floresta Brasileira Augusta, published her first book, and the first in Brazil to deal with women's intellectual equality and their capacity and right to be educated and participate in society on an equal basis with men, which was *Women's rights and men's injustice*. It was a translation of *Woman not Inferior to Man*, often attributed to Mary Wortley Montagu.

1833

- US, Ohio: The first co-educational American university, Oberlin College, was founded.

- Guatemala: Divorce was legalized; this was rescinded in 1840 and reintroduced in 1894.

1835

- US, Arkansas: Married women were allowed to own (but not control) property in their own name.

- Pitcairn Islands: The Pitcairn Islands granted women the right to vote.

1838

- US, Kentucky: Kentucky gave school suffrage (the right to vote at school meetings) to widows with children of school age.

- US, Iowa: Iowa was the first U.S. state to allow sole custody of a child to its mother in the event of a divorce.

1839

- US, Mississippi: Mississippi was the first U.S. state that gave married women limited property rights.

- Great Britain: The Custody of Infants Act 1839 made it possible for divorced mothers to be granted custody of their children under seven, but only if the Lord Chancellor agreed to it, and only if the mother was of good character.

- US, Mississippi: The Married Women's Property Act 1839 granted married women the right to own (but not control) property in their own name.

1840

- US, Texas: Married women were allowed to own property in their own name.

1841

- Bulgaria: The first secular girls school in Bulgaria was opened, making education and the profession of teacher available for women.

1842

- Sweden: Compulsory elementary school for both sexes was introduced.

1844

- US, Maine: Maine was the first U.S. state that passed a law to allow married women to own separate property in their own name (separate economy) in 1844.

- US, Maine: Maine passed Sole Trader Law which granted married women the ability to engage in business without the need for their husbands' consent.

- US, Massachusetts: Married women were granted separate economy.

1845

- Sweden: Equal inheritance for sons and daughters (in the absence of a will) became law.

- US, New York: Married women were granted patent rights.

1846

- Sweden: Trade- and crafts works professions were opened to all unmarried women.

1847

- Costa Rica: The first high school for girls opened, and the profession of teacher was opened to women.

1848

- US, State of New York: Married Women's Property Act grant married women separate economy.

- US, on June 14–15, third-party presidential candidate Gerrit Smith made women's suffrage a plank in the Liberty Party platform.

- Persia (now called Iran): The Conference of Badasht was held June–July.

- US, State of New York: A women's rights convention called the Seneca Falls Convention was held in July. It was the first American women's rights convention.

1849

- US: Elizabeth Blackwell, born in England, became the first female medical doctor in American history.

1850

- England: The first organized movement for English feminism was the Langham Place Circle of the 1850s, including among others Barbara Bodichon (née Leigh-Smith) and Bessie Rayner Parkes. They also campaigned for improved female rights in employment, and education.

- Haiti: The first permanent school for girls was opened.

- Iceland: Equal inheritance for men and women was required.

- US, California: Married Women's Property Act granted married women separate economy.

- US, Wisconsin: The Married Women's Property Act granted married women separate economy.

- US, Oregon: Unmarried women were allowed to own land.

- The feminist movement began in Denmark with the publication of the feminist book *Clara Raphael, Tolv Breve*, meaning "Clara Raphael, Twelve Letters," by Mathilde Fibiger.

1851

- Guatemala: Full citizenship was granted to economically independent women, but this was rescinded in 1879.

- Canada, New Brunswick : Married women were granted separate economy.

1852

- US, New Jersey: Married women were granted separate economy.

1853

- Colombia: Divorce was legalized; this was rescinded in 1856 and reintroduced in 1992.

- Sweden: The profession of teacher at public primary and elementary school was opened to both sexes.

1854

- Norway: Equal inheritance for men and women was required.

- US, Massachusetts: Massachusetts granted married women separate economy.

- Chile: The first public elementary school for girls was opened.

1855

- US, Iowa: The University of Iowa became the first coeducational public or state university in the United States.

- US, Michigan: Married women were granted separate economy.

1857

- Denmark: Legal majority was granted to unmarried women.

- Denmark: A new law established the right of unmarried women to earn their living in any craft or trade.

- UK: The Matrimonial Causes Act 1857 enabled couples to obtain a divorce through civil proceedings.

- Netherlands: Elementary education was made compulsory for both girls and boys.

- Spain: Elementary education was made compulsory for both girls and boys.

- US, Maine: Married women were granted the right to control their own earnings.

1858

- Russia: Gymnasiums for girls were opened.

- Sweden: Legal majority was granted to unmarried women if applied for; automatic legal majority was granted in 1863.

1859

- Canada West: Married women were granted separate economy.

- Denmark: The post of teacher at public school was opened to women.

- Russia: Women were allowed to audit university lectures, but this was retracted in 1863.

- Sweden: The posts of college teacher and lower official at public institutions were opened to women.

- US, Kansas: The Married Women's Property Act granted married women separate economy.

1860

- US, New York: New York passed a revised Married Women's Property Act which gave women shared ownership of their children, allowing them to have a say in their children's wills, wages, and granting them the right to inherit property.

1861

- South Australia: South Australia granted property-owning women the right to vote in local elections.

- US, Kansas: Kansas gave school suffrage to all women. Many U.S. states followed before the start of the 20th century.

1862

- Sweden: Restricted local suffrage was granted to women in Sweden. In 1919 suffrage was granted with restrictions, and in 1921 all restrictions were lifted.

1863

- Finland: In 1863, taxpaying women were granted municipal suffrage in the country side, and in 1872, the same reform was given to the cities.

1869

- United Kingdom: The UK granted women the right to vote in local elections.

- US, Wyoming: Wyoming granted women the right to vote, the first US state to do so.

1870

- US, Utah: The Utah territory granted women the right to vote, but it was revoked by Congress in 1887 as part of a national effort to rid the territory of polygamy. It was restored in 1895, when the right to vote and hold office was written into the constitution of the new state.

- England: The Married Women's Property Act was passed in 1870 and expanded in 1874 and 1882, giving English women control over their own earnings and property.

1871

- Denmark: In 1871 the worlds very first Women's Rights organization was founded by Mathilde Bajer and her husband Frederik Bajer, called Danish Women's Society (or Dansk Kvindesamfund. It still exists to this day).

- Netherlands: First female academic student Aletta Jacobs enrolls at a Dutch university (University of Groningen).

1872

- Finland: In 1872, taxpaying women were granted municipal suffrage in the cities.

1881

- Isle of Man: The right to vote was extended to unmarried women and widows who owned property, and as a result 700 women received the vote, comprising about 10% of the Manx electorate.

1884

- Canada: Widows and spinsters were the first women granted the right to vote within municipalities in Ontario, with the other provinces following throughout the 1890s.

1886

- US: All but six U.S. states allowed divorce on grounds of cruelty.

- Korea: Ewha Womans University, Korea's first educational institute for women, was founded in 1886 by Mary F. Scranton, an American missionary of the Methodist Episcopal Church.

1891

- Australia: The New South Wales Womanhood Suffrage League was founded.

1893

- US, Colorado: Colorado granted women the right to vote.

- New Zealand: New Zealand became the first self-governing country in the world in which all women had the right to vote in parliamentary elections.

- Cook Islands: The Cook Islands granted women the right to vote in island councils and a federal parliament.

1894

- South Australia: South Australia granted women the right to vote.

- United Kingdom: The United Kingdom extended the right to vote in local elections to married women.

1895

- US: Almost all U.S. states had passed some form of Sole Trader Laws, Property Laws, and Earnings Laws, granting married women the right to trade without their husbands' consent, own and/or control their own property, and control their own earnings.

1896

- US, Idaho: Idaho granted women the right to vote.

1900

- Western Australia: Western Australia granted women the right to vote.

- Belgium: Legal majority was granted to unmarried women.

- Egypt: A school for female teachers was founded in Cairo.

- France: Women were allowed to practice law.

- Korea: The post office profession was opened to women.

- Tunisia: The first public elementary school for girls was opened.

- Japan: The first women's university was opened.

- Baden, Germany: Universities opened to women.

- Sweden: Maternity leave was granted for female industrial workers.

1901

- Bulgaria: Universities opened to women.

- Cuba: Universities opened to women.

- Denmark: Maternity leave was granted for all women.

- Sweden: The first Swedish law regarding parental leave was instituted in 1900. This law only affected women who worked as wage-earning factory workers and simply required that employers not allow women to work in the first four weeks after giving birth.

- Commonwealth of Australia: The First Parliament was not elected with a uniform franchise. The voting rights were based on existing franchise laws in each of the States. Thus, in

South Australia and Western Australia women had the vote, in South Australia Aborigines (men and women) were entitled to vote and in Queensland and Western Australia Aborigines were explicitly denied voting rights.

1902

- China: Foot binding was outlawed in 1902 by the imperial edicts of the Qing Dynasty, the last dynasty in China, which ended in 1911.

- El Salvador: Married women were granted separate economy.

- El Salvador: Legal majority was granted to married women.

- New South Wales: New South Wales granted women the right to vote in state elections.

- England: A delegation of women textile workers from Northern England presented a petition to Parliament with 37,000 signatures demanding votes for women.

1903

- Bavaria, Germany: Universities opened to women.

- Sweden: Public medical offices opened to women.

- Australia: Tasmania granted women the right to vote.

- England: The Women's Social and Political Union was founded.

1904

- Nicaragua: Married women were granted separate economy.

- Nicaragua: Legal majority was granted to married women.

- Württemberg, Germany: Universities opened to women.

- England: The suffragette Dora Montefiore refused to pay her taxes because women could not vote.

1905

- Australia: Queensland granted women the right to vote.

- Iceland: Educational institutions opened to women.

- Russia: Universities opened to women.

- England: On October 10, Christabel Pankhurst and Annie Kenney became the first women to be arrested in the fight for women's suffrage.

1906

- Finland granted women the right vote. It was the first country in Europe to do so.

- Honduras: Married women were granted separate economy.

- Honduras: Legal majority was granted to married women.

- Honduras: Divorce was legalized.

- Korea: The profession of nurse was allowed for women.

- Nicaragua: Divorce was legalized.

- Sweden : Municipal suffrage, since 1862 granted to unmarried women, was granted to married women.

- Saxony, Germany: Universities opened to women.

- England: A delegation of women from both the Women's Social and Political Union and the National Union of Women's Suffrage Societies met with the Prime Minister, Sir Henry Campbell-Bannerman.

- England: The word suffragette, intended as an insult to women in the Women's Social and Political Union, was used for the first time, by the Daily Mail.

- Britain: The National Federation of Women Workers was established by Mary Reid MacArthur.

1907

- France: Married women were given control of their income.

- France: Women were allowed guardianship of children.

- Norway: Women were granted the right to stand for election, although this was subject to restrictions until 1913.

- Finland: The first female members of parliament in world history were elected in Finland in 1907.

- Uruguay: Divorce was legalized.

- England: The National Union of Women's Suffrage Societies organized its first national demonstration, which became known as the "Mud March" because of the terrible weather at the time.

- England: Emmeline Pethick-Lawrence and her husband Frederick launched the suffragette newspaper "Votes for Women".

- England: The Women's Freedom League was formed when Charlotte Despard and others broke away from the Women's Social and Political Union.

- England: The Qualification of Women Act 1907 allowed women to be elected as mayors and to borough and city councils.

1908

- Belgium: Women were allowed to act as legal witnesses in court.

- Denmark: Unmarried women were made legal guardians of their children.

- Peru: Universities opened to women.

- Prussia, Alsace-Lorraine and Hesse, Germany: Universities opened to women.

- Denmark: Denmark granted women over 25 the right to vote in local elections.

- Australia: Victoria granted women the right to vote in state elections.

- England: On January 17, suffragettes chained themselves to the railings of 10 Downing Street. Emmeline Pankhurst was imprisoned for the first time. The Women's Social and Political Union also introduced their stone-throwing campaign.

1909

- Sweden: Women were granted eligibility to municipal councils.

- Sweden: The phrase "Swedish man" was removed from the application forms to public offices and women were thereby approved as applicants to most public professions.

- Mecklenburg, Germany: Universities opened to women.

- England: In July, Marion Wallace Dunlop became the first imprisoned suffragette to go on a hunger strike. As a result, force-feeding was introduced.

- Women were first elected to the procurer of the Bahá'í Local Spiritual Assembly of Chicago – the Bahai Temple Unity. Of the nine members elected by secret ballot three were women with Corinne True (later appointed as a Hand of the Cause) serving as an officer.

1910

- Denmark: The Socialist International, meeting in Copenhagen, established a Women's Day, international in character, to honor the movement for women's rights and to assist in achieving universal suffrage for women.

- US, Washington: Washington granted women the right to vote.

- Ecuador: Divorce was legalized.

- England: November 18 was "Black Friday", when the suffragettes and police clashed violently outside Parliament after the failure of the first Conciliation Bill. Ellen Pitfield, one of the suffragettes, later died from her injuries.

1911

- England: Dame Ethel Smyth composed "The March of the Women", the suffragette song.

- Portugal: Legal majority was granted to married women (rescinded in 1933.)

- Portugal: Divorce was legalized.

- US, California: California granted women the right to vote.

- Austria, Denmark, Germany and Switzerland: International Women's Day was marked for the first time in Austria, Denmark, Germany and Switzerland on the 19th of March. More than one million women and men attended IWD rallies campaigning for women's rights to work, vote, be trained, hold public office and be free from discrimination.

- South Africa: Olive Schreiner published Women and Labor.

1912

- US, Oregon, Kansas, Arizona: Oregon, Kansas, and Arizona granted women the right to vote.

- England: Sylvia Pankhurst established her East London Federation of Suffragettes.

- The all-male administrative bodies in the United States of the Bahá'í Faith were completely dissolved by `Abdu'l-Bahá during his visit to America replacing them with integrated institutions.

- Palestine: During the periods her brother was away in America, Bahíyyih Khánum was empowered as the acting head of the Bahá'í Faith, which was a rare position for a woman to be in at that time.

1913

- Russia: In 1913 Russian women observed their first International Women's Day on the last Sunday in February. Following discussions, International Women's Day was transferred to 8 March and this day has remained the global date for International Women's Day ever since.

- US, Alaska: Alaska granted women the right to vote.

- Norway: Norway granted women the right to vote.

- Japan: Public universities opened to women.

- England: The suffragette Emily Davison was killed by the King's horse at the Epsom Derby.

- England: 50,000 women taking part in a pilgrimage organized by the National Union of Women's Suffrage Societies arrived in Hyde Park on July 26.

1914

- Russia: Married women were allowed their own internal passport.

- US, Montana, Nevada: Montana and Nevada granted women the right to vote.

- England: The suffragette Mary Richardson entered the National Gallery and slashed the Rokeby Venus.

1915

- Denmark: Denmark granted women the right to vote.

- Iceland: Iceland granted women the right to vote, subject to conditions and restrictions.

- US: In 1915 the American Medical Association began to admit women as members.

- Wales: The first Women's Institute in Britain was founded in North Wales at Llanfairpwll.

1916

- Canada: Alberta, Manitoba and Saskatchewan granted women the right to vote.

- US: Margaret Sanger opened America's first birth control clinic in 1916.

- England: The Cat and Mouse Act was introduced for suffragettes who refused to eat.

1917

- Cuba: Married women were granted separate economy.

- Cuba: Legal majority was granted to married women.

- Netherlands: Women were granted the right to stand for election.

- Mexico: Legal majority for married women.

- Mexico: Divorce was legalized.

- US, New York: New York granted women the right to vote.

- Belarus: Belarus granted women the right to vote.

- Russia: The Russian SFSR granted women the right to vote.

1918

- Cuba: Divorce was legalized.

- Russia: The first Constitution of the new Soviet State (the Russian Socialist Federative Soviet Republic) declared that "women have equal rights to men."

- Thailand: Universities opened to women.

- England: In 1918 Marie Stopes, who believed in equality in marriage and the importance of women's sexual desire, published *Married Love*, a sex manual that, according to a survey of American academics in 1935, was one of the 25 most influential books of the previous 50 years, ahead of *Relativity* by Albert Einstein, *Mein Kampf* by Adolf Hitler, *Interpretation of Dreams* by Sigmund Freud and *The Economic Consequences of the Peace* by John Maynard Keynes.

- US, Michigan, South Dakota, Oklahoma: Michigan, South Dakota, and Oklahoma granted women the right to vote.

- Austria: Austria granted women the right to vote.

- Canada: Canada granted women the right to vote on the federal level (the last province to enact women's suffrage was Quebec in 1940.)

- United Kingdom: The Representation of the People Act was passed which allowed women over the age of 30 who met a property qualification to vote. Although 8.5 million women met this criteria, it only represented 40 per cent of the total population of women in the UK. The same act extended the vote to all men over the age of 21.

- United Kingdom: The Parliament (Qualification of Women) Act 1918 was passed allowing women to stand as Members of Parliament.

- Czechoslovakia: Czechoslovakia granted women the right to vote.

1919

- Germany: Germany granted women the right to vote.

- Azerbaijan: Azerbaijan granted women the right to vote.

- Italy: Women gained more property rights, including control over their own earnings, and access to some legal positions.

- Great Britain: The Sex Disqualification (Removal) Act 1919 became law. In a broad opening statement it specified that, "[a] person shall not be disqualified by sex or marriage from the exercise of any public function, or from being appointed to or holding any civil or judicial office or post, or from entering or assuming or carrying on any civil profession or vocation". The Act did provide employment opportunities for individual women and many were appointed as magistrates, but in practice it fell far short of the expectations of the women's movement. Senior positions in the civil service were still closed to women and they could be excluded from juries if evidence was likely to be too "sensitive".

- Luxembourg: Luxembourg granted women the right to vote.

- Canada: Women were granted the right to be candidates in federal elections.

- Netherlands: The Netherlands granted women the right to vote. The right to stand in election was granted in 1917.

- New Zealand: New Zealand allowed women to stand for election into parliament.

- England: Nancy Astor became the first woman to take her seat in the House of Commons.

1920

- China: The first female students were accepted in Peking University, soon followed by universities all over China.

- Haiti: The apothecary profession was opened to women.

- Korea: The profession of telephone operator, as well as several other professions, such as store clerks, were opened to women.

- Sweden: Legal majority was granted to married women and equal marriage rights were granted to women.

- US: The 19th Amendment was signed into law, granting all American women the right to vote.

- England: Oxford University opened its degrees to women.

1921

- England: The Six Point Group was founded by Lady Rhondda to push for women's social, political, occupational, moral, economic, and legal equality.

1922

- China: International Women's Day was celebrated in China from 1922 on.

- United Kingdom: The Law of Property Act 1922 was passed, giving wives the right to inherit property equally with their husbands.

- England: The Infanticide Act was passed, ending the death penalty for women who killed their children if the women's minds were found to be unbalanced.

1923

- Nicaragua: Elba Ochomogo became the first woman to obtain a university degree in Nicaragua.

- England: The Matrimonial Causes Act gave women the right to petition for divorce on the grounds of adultery.

1925

- UK: The Guardianship of Infants Act gave parents equal claims over their children.

1928

- UK: The right to vote was granted to all UK women equally with men in 1928.

1934

- Turkey: Women gained the right to vote and to become a nominee to be elected equally in 1934 after reformations for a new civil law.

Feminism in Culture

Feminism has affected culture in many ways, and has famously been theorised in relation to culture by Angela McRobbie, Laura Mulvey and others. Timothy Laurie and Jessica Kean have argued that "one of feminism's most important innovations has been to seriously examine the ways women receive popular culture, given that so much pop culture is made by and for men." This is reflected in a variety of forms, including literature, music, film and other screen cultures.

Women's Writing

Women's writing came to exist as a separate category of scholarly interest relatively recently. In the West, second-wave feminism prompted a general reevaluation of women's historical contributions, and various academic sub-disciplines, such as Women's history (or herstory) and women's writing, developed in response to the belief that women's lives and contributions have been underrepresented as areas of scholarly interest. Virginia Blain et al. characterize the growth in interest since 1970 in women's writing as "powerful". Much of this early period of feminist literary scholarship was given over to the rediscovery and reclamation of texts written by women. Studies such as Dale Spender's *Mothers of the Novel* (1986) and Jane Spencer's *The Rise of the Woman Novelist* (1986) were ground-breaking in their insistence that women have always been writing. Commensurate with this growth in scholarly interest, various presses began the task of reissuing long-out-of-print texts. Virago Press began to publish its large list of nineteenth- and early-twentieth-century novels in 1975 and became one of the first commercial presses to join in the project of reclamation. In the 1980s, Pandora Press, responsible for publishing Spender's study, issued a companion line of eighteenth-century novels written by women. More recently, Broadview Press has begun to issue eighteenth- and nineteenth-century works, many hitherto out of print, and the University of Kentucky has a series of republications of early women's novels. There has been commensurate growth in the area of biographical dictionaries of women writers due to a perception, according to one editor, that "most of our women are not represented in the 'standard' reference books in the field".

Virginia Woolf.

Science Fiction

In the 1960s, the genre of science fiction combined its sensationalism with political and technological critiques of society to produce feminist science fiction. With the advent of feminism, questioning women's roles became fair game to this "subversive, mind expanding genre". Two early texts are Ursula K. Le Guin's *The Left Hand of Darkness* (1969) and Joanna Russ' *The Female Man* (1970). They serve to highlight the socially constructed nature of gender roles by creating utopias that do away with gender. Both authors were also pioneers in feminist criticism of science fiction in the 1960s and '70s, in essays collected in *The Language of the Night* (Le Guin, 1979) and *How To Suppress Women's Writing* (Russ, 1983). Another major work of feminist science fiction has been *Kindred* by Octavia Butler.

Women's Films

The term "women's cinema" usually refers to the work of women film directors. It can also designate the work of other women behind the camera such as cinematographers and screenwriters. Although the participation of women film editors, costume designers, and production designers is usually not considered to be decisive enough to justify the term "women's cinema", it does have a large influence on the visual impression of any movie.

In a film from popular culture although not in women's film, an early reference to the "feminist movement" is heard from Katharine Hepburn in the 1942 movie *Woman of the Year*.

Women's Music

Women's music (or womyn's music or wimmin's music) is the music by women, for women, and about women. The genre emerged as a musical expression of the second-wave feminist movement as well as the labor, civil rights, and peace movements. The movement was started by lesbians such as Cris Williamson, Meg Christian, and Margie Adam, African-American women activists such as Bernice Johnson Reagon and her group Sweet Honey in the Rock, and peace activist Holly Near. Women's music also refers to the wider industry of women's music that goes beyond the performing artists to include studio musicians, producers, sound engineers, technicians, cover artists, distributors, promoters, and festival organizers who are also women.

Riot Grrrl Movement

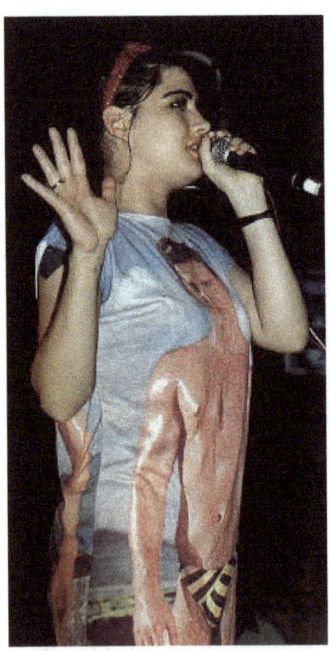

Kathleen Hanna was the lead singer of Bikini Kill, a riot grrrl music band formed in 1990.

Riot grrrl (or *riot grrl*) is an underground feminist punk movement that started in the 1990s and is often associated with third-wave feminism (it is sometimes seen as its starting point). It was grounded in the DIY philosophy of punk values. Riot grrrls took an anti-corporate stance of self-sufficiency and self-reliance. Riot grrrls' emphasis on universal female identity and separatism often appears more closely allied with second-wave feminism than with the third wave. Riot grrrl bands often address issues such as rape, domestic abuse, sexuality, and female empowerment. Some bands associated with the movement are Bikini Kill, Bratmobile, Excuse 17, Free Kitten, Heavens to Betsy, Huggy Bear, L7, and Team Dresch. In addition to a music scene, riot grrrl is also a subculture; zines, the DIY ethic, art, political action, and activism are part of the movement. Riot grrrls hold meetings, start chapters, and support and organize women in music.

The riot grrrl movement sprang out of Olympia, Washington, and Washington, D.C., in the early 1990s. It sought to give women the power to control their voices and artistic expressions. Riot grrrls took a growling double or triple r, placing it in the word *girl* as a way to take back the derogatory use of the term.

The riot grrrls' links to social and political issues are where the beginnings of third-wave feminism can be seen. The music and zine writings are strong examples of "cultural politics in action, with strong women giving voice to important social issues though an empowered, a female oriented community, many people link the emergence of the third-wave feminism to this time". The movement encouraged and made "adolescent girls' standpoints central", allowing them to express themselves fully.

Pornography

The feminist sex wars is a term for the acrimonious debates within the feminist movement in the late 1970s through the 1980s around the issues of feminism, sexuality, sexual representation, pornography, sadomasochism, the role of transwomen in the lesbian community, and other sexual issues. The feminist debate on porn pitted anti-pornography feminism against sex-positive feminism, and parts of the feminist movement were deeply divided by these debates.

Anti-pornography Movement

Anti-pornography feminists, such as Catharine MacKinnon, Andrea Dworkin, Robin Morgan, and Dorchen Leidholdt, put pornography at the center of a feminist explanation of women's oppression.

Some feminists, such as Diana Russell, Andrea Dworkin, Catharine MacKinnon, Susan Brownmiller, Dorchen Leidholdt, Ariel Levy, Robin Morgan, and Page Mellish, argue that pornography is degrading of women and complicit in violence against women both in its production (whereby, they charge, abuse and exploitation of women performing in pornography is rampant) and in its consumption (whereby, they charge, pornography eroticizes the domination, humiliation, and coercion of women and reinforces sexual and cultural attitudes that are complicit in rape and sexual harassment).

Beginning in the late 1970s, anti-pornography radical feminists formed organizations such as Women Against Pornography and Feminists Fighting Pornography that provided educational events, including slide-shows, speeches, and guided tours of the sex industry in Times Square, New York City, in order to raise awareness of the content of pornography and the sexual subculture in pornography shops and live sex shows. Andrea Dworkin and Robin Morgan began articulating a vehemently anti-porn stance based in radical feminism beginning in 1974 and anti-porn feminist groups, such as Women Against Violence in Pornography and Media in San Francisco, became highly active in various U.S. cities during the late 1970s.

Sex-positive Movement

Sex-positive feminism is a movement that was formed in order to address issues of women's sexual pleasure, freedom of expression, sex work, and inclusive gender identities. Ellen Willis' 1981 essay, "Lust Horizons: Is the Women's Movement Pro-Sex?" is the origin of the term, "pro-sex feminism"; the more commonly used variant, "sex positive feminism" arose soon after.

Although some sex-positive feminists, such as Betty Dodson, were active in the early 1970s, much of sex-positive feminism largely began in the late 1970s and 1980s as a response to the increasing emphasis in radical feminism on anti-pornography activism.

Sex-positive feminists are also strongly opposed to radical feminist calls for legislation against pornography, a strategy they decried as censorship, and something that could, they argued, be used by social conservatives to censor the sexual expression of women, gay people, and other sexual minorities. The initial period of intense debate and acrimony between sex-positive and anti-pornography feminists during the early 1980s is often referred to as the feminist sex wars. Other sex-positive feminists became involved not in opposition to other feminists but in direct response to what they saw as patriarchal control of sexuality.

Sex Work and Sex Industry

Feminist views on sex work and prostitution vary. Feminist supporters of sex worker rights and decriminalization argue that women's right to control their own bodies and sexuality includes the right to engage in consensual sexual commerce. They also argue that criminalization and social stigmatization of sex work and sex workers only worsens the existing marginalization and victimization that sex workers are often subjected to. On the other hand, feminist opponents of prostitution argue that prostitution is so tangled with forced prostitution, human trafficking, exploitation, and violence as to be inseparable from these ills in practice. They also argue that prostitution and other forms of sex work are inherently a product of patriarchy and sexism, and that the presence even of consensual sex work is harmful to society and women in particular. While feminists across all positions generally agree that direct criminalization of women in prostitution should be ended, there is little or no consensus on much else on the topics of legal approaches to the sex trade, the status of sex workers, or the nature of sex work itself.

Feminist Psychology

Feminist psychology is a form of psychology centered on social structures and gender. Feminist psychology critiques historical psychological research as done from a male perspective with the view that males are the norm. Feminist psychology is oriented on the values and principles of feminism. It incorporates gender and the ways women are affected by issues resulting from it.

Gender issues can include the way people identify their gender (male, female, genderqueer; transgender or cisgender), how they have been affected by societal structures related to gender (gender hierarchy), the role of gender in the individual's life (such as stereotypical gender roles), and any other gender related issues. The objective behind this field of study is to understand the individual within the larger social and political aspects of society. Feminist psychology puts a strong emphasis on women's rights. Psychoanalysis took shape as a clinical or therapeutic method, feminism as a political strategy (Buhle, 1998).

History

Feminist Psychoanalysis

The term feminist psychology was originally coined by Karen Horney. In her book, *Feminine Psychology*, which is a collection of articles Horney wrote on the subject from 1922–1937, she addresses previously held beliefs about women, relationships, and the effect of society on female psychology.

Functionalism, Darwinism and the Psychology of Women

The beginning of psychology research presents very little in the way of female psychology. Many women did not fight against oppression because they did not realize they were oppressed in the first place (Ruck, 2015). Once the functionalist movement came about in the United States, academic psychology's study of sex difference and a prototypic psychology of woman were developed.

Anti-feminism After WWII

In 1942 Edward Strecker made "mom-ism" an official pathological syndrome under the APA. He believed that the country was under threat because mothers weren't emotionally disconnecting from their children at a young enough age, and the matriarchy was making young men weak and losing their "man power". This fueled that anti-feminist movement; women were in need of psychotherapy to aid their mental illness and further prevent the spread of maternalism. The psychological damage on the family would be severe if a woman chose a career to satisfy her needs as opposed to her feminine domestic role assigned by society – a woman's happiness was not important, she must follow her role. The effect of women having independent thoughts and a thirst for exploring her options was a huge threat to gender, as it resulted in masculinized women and feminized men, apparently confounding the nation's youth and dooming their future. Constantinople and Bem both agreed that men and women possess masculinity and femininity, and that having both is being *psychologically androgynous* and a cause to be psychologically fixed or evaluated.

Gender Research in the 1960s and 1970s

Edith Greenglass states that in 1972, the field of psychology was still male-dominated, women were totally excluded. The use of the word women in conjunction with psychology was forbidden, men refused to be excluded from the narrative. In her experience of teaching class, or being assistant professors, they had to phrase it in the interest of human beings or gender. Unger's paper "Toward a Redefinition of Sex and Gender" said that the use of gender showed the separation of biological and psychological sex. Psychology of women is feminist because it says women are different from men and that women's behavior cannot be understood outside of context. Feminists in turn compelled psychoanalysts to consider the implications of one of Freud's own, most uncompromising propositions: "that human beings consist of men and women and that this distinction is the most significant one that exists" (Buhl, 1998). In *Liberating Minds: Consciousness-Raising as a Bridge Between Feminism and Psychology in 1970s Canada*, Nora Ruck leads with, "U.S. radical feminist Irene Peslikis warned that equating women's liberating with individual therapy prevented women from truly understanding and fighting the roots of their oppression". Canada was one of the few countries with an academic category within psychology for feminism. They relied on CR (consciousness raising) groups to build their movement. Ruck describes the process of these CR groups by "bridging the tensions" between the personal and political. The development of CR as a political method in its own right is widely attributed to the New York-based radical feminist collective "Redstockings" (Echols, 1989). CR is also closely tied with radical feminism, which aims to weed out discrimination and segregation based on sex, and through a grassroots movement like socialist feminism, maintains that women's oppression is not a by-product of capitalist oppression but a "primary cause" (Koedt, 1968).

Joining the Workforce

Women were excluded from Freud's definition of mental health (the ability to love and to work) because women wanting jobs was attributed to a masculinity complex or envy of men. Between 1970 and 1980 the percentage of women working outside the home had risen from 43 to 51. Although women reported having difficulty juggling the roles of mother and provider, they found a way to be fulfilled void of childbearing (Buhle, 1998).

Organizations

Association for Women in Psychology (AWP)

The Association for Women in Psychology (AWP) was created in 1969 in response to the American Psychological Association's apparent lack of involvement in the Women's Liberation Movement. The organization formed with the purpose of fighting for and raising awareness of feminist issues within the field of psychology. The association focused its efforts toward feminist representation in the APA and finally succeeded in 1973 with the establishment of APA Division 35 (the Society for the Psychology of Women).

Society for the Psychology of Women

APA Division 35, the Society for the Psychology of Women, was established in 1973. It was created to provide a place for all people interested in the psychology of women to access information and resources in the field. SWP works to incorporate feminist concerns into the teaching and practice of psychology. Div 35 also runs a number of committees, projects, and programs.

Section on Women and Psychology (SWAP)

The Canadian Psychological Association (CPA) has a section on Women and Psychology (SWAP), which is meant "to advance the status of women in psychology, promote quity for women in general, and to educate psychologists and the public on topics relevant to women and girls." SWAP supports projects such as Psychology's Feminist Voices. The Journal of Diversity in Higher Education expresses that female psychologists are often considered to be inefficient due to their low contribution in scientific productivity. Hence, women tend to dominate in low level positions than their male counterparts even if they acquire their doctoral degrees. "They did not show any acknowledgement or appreciation that there was a difference and that there was a need for it, and that was around the time that we were giving a course here interdisciplinary, not in psychology. I still didn't have a course here because they wouldn't let me do it. And the men pretty well called the shots when they told you, you can't do it, you just, you don't do it." (Greenglass, 2005).

The Psychology of Women Section (BPS)

The Psychology of Women Section (BPS), of the British Psychological Society was created in 1988 to draw together everyone with an interest in the psychology of women, to provide a forum to support research, teaching and professional practice, and to raise an awareness of gender issues and gender inequality in psychology as profession and as practice. POWS is open to all members of the British Psychological Society.

Current Research

Emotion

A major topic of study within feminist psychology is that of gender differences in emotion. In general, feminist psychologists view emotion as culturally controlled and state that the differences lie in the expression of emotion rather than the actual experience. The way a person shows his or her emotions is defined by socially enforced display rules which guide the acceptable forms of expression for particular people and feelings.

Stereotypes of emotion view women as the more emotional sex. However, feminist psychologists point out that women are only viewed as experiencing passive emotions such as sadness, happiness, fear, and surprise more strongly. Conversely, men are viewed as more likely to express emotions of a more dominant nature, such as anger. Feminist psychologists believe that men and women are socialized throughout their lifetimes to view and express emotions differently. From infancy mothers use more facial expression when speaking to female babies and use more emotion words in conversation with them as they get older.

Girls and boys are further socialized by peers where girls are rewarded for being sensitive and emotional and boys are rewarded for dominance and lack of most emotional expression. Psychologists have also found that women, overall, are more skilled at decoding emotion using non-verbal cues. These signals include facial expression, tone of voice, and posture. Studies have shown gender differences in decoding ability beginning as early as age $3\frac{1}{2}$. The book *Man and Woman, Boy and Girl* looks at intersex patients in explaining why social factors are more important than biological factors in gender identity and gender roles and brought nature vs nurture issues back into the spotlight (Money & Ehrhardt, 1972).

Leadership

Social scientists in many disciplines study aspects of the "glass ceiling effect", the invisible yet powerful barriers that prevent many women from moving beyond a certain level in the workplace and other public institutions. According to the U.S. Department of Labor, women in the United States comprised 47% of the workforce in 2010. However, there are only a small amount of women with high held positions in corporations. Women constitute only 5% of Fortune 500 CEOs (in 2014) and 19% of board members of S&P500 companies (in 2014), and 26% of college presidents. In 2017 U.S. government bodies, women comprise 19.1% of U.S. Representatives, 21% of U.S. Senators, 8% of state governors, and similarly low percentages of state elected officials. Women of color have lower representation than white women. The U.S. lags behind other countries in gender parity in government representation; according to the Global Gender Gap Report of 2014, the U.S. ranked 33 out of 49 so-called "high-income" countries, and 83rd out of the 137 countries surveyed. "Women affiliated with the American Academy of Psychoanalysis were among the first to pursue such subjects as women's fear of success and inclinations toward neurotic dependency. They acknowledged the cultural forces inhibiting women's progress in nondomestic realms, particularly the pressures inherent in a male-dominated society" (Buhl, 1998). Much scholarship focuses on structural features inhibiting women's progress in public spheres, rather than locating the source of the issue on women themselves.

In addition, women experience a "sticky floor effect". The sticky floor effect happens when women have no job path or ladder to higher positions. When women have children they experience a roadblock called the maternal wall. The maternal wall is when women receive less desirable assignments and less opportunities for advancement after they have a child. The patriarchy labels women as "nourishing facilitators" making them not mentally strong enough to take part in the aggressive male-dominated workforce without taking psychological and emotional hits (Buhl, 1998). When women begin working at a company, their advancement can be limited by not having a senior level employee taking an active role in the development and career planning of junior employees. There are a lack of female mentors to assist new female employees because there are less women than men in higher level company positions. A woman with a male mentor could experience difficulty in gaining bonding and advice from out of work experiences. This is because men play basketball or golf and typically exclude women from these endeavors. Other factors limiting leadership for women are cultural differences, stereotypes, and perceived threats. If women show a small amount of sensitivity, they are stereotyped as being overly emotional. Generally, employers do not accept sensitive, soft people as being able to tackle tough decisions or handle leadership roles. However, if a woman displays male traits she is portrayed as mean, butch, and aggressive. Women are viewed as less competent when they showcase non-"feminine" traits and are not taken seriously. These women don't brag about their accomplishments and feel guilty for being able to go beyond stereotypes of feminine emotion and thought in order to become masculine in their jobs, just to be successful or try and be equal to men. Career women, whose professional status depends on the appropriation of masculine traits, frequently suffer from depression (Buhl, 1998). Recent research has connected the concept of stereotype threat with girls' motivations to avoid success as an individual difference, girls might avoid participation in certain male-dominated fields due to real and perceived obstacles to success in those fields, although there is little that can be proven (e.g., Spencer et al. 1999).

Another factor leading to discrimination and stress are cultural differences between managers and workers. For example, if a manager is white and has an employee of color, stress may be created if they do not understand or respect each other. Without trust and respect, advancement is unlikely. Our depiction of gender identity is white and middle class. White women are described as intelligent, manipulative, and privileged by Black women, who are described as strong, determined, and having attitude (Burack, 2002). "There it is, White fear of Black anger", was written in Ladies Home Journal (Edwards 1998: 77). Regarding perceived threats at work, it is not a matter of sexual harassment or harassment in general. The threat is the fact that women could possibly take over. The more women working in a place of employment, the increased threat a man feels over job security. In a study of 126 male managers, when asked to estimate the number of women working at their place of employment and whether or not they felt men were disadvantaged. Men who believed there were many women felt threatened about the security of their job (Beaton et al., 1996). Alice Eagly and Blair Johnson (1990) discovered that men and women have different small differences in their styles of leadership. Women in power were seen as interpersonal and more democratic, whereas men were seen as task-oriented and more autocratic. In reality, men and women are equally effective in their styles of leadership. A study by Alice Eagly (Eagly, Karau, & Makhijani, 1995) found no overall differences in the effectiveness of male and female leaders in facilitating accomplishment of their group goals.

Violence

Herman (1996) has shown that feminists relied on the psychological notion of "trauma" to criticize institutions like the family, to protect the children, to argue for revised policies, and to fight against male violence against women and children. Feminists argue that gender-based violence occurs frequently in the forms of domestic violence, sexual harassment, childhood sexual abuse, sexual assault, and rape. Violence towards women can be physical or psychological and is not limited by race, economic status, age, ethnicity, or location. Women can be abused by strangers but often the abuser is someone the woman knows. Violence can have both short- and long-term effects on women, and they react to the abuse in various ways. Some women express emotions such as fear, anxiety, and anger. Others choose to deny it occurred and conceal their feelings. Often, women blame themselves for what happened and try to justify that they somehow deserved it. Among victims of violence, psychological disorders such as post traumatic stress disorder and depression are common. In addition to the psychological ramifications, many women also sustain physical injuries from the violence that require medical attention.

Relational-cultural Theory

Relational-cultural theory is based on the work of Jean Baker Miller, whose book *Toward a New Psychology of Women* proposes that "growth-fostering relationships are a central human necessity and that disconnections are the source of psychological problems." Inspired by Betty Friedan's *Feminine Mystique*, and other feminist classics from the 1960s, relational-cultural theory proposes that "isolation is one of the most damaging human experiences and is best treated by reconnecting with other people", and that therapists should "foster an atmosphere of empathy and acceptance for the patient, even at the cost of the therapist's neutrality". The theory is based on clinical observations and sought to prove that "there was nothing wrong with women, but rather with the way modern culture viewed them".

Feminist Therapy

Feminist therapy is a type of therapy based on viewing individuals within their sociocultural context. The main idea behind this therapy is that the psychological problems of women and minorities are often a symptom of larger problems in the social structure in which they live. There is a general agreement that women are more frequently diagnosed with internalizing disorders such as depression, anxiety, and eating disorders than men. Feminist therapists dispute earlier theories that this is a result of psychological weakness in women and instead view it as a result of encountering more stress because of sexist practices in our culture. A common misconception is that feminist therapists are only concerned with the mental health of women. While this is certainly a central component of feminist theory, feminist therapists are also sensitive to the impact of gender roles on individuals regardless of sex. Goldman found the connection between psychoanalysis and feminism as the recognition of sexuality as preeminent in the makeup of women as well as men. Freud found that men's ideology was forced onto women in order to sexually repress them, connecting the public and private spheres for the subjugation of women (Buhle, 1998). The goal of feminist therapy is the empowerment of the client. Generally, therapists avoid giving specific diagnoses or labels and instead focus on problems within the context of living in a sexist culture. Clients are sometimes trained to be more assertive and encouraged to understand their problems with the intent of changing or challenging their circumstances. Feminist therapists view lack of power as a major issue in the psychology of women and minorities. Accordingly, the client-therapist relationship is meant to be as egalitarian as possible with both sides communicating on equal ground and sharing experiences.

Feminist therapy is different than other types of therapy in that it goes beyond the idea that men and women should be treated equally in the therapeutic relationship. Feminist therapy incorporates political values to a greater extent than many other types of therapy. Also, feminist therapy encourages social change as well as personal change in order to improve the psychological state of the client and society.

Issues with Traditional Therapies

Gender Biases

Many traditional therapies assume that women should follow sex-roles in order to be mentally healthy. They believe gender differences are biologically based and encourage female clients to be submissive, expressive, and nurturant in order to achieve fulfillment (Worell & Remer, 1992). Psychotherapy is a male-dominated practice and supports women's adjustment to stereotypical gender roles instead of women's liberation (Kim & Rutherford, 2015). This may be done unconsciously by the therapist – for example, they may encourage a female to be a nurse, when they would have encouraged a male client of the same abilities to be a doctor, but there is the risk that the goals and outcomes of therapy will be evaluated differently in accordance with the therapist's beliefs and values. Inequality between the sexes and restrictions on sex roles are perpetuated by evolutionary psychology, but we could understand the role of gender in scientific communities by using feminist research strategies and admitting to gender bias (Fehr, 2012).

Androcentrism

Traditional therapies are based on the assumption that being male is the norm. Male traits are seen as the default, and stereotypically male traits are seen as more highly valued (Worell & Remer, 1992; Hegarty & Buechel, 2006). Men are considered the standard of comparison when comparing gender differences, with feminine traits viewed as a deviation from the norm and a deficiency on the part of women (Hegarty & Buechel, 2006).) Psychological theories of female development were written by men who are completely uniformed by women's actual experiences and the conditions under which they lived (Kim & Rutherford, 2015).

Intrapsychic Assumptions

Traditional therapies place little emphasis on sociopolitical influences, focusing instead on the client's internal functioning. This can lead therapists to blame clients for their symptoms, even if the client may in fact be coping admirably in a difficult and oppressive situation (Worell & Remer, 1992). Another possible issue can arise if therapists pathologize normal responses to oppressive environments (Goodman & Epstein, 2007).

Principles of Empowerment

The Personal is Political

This principle stems from the belief that psychological symptoms are caused by the environment. The goal of the therapist is to separate the external from the internal so the client can become aware of the socialization and oppression they have experienced, and attribute their problems to the appropriate causes (Worrel & Remer, 1992).). Feminist stance is largely marginalized and seen as standing outside of mainstream psychiatry, and there is the power-based distribution of knowledge, which gives therapists the ability to label women's disorders without knowing their lived experiences (Sawicki, 1991).

Therapists do not view their client's cognitions or behaviors as maladaptive – indeed, symptoms of depression or PTSD are often considered to be the normal, rational response to oppression and discrimination (Goodman & Epstein, 2007). Traditional therapies place little emphasis on sociopolitical influences, focusing instead on the client's internal functioning. This can lead therapists to blame clients for their symptoms, even if the client may in fact be coping admirably in a difficult and oppressive situation (Worell & Remer, 1992). Another possible issue can arise if therapists pathologize normal responses to oppressive environments (Goodman & Epstein, 2007).

Egalitarian Relationships

Feminist therapists consider power inequalities to be a major contributing factor to the struggles of women, and as such criticize the traditional therapist role as an authority figure. Feminist therapists believe interpersonal relationships should be based in equality, and view the client as the "expert" in their own experiences. Therapists emphasize collaboration, and use techniques such as self-disclosure to reduce the power differential (Worrel & Remer, 1992).

Value the Female Perspective

The goal of feminist therapy is to re-value feminine characteristics and perspectives. Often, women are criticized for breaking gender norms while simultaneously being devalued for acting feminine. In order to break this double bind, therapists encourage women to value the female perspective and self-define themselves and their roles. In doing so, clients can value their own characteristics, bond with other women, and embrace traits that had previously been discouraged (Worrel & Remer, 1992).

Techniques

Sex Role Analysis

One component of feminist therapy involves a critique of cultural conditioning that produces and maintains socially biased structures (Ballou & Gabalac, 1985). From birth, women are taught which behaviors are appropriate, and face sanctions if they fail to conform. These gender stereotypes are taught explicitly or implicitly by the family, media, school, and the workplace, and lead to gender-related belief systems and self-imposed expectations (Worell & Remer, 1992).

Before women can be free of these expectations, they need to gain an understanding of the social systems that molded and encouraged these gender stereotypes, and how this system impacted their mental health. First, women work to identify the gendered messages they've received, as well as the consequences. Then, women explore how these messages have been internalized, and decide which rules they would like to follow and which behaviors they would prefer to change (Worrel & Remer, 1992).

Power Analysis

Power systems are organized groups that have legitimized status, that are sanctioned by custom or law, that have the power to set the standards for society. In Western society, women are expected to conform to the power systems that place them as submissive and inferior to men (Ballou & Gabalac, 1985). Types of power include the legal, physical, financial, and institutional ability to exert change. Often, men control direct power via concrete resources, while women are left to use indirect means and interpersonal resources. Also, sex-roles and institutionalized sexism play a role in limiting the power women have (Worrel & Remer, 1992).

Power analysis is the technique used to examine the power differential between women and men, and to empower women to challenge the interpersonal and institutional inequalities they face (Worrel & Remer, 1992).

Assertiveness Training

Traditionally, assertiveness is a masculine trait, so frequently women struggle with learning to stand up for their rights. Feminist therapists work to help women distinguish assertive behaviors from passive or aggressive ones, overcome beliefs that tell women they cannot be assertive, and help women rehearse assertiveness skills through role play (Worrel & Remer, 1992).

Application to Other Theories

Cognitive-behavioral Therapy

The biggest feminist critique of cognitive-behavioral therapy is that the theory fails to focus on how behaviors are learned from society (NetCE, 2014). Often, the focus is on encouraging women to change their "maladaptive" responses and conform to normative standards. By putting the onus on the woman to change her thoughts and behaviors, instead of changing the environmental factors that give rise to the problems, the theory fails to question the social norms that condone the oppression of women (Brown & Ballou, 1992). Despite this, feminist therapists do use cognitive-behavioral techniques to help women change their beliefs and behaviors, in particular using techniques such as sex-role analysis or assertiveness training (Brown & Ballou, 1993; NetCE, 2014).

Psychoanalytic Therapy

Many psychoanalytic concepts are considered by feminist therapists to be sexist and culturally-bound (NetCE, 2014). However, feminist psychoanalysis adapts many of the ideas of traditional psychotherapy, including the focus on early childhood experiences and the idea of transference. Specifically, therapists serve as a mother figure and help clients connect emotionally with others while maintaining an individuated sense of self (NetCE, 2014).

Family Systems Therapy

The main critique of family systems therapy is the endorsement of power imbalances and traditional gender roles. For example, family systems therapists often respond to men and women differently, for example placing more importance on the man's career or placing the responsibility for childcare and housework on the mother (Braverman, 1988).

Feminist therapists strive to make the discussion of gender roles explicit in therapy, as well as focusing on the needs of and empowering the woman in her relationship (Braverman, 1988). Therapists help couples examine how gender role beliefs and power dynamics lead to conflict. The focus is on encouraging more egalitarian relationships and affirming the women's experiences (NetCE, 2014).

Core Issues Covered in Therapy

Rape/Domestic Violence

A feminist approach to dealing with rape or domestic abuse is focused on empowerment. Therapists help clients analyze societal messages about rape or domestic abuse that encourage a victim-blaming attitude, and try to help clients get past shame, guilt, and self-blame. Often, women do not know the true definitions of abuse or rape, and don't immediately identify themselves as victims (Worrel & Remer, 1992).

Survivors often face negative reactions from others that lead to re-victimization when trying to seek help, so therapists can help the woman navigate the medical and legal services if she wishes. At all times, although safety is the main concern, the therapist empowers the woman to explore her options and make her own decisions (for example, to leave the relationship or stay following an attack) (Worrel & Remer, 1992).

It is emphasized that any symptoms are in fact normal responses to the traumatic effect, and the women is not pathologized. Both rape and domestic violence are not viewed as something one can recover from, but are instead viewed as experiences that one can integrate into one's life story as one restructures one's self-esteem and self-confidence (Worrel & Remer, 1992).

Career Counseling

Occupational choice is a main theme in feminist counseling. Women are more likely to earn less than men, and are overrepresented in lower-status occupations (Worrel & Remer, 1992). Several factors influence this career trajectory, including gender-role stereotyping of which jobs are appropriate for men and women. Women are often pointed towards nurturing jobs, while leadership jobs are reserved for men (Worrel & Remer, 1992).

Institutionalized sexism in the educational system often encourages girls to study traditionally feminine subjects while discouraging them from studying math and science. Discriminatory hiring practices also reflect the attitude that men should be the breadwinner and women are a riskier choice because their work will be disrupted once they have children (Worrel & Remer, 1992).

These societal messages often lead to internalized negative messages, including lower self-confidence and self-esteem, lower levels of assertiveness and willingness to negotiate, and the *imposter syndrome*, where women believe they do not deserve success and are merely lucky (Worrel & Remer, 1992).

When women do seek nontraditional employment, they are placed in a double bind, where they are expected to be competent at their job while simultaneously being feminine. Especially for women in male-dominated fields, trying to be competent and successful as a woman is difficult (Howard, 1986).

Feminist Therapists

Feminist therapists work with women in search of counseling, as well as men, for help in alleviating a variety of mental health concerns. Feminist therapists have an interest in gender and how multiple social identities can impact an individual's functioning. Psychologists or therapists who identify with the feminism, the belief that women and men are equals, and/or feminist psychological theory may call themselves feminist therapists. Currently, there are not many postdoctoral training programs in feminist psychology, but models for this training are being developed and modified for institutions to start offering them. Most of this training is modeled around gender-fair counseling techniques.

Feminist Theory

Feminist theory is the extension of feminism into theoretical, fictional, or philosophical discourse. It aims to understand the nature of gender inequality. It examines women's and men's social roles, experience, interests, chores, and feminist politics in a variety of fields, such as anthropology and sociology, communication, psychoanalysis, home economics, literature, education, and philosophy.

Feminist theory focuses on analyzing gender inequality. Themes explored in feminism include discrimination, objectification (especially sexual objectification), oppression, patriarchy, stereotyping, art history and contemporary art, and aesthetics.

History

Feminist theories first emerged as early as 1794 in publications such as A Vindication of the Rights of Woman by Mary Wollstonecraft, "The Changing Woman", "Ain't I a Woman", "Speech after Arrest for Illegal Voting", and so on. "The Changing Woman" is a Navajo Myth that gave credit to a woman who, in the end, populated the world. In 1851, Sojourner Truth addressed women's rights issues through her publication, "Ain't I a Woman". Sojourner Truth addressed the issue of women having limited rights due to men's flawed perception of women. Truth argued that if a woman of color can perform tasks that were supposedly limited to men, then any woman of any color could perform those same tasks. After her arrest for illegally voting, Susan B. Anthony gave a speech within court in which she addressed the issues of language within the constitution documented in her publication, "Speech after Arrest for Illegal voting" in 1872. Anthony questioned the authoritative principles of the constitution and its male gendered language. She raised the question of why women are accountable to be punished under law but they cannot use the law for their own protection (women could not vote, own property, nor themselves in marriage). She also critiqued the constitution for its male gendered language and questioned why women should have to abide by laws that do not specify women.

Nancy Cott makes a distinction between *modern feminism* and its antecedents, particularly the struggle for suffrage. In the United States she places the turning point in the decades before and after women obtained the vote in 1920 (1910–1930). She argues that the prior *woman movement* was primarily about woman as a *universal* entity, whereas over this 20-year period it transformed itself into one primarily concerned with social differentiation, attentive to *individuality* and diversity. New issues dealt more with woman's condition as a social construct, gender identity, and relationships within and between genders. Politically this represented a shift from an ideological alignment comfortable with the right, to one more radically associated with the left.

Susan Kingsley Kent says that Freudian patriarchy was responsible for the diminished profile of feminism in the inter-war years, others such as Juliet Mitchell consider this to be overly simplistic since Freudian theory is not wholly incompatible with feminism. Some feminist scholarship shifted away from the need to establish the origins of family, and towards analyzing the process of patriarchy. In the immediate postwar period, Simone de Beauvoir stood in opposition to an image of "the woman in the home". De Beauvoir provided an existentialist dimension to feminism with the publication of *Le Deuxième Sexe* (The Second Sex) in 1949. As the title implies, the starting point is the implicit inferiority of women, and the first question de Beauvoir asks is "what is a woman"?. Woman she realizes is always perceived of as the "other", "*she is defined and differentiated with reference to man and not he with reference to her*". In this book and her essay, "*Woman: Myth & Reality*", de Beauvoir anticipates Betty Friedan in seeking to demythologise the male concept of woman. "*A myth invented by men to confine women to their oppressed state. For women it is not a question of asserting themselves as women, but of becoming full-scale human beings.*" "One is not born, but rather becomes, a woman", or as Toril Moi puts it "a woman defines herself through the way she lives her embodied situation in the world, or in other words, through the way in which she makes something of what the world makes of her". Therefore, woman must regain subject, to escape her defined role as "other", as a Cartesian point of departure. In her examination of myth, she appears as one who does not accept any special privileges for women. Ironically, feminist philosophers have had to extract de Beauvoir herself from out of the shadow of Jean-Paul Sartre to fully appreciate her. While more philosopher and novelist than activist, she did sign one of the *Mouvement de Libération des Femmes* manifestos.

The resurgence of feminist activism in the late 1960s was accompanied by an emerging literature of concerns for the earth and spirituality, and environmentalism. This in turn created an atmosphere conducive to reigniting the study of and debate on matricentricity, as a rejection of determinism, such as Adrienne Rich and Marilyn French while for socialist feminists like Evelyn Reed, patriarchy held the properties of capitalism. Feminist psychologists, such as Jean Baker Miller, sought to bring a feminist analysis to previous psychological theories, proving that "there was nothing wrong with women, but rather with the way modern culture viewed them".

Elaine Showalter describes the development of feminist theory as having a number of phases. The first she calls "feminist critique" – where the feminist reader examines the ideologies behind literary phenomena. The second Showalter calls "Gynocritics" – where the "woman is producer of textual meaning" including "the psychodynamics of female creativity; linguistics and the problem of a female language; the trajectory of the individual or collective female literary career and literary history". The last phase she calls "gender theory" – where the "ideological inscription and the literary effects of the sex/gender system" are explored". This model has been criticized by Toril Moi who sees it as an essentialist and deterministic model for female subjectivity. She also criticized it for not taking account of the situation for women outside the west. From the 1970s onwards, psychoanalytical ideas that have been arising in the field of French feminism have gained a decisive influence on feminist theory. Feminist psychoanalysis deconstructed the phallic hypotheses regarding the Unconscious. Julia Kristeva, Bracha Ettinger and Luce Irigaray developed specific notions concerning unconscious sexual difference, the feminine and motherhood, with wide implications for film and literature analysis.

Disciplines

There are a number of distinct feminist disciplines, in which experts in other areas apply feminist techniques and principles to their own fields. Additionally, these are also debates which shape feminist theory and they can be applied interchangeably in the arguments of feminist theorists.

Bodies

In western thought, the body has been historically associated solely with women, whereas men have been associated with the mind. Susan Bordo, a modern feminist philosopher, in her writings elaborates the dualistic nature of the mind/body connection by examining the early philosophies of Aristotle, Hegel and Descartes, revealing how such distinguishing binaries such as spirit/matter and male activity/female passivity have worked to solidify gender characteristics and categorization. Bordo goes on to point out that while men have historically been associated with the intellect and the mind or spirit, women have long been associated with the body, the subordinated, negatively imbued term in the mind/body dichotomy. The notion of the body (but not the mind) being associated with women has served as a justification to deem women as property, objects, and exchangeable commodities (among men). For example, women's bodies have been objectified throughout history through the changing ideologies of fashion, diet, exercise programs, cosmetic surgery, childbearing, etc. This contrasts to men's role as a moral agent, responsible for working or fighting in bloody wars. The race and class of a woman can determine whether her body will be treated as decoration and protected, which is associated with middle or upper-class women's bodies. On the other hand, the other body is recognized for its use in labor and exploitation which is generally associated with women's bodies in the working-class or with women of color. Second-wave feminist activism has argued for reproductive rights and choice, women's health (movement), and lesbian rights (movement) which are also associated with this Bodies debate.

The Standard and Contemporary Sex and Gender System

The standard sex and gender model consists of ideologies based on the sex and gender of every individual and serve as "norms" for societal life. The model claims that the sex of a person is the physical body that the individual is born with, strictly existing within a male/female dichotomy giving importance to the genitals and the chromosomes which make the organism male or female. The standard model defines gender as a social understanding/ideology that defines what behaviors, actions, and appearances are proper for males and females living in society.

The contemporary sex and gender model corrects and broadens the horizons of the sex and gender ideologies. It revises the ideology of sex in that an individual's sex is actually a social construct which is not limited to either male or female. This can be seen by the Intersex Society of North America which explains that, "nature doesn't decide where the category of 'male' ends and the category of 'intersex' begins, or where the category of 'intersex' ends and the category of 'female' begins. Humans decide. Humans (today, typically doctors) decide how small a penis has to be, or how unusual a combination of parts has to be, before it counts as intersex". Therefore, sex is not a biological/natural construct but a social one instead since, society and doctors decide on what it means to be male, female, or intersex in terms of sex chromosomes and genitals, in addition to their personal judgment on who or how one passes as a specific sex. The ideology of gender remains a social construct but is not as strict and fixed. Instead, gender is easily malleable, and is forever changing. One example of where the standard definition of gender alters with time happens to be depicted in Sally Shuttleworth's *Female Circulation* in which the, "abasement of the woman, reducing her from an active participant in the labor market to the passive bodily existence to be controlled by male expertise is indicative of the ways in which the ideological deployment of gender roles operated to facilitate and sustain the changing structure of familial and market relations in Victorian England". In other words, this quote shows what it meant growing up into the roles of a female (gender/roles) changed from being a homemaker to being a working woman and then back to being passive and inferior to males. In conclusion, the contemporary sex gender model is accurate because both sex and gender are rightly seen as social constructs inclusive of the wide spectrum of sexes and genders and in which nature and nurture are interconnected.

Epistemologies

The generation and production of knowledge has been an important part of feminist theory and is at the centre of discussions on feminist epistemology. This debate proposes such questions as "Are there 'women's ways of knowing' and 'women's knowledge'?" And "How does the knowledge women produce about themselves differ from that produced by patriarchy?" Feminist theorists have also proposed the "feminist standpoint knowledge" which attempts to replace "the view from nowhere" with the model of knowing that expels the "view from women's lives". A feminist approach to epistemology seeks to establish knowledge production from a woman's perspective. It theorizes that from personal experience comes knowledge which helps each individual look at things from a different insight.

Central to feminism is that women are systematically subordinated, and bad faith exists when women surrender their agency to this subordination, e.g., acceptance of religious beliefs that a man is the dominant party in a marriage by the will of God; Simone de Beauvoir labels such women "mutilated" and "immanent".

Intersectionality

Intersectionality is the examination of various ways in which people are oppressed, based on the relational web of dominating factors of race, sex, class, nation and sexual orientation. Intersectionality "describes the simultaneous, multiple, overlapping, and contradictory systems of power that shape our lives and political options". While this theory can be applied to all people, and more particularly all women, it is specifically mentioned and studied within the realms of black feminism. Patricia Hill Collins argues that black women in particular, have a unique perspective on the oppression of the world as unlike white women, they face both racial and gender oppression simultaneously, among other factors. This debate raises the issue of understanding the oppressive lives of women that are not only shaped by gender alone but by other elements such as racism, classism, ageism, heterosexism, ableism etc.

Language

In this debate, women writers have addressed the issues of masculinized writing through male gendered language that may not serve to accommodate the literary understanding of women's lives. Such masculinized language that feminist theorists address is the use of, for example, "God the Father" which is looked upon as a way of designating the sacred as solely men (or, in other words, biblical language glorifies men through all of the masculine pronouns like "he" and "him" and addressing God as a "He"). Feminist theorists attempt to reclaim and redefine women through re-structuring language. For example, feminist theorists have used the term "womyn" instead of "women". Some feminist theorists find solace in changing titles of unisex jobs (for example, police officer versus policeman or mail carrier versus mailman). Some feminist theorists have reclaimed and redefined such words as "dyke" and "bitch" and others have invested redefining knowledge into feminist dictionaries.

Psychology

Feminist psychology is a form of psychology centered on societal structures and gender. Feminist psychology critiques the fact that historically psychological research has been done from a male perspective with the view that males are the norm. Feminist psychology is oriented on the values and principles of feminism. It incorporates gender and the ways women are affected by issues resulting from it. Ethel Dench Puffer Howes was one of the first women to enter the field of psychology. She was the Executive Secretary of the National College Equal Suffrage League in 1914.

One major psychological theory, *relational-cultural theory*, is based on the work of Jean Baker Miller, whose book *Toward a New Psychology of Women* proposes that "growth-fostering relationships are a central human necessity and that disconnections are the source of psychological problems". Inspired by Betty Friedan's *Feminine Mystique*, and other feminist classics from the 1960s, relational-cultural theory proposes that "isolation is one of the most damaging human experiences and is best treated by reconnecting with other people", and that a therapist should "foster an atmosphere of empathy and acceptance for the patient, even at the cost of the therapist's neutrality". The theory is based on clinical observations and sought to prove that "there was nothing wrong with women, but rather with the way modern culture viewed them".

Psychoanalysis

Psychoanalytic feminism and feminist psychoanalysis are based on Freud and his psychoanalytic theories, but they also supply an important critique of it. It maintains that gender is not biological but is based on the psycho-sexual development of the individual, but also that sexual difference and gender are different notions. Psychoanalytical feminists believe that gender inequality comes from early childhood experiences, which lead men to believe themselves to be masculine, and women to believe themselves feminine. It is further maintained that gender leads to a social system that is dominated by males, which in turn influences the individual psycho-sexual development. As a solution it was suggested by some to avoid the gender-specific structuring of the society coeducation. From the last 30 years of the 20th Century, the contemporary French psychoanalytical theories concerning the feminine, that refer to sexual difference rather than to gender, with psychoanalysts like Julia Kristeva,Maud Mannoni, Luce Irigaray, and Bracha Ettinger, have largely influenced not only feminist theory but also the understanding of the subject in philosophy and the general field of psychoanalysis itself. These French psychoanalysts are mainly post-Lacanian. Other feminist psychoanalysts and feminist theorists whose contributions have enriched the field through an engagement with psychoanalysis are Jessica Benjamin, Jacqueline Rose, Ranjana Khanna, and Shoshana Felman.

Girl with doll.

Literary Theory

Feminist literary criticism is literary criticism informed by feminist theories or politics. Its history has been varied, from classic works of female authors such as George Eliot, Virginia Woolf, and Margaret Fuller to recent theoretical work in women's studies and gender studies by "third-wave" authors.

In the most general, feminist literary criticism before the 1970s was concerned with the politics of women's authorship and the representation of women's condition within literature. Since the arrival of more complex conceptions of gender and subjectivity, feminist literary criticism has taken a variety of new routes. It has considered gender in the terms of Freudian and Lacanian psycho-analysis, as part of the deconstruction of existing power relations.

Film Theory

Film theory is often dominated by feminism being played a major antagonist side of the film or made fun of. Feminists have taken many different approaches to the analysis of cinema. These include discussions of the function of women characters in particular film narratives or in particular genres, such as film noir, where a female character can often be seen to embody a subversive sexuality that is dangerous to males and is ultimately punished with death. In considering the way that films are put together many feminist film critics, such as Laura Mulvey, have pointed to the "male gaze" that predominates in classical Hollywood film making. Through the use of various film techniques, such as shot reverse shot, the viewers are led to align themselves with the point of view of a male protagonist. Notably, women function as objects of this gaze far more often than as proxies for the spectator. Feminist film theory of the last twenty years is heavily influenced by the general transformation in the field of aesthetics, including the new options of articulating the gaze, offered by psychoanalytical French feminism, like the matrixial gaze.

Art History

Linda Nochlin and Griselda Pollock are prominent art historians writing on contemporary and modern artists and articulating Art history from a feminist perspective since the 1970s. Pollock works with French psychoanalysis, and in particular with Kristeva's and Ettinger's theories, to offer new insights into art history and contemporary art with special regard to questions of trauma and trans-generation memory in the works of women artists. Other prominent feminist art historians include: Norma Broude and Mary Garrard; Amelia Jones; Mieke Bal; Carol Duncan; Lynda Nead; Lisa Tickner; Tamar Garb; Hilary Robinson; Katy Deepwell.

History

Feminist history refers to the re-reading and re-interpretation of history from a feminist perspective. It is not the same as the history of feminism, which outlines the origins and evolution of the feminist movement. It also differs from women's history, which focuses on the role of women in historical events. The goal of feminist history is to explore and illuminate the female viewpoint of history through rediscovery of female writers, artists, philosophers, etc., in order to recover and demonstrate the significance of women's voices and choices in the past.

Geography

Feminist geography is often considered part of a broader postmodern approach to the subject which is not primarily concerned with the development of conceptual theory in itself but rather focuses on the real experiences of individuals and groups in their own localities, upon the geographies that they live in within their own communities. In addition to its analysis of the real world, it also critiques existing geographical and social studies, arguing that academic traditions are delineated by patriarchy, and that contemporary studies which do not confront the nature of previous work reinforce the male bias of academic study.

Philosophy

The Feminist philosophy refers to a philosophy approached from a feminist perspective. Feminist philosophy involves attempts to use methods of philosophy to further the cause of the feminist movements, it also tries to criticize and/or reevaluate the ideas of traditional philosophy from within a feminist view. This critique stems from the dichotomy Western philosophy has conjectured with the mind and body phenomena. There is no specific school for feminist philosophy like there has been in regard to other theories. This means that Feminist philosophers can be found in the analytic and continental traditions, and the different viewpoints taken on philosophical issues with those traditions. Feminist philosophers also have many different viewpoints taken on philosophical issues within those traditions. Feminist philosophers who are feminists can belong to many different varieties of feminism. The writings of Judith Butler, Rosi Braidotti, Donna Haraway, Bracha Ettinger and Avital Ronell are the most significant psychoanalytically informed influences on contemporary feminist philosophy.

Sexology

Feminist sexology is an offshoot of traditional studies of sexology that focuses on the intersectionality of sex and gender in relation to the sexual lives of women. Feminist sexology shares many principles with the wider field of sexology; in particular, it does not try to prescribe a certain path or "normality" for women's sexuality, but only observe and note the different and varied ways in which women express their sexuality. Looking at sexuality from a feminist point of view creates connections between the different aspects of a person's sexual life.

From feminists' perspectives, sexology, which is the study of human sexuality and sexual relationship, relates to the intersectionality of gender, race and sexuality. Men have dominant power and control over women in the relationship, and women are expected to hide their true feeling about sexual behaviors. Women of color face even more sexual violence in the society. Some countries in Africa and Asia even practice female genital cutting, controlling women's sexual desire and limiting their sexual behavior. Moreover, Bunch, the women's and human rights activist, states that the society used to see lesbianism as a threat to male supremacy and to the political relationships between men and women. Therefore, in the past, people viewed being a lesbian as a sin and made it death penalty. Even today, many people still discriminate homosexuals. Many lesbians hide their sexuality and face even more sexual oppression.

Compulsory Heterosexuality

The feminist theory touches upon the intersectionality of many disciplines such as race, gender, sex, socioeconomic status, etc. According to the writings of Adrienne Rich, there is revelation on the topic of compulsory heterosexuality. Rich argues that the feminist theory has in some ways overlooked and marginalized the topic of sexuality, specifically lesbian experience. The sexuality of women is a topic that is generally associated with feminist theory; however there is not much focus on the life and experience of those women who do not fit the traditional heterosexual standards. Although feminist theory considers intersectionality of many topics, lesbian experience is often set to the side. In many aspects of feminist theory, there is a slight reference of compulsory heterosexuality. Compulsory heterosexuality is the assumption that it is traditionally "normal" or favorable to be heterosexual. However, in the aspects of women's sexuality, it is completely possible to be free and feminist, and not heterosexual. This, in many ways relates to the patriarchal perspective of women and their sexuality. By denying one gender the freedom to their sexuality, the concept of compulsory heterosexuality is enforced; thus marginalizing women's sexuality and the lesbian experience overall.

Monosexual Paradigm

Monosexual Paradigm is a term coined by Blasingame, a self-identified African American, bisexual female. Blasingame used this term to address the lesbian and gay communities who turned a blind eye to the dichotomy that oppressed bisexuals from both heterosexual and homosexual communities. This oppression negatively affects the gay and lesbian communities more so than the heterosexual community due to its contradictory exclusiveness of bisexuals. Blasingame argued that in reality dichotomies are inaccurate to the representation of individuals because nothing is truly black or white, straight or gay. Her main argument is that biphobia is the central message of two roots; internalized heterosexism and racism. Internalized heterosexism is described in the monosexual paradigm in which the binary states that you are either straight or gay and nothing in between. Gays and lesbians accept this internalized heterosexism by morphing into the monosexial paradigm and favoring single attraction and opposing attraction for both sexes. Blasingame described this favoritism as an act of horizontal hostility, where oppressed groups fight amongst themselves. Racism is described in the monosexual paradigm as a dichotomy where individuals are either black or white, again nothing in between. The issue of racism comes into fruition in regards to the bisexuals coming out process, where risks of coming out vary on a basis of anticipated community reaction and also in regards to the norms among bisexual leadership, where class status and race factor predominately over sexual orientation.

Politics

Feminist political theory is a recently emerging field in political science focusing on gender and feminist themes within the state, institutions and policies. It questions the "modern political theory, dominated by universalistic liberalist thought, which claims indifference to gender or other identity differences and has therefore taken its time to open up to such concerns".

Economics

Feminist economics broadly refers to a developing branch of economics that applies feminist insights and critiques to economics. Research under this heading is often interdisciplinary, critical, or heterodox. It encompasses debates about the relationship between feminism and economics on many levels: from applying mainstream economic methods to under-researched "women's" areas, to questioning how mainstream economics values the reproductive sector, to deeply philosophical critiques of economic epistemology and methodology.

One prominent issue that feminist economists investigate is how the gross domestic product (GDP) does not adequately measure unpaid labor predominantly performed by women, such as housework, childcare, and eldercare. Feminist economists have also challenged and exposed the rhetorical approach of mainstream economics. They have made critiques of many basic assumptions of mainstream economics, including the *Homo economicus* model. In the *Houseworker's Handbook* Betsy Warrior presents a cogent argument that the reproduction and domestic labor of women form the foundation of economic survival; although, unremunerated and not included in the GDP.

According to Warrior: "Economics, as it's presented today, lacks any basis in reality as it leaves out the very foundation of economic life. That foundation is built on women's labor; first her reproductive labor which produces every new laborer (and the first commodity, which is mother's milk and which nurtures every new "consumer/laborer"); secondly, women's labor composed of cleaning, cooking, negotiating social stability and nurturing, which prepares for market and maintains each laborer. This constitutes women's continuing industry enabling laborers to occupy every position in the work force. Without this fundamental labor and commodity there would be no economic activity." Warrior also notes that the unacknowledged income of men from illegal activities like arms, drugs and human trafficking, political graft, religious emoluments and various other undisclosed activities provide a rich revenue stream to men, which further invalidates GDP figures. Even in underground economies where women predominate numerically, like trafficking in humans, prostitution and domestic servitude, only a tiny fraction of the pimp's revenue filters down to the women and children he deploys. Usually the amount spent on them is merely for the maintenance of their lives and, in the case of those prostituted, some money may be spent on clothing and such accouterments as will make them more salable to the pimp's clients. For instance, focusing on just the U.S., according to a government sponsored report by the Urban Institute in 2014, "A street prostitute in Dallas may make as little as $5 per sex act. But pimps can take in $33,000 a week in Atlanta, where the sex business brings in an estimated $290 million per year."

Proponents of this theory have been instrumental in creating alternative models, such as the capability approach and incorporating gender into the analysis of economic data to affect policy. Marilyn Power suggests that feminist economic methodology can be broken down into five categories.

Legal Theory

Feminist legal theory is based on the feminist view that law's treatment of women in relation to men has not been equal or fair. The goals of feminist legal theory, as defined by leading theorist Claire Dalton, consist of understanding and exploring the female experience, figuring out if law and institutions oppose females, and figuring out what changes can be committed to. This is to be accomplished through studying the connections between the law and gender as well as applying feminist analysis to concrete areas of law.

Feminist legal theory stems from the inadequacy of the current structure to account for discrimination women face, especially discrimination based on multiple, intersecting identities. Kimberlé Crenshaw's work is central to feminist legal theory, particularly her article *Demarginalizing the Intersection of Race and Sex: A Black Feminist Critique of Antidiscrimination Doctrine, Feminist Theory, and Antiracist Politics*. *DeGraffenreid v General Motors* is an example of such a case. In this instance, the court ruled the plaintiffs, five Black women who were employees of General Motors, were not eligible to file a complaint on the grounds they, as black women, were not "a special class to be protected from discrimination". The ruling in *DeGraffenreid* against the plaintiff revealed the courts inability to understand intersectionality's role in discrimination. *Moore v Hughes Helicopters, Inc.* is another ruling, which serves to reify the persistent discrediting of intersectionality as a factor in discrimination. In the case of *Moore*, the plaintiff brought forth statistical evidence revealing a disparity in promotions to upper-level and supervisory jobs between men and women and, to a lesser extent, between Black and white men. Ultimately, the court denied the plaintiff the ability to represent all Blacks and all females. The decision dwindled the pool of statistical information the plaintiff could pull from and limited the evidence only to that of Black women, which is a ruling in direct contradiction to *DeGraffenreid*. Further, because the plaintiff originally claimed discrimination as a Black female rather than, more generally, as a female the court stated it had concerns whether the plaintiff could "adequately represent white female employees". *Payne v Travenol* serves as yet another example of the courts inconsistency when dealing with issues revolving around intersections of race and sex. The plaintiffs in *Payne*, two Black females, filed suit against Travenol on behalf of both Black men and women on the grounds the pharmaceutical plant practiced racial discrimination. The court ruled the plaintiffs could not adequately represent Black males, however, they did allow the admittance of statistical evidence, which was inclusive of all Black employees. Despite the more favorable outcome after it was found there was extensive racial discrimination, the courts decided the benefits of the ruling – back pay and constructive seniority – would not be extended to Black males employed by the company. *Moore* contends Black women cannot adequately represent white women on issues of sex discrimination, *Payne* suggests Black women cannot adequately represent Black men on issues of race discrimination, and *DeGraffenreid* argues Black women are not a special class to be protected. The rulings, when connected, display a deep-rooted problem in regards to addressing discrimination within the legal system. While the cases of *DeGraffenreid* (1976), *Moore* (1983), and *Payne* (1976) are not recent accounts; they provide proof of the courts inconsistency in procedures and rulings on the basis of sex and race, which serves to reinforce the need for Feminist legal theory to not only be further developed, but also applied.

Communication Theory

Feminist communication theory has evolved over time and branches out in many directions. Early theories focused on the way that gender influenced communication and many argued that language was "MAN made". This view of communication promoted a "deficiency model" asserting that characteristics of speech associated with women were negative and that men "set the standard for competent interpersonal communication". These early theories also suggested that ethnicity, cultural and economic backgrounds also needed to be addressed. They looked at how gender intersects with other identity constructs, such as class, race, and sexuality. Feminist theorists, especially those considered to be liberal feminists, began looking at issues of equality in education and employment. Other theorists addressed political oratory and public discourse. The recovery project brought to light many women orators who had been "erased or ignored as significant contributors". Feminist communication theorists also addressed how women were represented in the media and how the media "communicated ideology about women, gender, and feminism".

Feminist communication theory also encompasses access to the public sphere, whose voices are heard in that sphere, and the ways in which the field of communication studies has limited what is regarded as essential to public discourse. The recognition of a full history of women orators overlooked and disregarded by the field has effectively become an undertaking of recovery, as it establishes and honors the existence of women in history and lauds the communication by these historically significant contributors. This recovery effort, begun by Andrea Lunsford, Professor of English and Director of the Program in Writing and Rhetoric at Stanford University and followed by other feminist communication theorists also names women such as Aspasia, Diotima, and Christine de Pisan, who were likely influential in rhetorical and communication traditions in classical and medieval times, but who have been negated as serious contributors to the traditions.

Feminist communication theorists are also concerned with attempting to explain the methods used by those with power to prohibit women like Maria W. Stewart, Sarah Moore Grimké, and Angelina Grimké, and more recently, Ella Baker and Anita Hill, from achieving a voice in political discourse and consequently being driven from the public sphere. Theorists in this vein are also interested in the unique and significant techniques of communication employed by these women and others like them to surmount some of the oppression they experienced.

Design

Technical writers have concluded that visual language can convey facts and ideas clearer than almost any other means of communication. According to the feminist theory, "gender may be a factor in how human beings represent reality."

Men and women will construct different types of structures about the self, and, consequently, their thought processes may diverge in content and form. This division depends on the self-concept, which is an "important regulator of thoughts, feelings and actions" that "governs one's perception of reality".

With that being said, the self-concept has a significant effect on how men and women represent reality in different ways.

Recently, "technical communicators' terms such as 'visual rhetoric,' 'visual language,' and 'document design' indicate a new awareness of the importance of visual design".

Deborah S. Bosley explores this new concept of the "feminist theory of design" by conducting a study on a collection of undergraduate males and females who were asked to illustrate a visual, on paper, given to them in a text. Based on this study, she creates a "feminist theory of design" and connects it to technical communicators.

In the results of the study, males used more angular illustrations, such as squares, rectangles and arrows, which are interpreted as a "direction" moving away from or a moving toward, thus suggesting more aggressive positions than rounded shapes, showing masculinity.

Females, on the other hand, used more curved visuals, such as circles, rounded containers and bending pipes. Bosley takes into account that feminist theory offers insight into the relationship between females and circles or rounded objects. According to Bosley, studies of women and leadership indicate a preference for nonhierarchical work patterns (preferring a communication "web" rather than a communication "ladder"). Bosley explains that circles and other rounded shapes, which women chose to draw, are nonhierarchical and often used to represent inclusive, communal relationships, confirming her results that women's visual designs do have an effect on their means of communications.

Based on these conclusions, this "feminist theory of design" can go on to say that gender does play a role in how humans represent reality.

Black Feminist Criminology

Black feminist criminology theory is a concept created by Hillary Potter in the 1990s and a bridge that integrates Feminist theory with criminology. It is based on the integration of Black feminist theory and critical race theory.

For years, Black women were historically overlooked and disregarded in the study of crime and criminology; however, with a new focus on Black feminism that sparked in the 1980s, Black feminists began to contextualize their unique experiences and examine why the general status of Black women in the criminal justice system was lacking in female specific approaches. Potter explains that because Black women usually have "limited access to adequate education and employment as consequences of racism, sexism, and classism", they are often disadvantaged. This disadvantage materializes into "poor responses by social service professionals and crime-processing agents to Black women's interpersonal victimization". Most crime studies focused on White males/females and Black males. Any results or conclusions targeted to Black males were usually assumed to be the same situation for Black females. This was very problematic since Black males and Black females differ in what they experience. For instance, economic deprivation, status equality between the sexes, distinctive socialization patterns, racism, and sexism should all be taken into account between Black males and Black females. The two will experience all of these factors differently; therefore, it was crucial to resolve this dilemma.

Black feminist criminology is the solution to this problem. It takes four factors into account: One, it observes the social structural oppression of Black women. Two, it recognizes the Black community and its culture. Three, it looks at Black intimate and familial relations. And four, it looks at the Black woman as an individual. These four factors will help distinguish Black women from Black males into an accurate branch of learning in the criminal justice system.

Criticisms

It has been said that Black feminist criminology is still in its "infancy stage"; therefore, there is little discussion or studies that disprove it as an affective feminist perspective. In addition to its age, Black feminist criminology has not actively accounted for role of religion and spirituality in Black women's "experience with abuse".

Feminist Science and Technology Studies

Feminist science and technology studies (STS) refers to the transdisciplinary field of research on the ways gender and other markers of identity intersect with technology, science, and culture. The practice emerged from feminist critique on the masculine-coded uses of technology in the fields of natural, medical, and technical sciences, and its entanglement in gender and identity. A large part of feminist technoscience theory explains science and technologies to be linked and should be held accountable for the social and cultural developments resulting from both fields.

Some key issues feminist technoscience studies address include:

1. The use of feminist analysis when applied to scientific ideas and practices.

2. Intersections between race, class, gender, science, and technology.

3. The implications of situated knowledges.

4. Politics of gender on how to understand agency, body, rationality, and the boundaries between nature and culture.

Feminist Legal Theory

Feminist legal theory, also known as feminist jurisprudence, is based on the belief that the law has been fundamental in women's historical subordination. The project of feminist legal theory is twofold. First, feminist jurisprudence seeks to explain ways in which the law played a role in women's former subordinate status. Second, feminist legal theory is dedicated to changing women's status through a reworking of the law and its approach to gender.

History

The term *feminist jurisprudence* was coined in 1977 by Ann Scales during the planning process for Celebration 25, a party and conference held in 1978 to celebrate the twenty-fifth anniversary of the first women graduating from Harvard Law School. The term was first published in 1978 in the first issue of the Harvard Women's Law Journal.

In 1984 Martha Fineman founded the Feminism and Legal Theory Project at the University of Wisconsin Law School to explore the relationships between feminist theory, practice, and law, which has been instrumental in the development of feminist legal theory.

Main Approaches

Some approaches to feminist jurisprudence are:

- the liberal equality model;
- the sexual difference model;
- the dominance model;
- and the postmodern or anti-essentialist model.

Each model provides a distinct view of the legal mechanisms that contribute to women's subordination, and each offers a distinct method for changing legal approaches to gender.

The Liberal Equality Model

The liberal equality model operates from within the liberal legal paradigm and generally embraces liberal values and the rights-based approach to law, though it takes issue with how the liberal framework has operated in practice. This model focuses on ensuring that women are afforded genuine equality—as opposed to the nominal equality often given them in the traditional liberal framework—and seeks to achieve this either by way of a more thorough application of liberal values to women's experiences or the revision of liberal categories to take gender into account. Susan Okin (1946–2004), for example, has critiqued liberal approaches to justice.

The Sexual Difference Model

The difference model emphasizes the significance of gender differences and holds that these differences should not be obscured by the law, but should be taken into account by it. Only by taking into account differences can the law provide adequate remedies for women's situation, which is in fact distinct from men's. The difference model is in direct opposition to the sameness account which holds that women's sameness with men should be emphasized. To the sameness feminist, employing women's differences in an attempt to garner greater rights is ineffectual to that end and places emphasis on the very characteristics of women that have historically precluded them from achieving equality with men (for example, the protective laws).

The Dominance Model

The dominance model rejects liberal feminism and views the legal system as a mechanism for the perpetuation of male dominance. It thus joins certain strands of critical legal theory, which also consider the potential for law to act as an instrument for domination.

In the account of dominance proposed by Catherine MacKinnon, sexuality is central to the dominance. MacKinnon argues that women's sexuality is socially constructed by male dominance and the sexual domination of women by men is a primary source of the general social subordination of women.

The Anti-essentialist Model

Feminists from the postmodern camp have deconstructed the notions of objectivity and neutrality, claiming that every perspective is socially situated. Anti-essentialist and intersectionalist critiques of feminists have objected to the idea that there can be any universal women's voice and have criticized feminists, as did Black feminism, for implicitly basing their work on the experiences of white, middle class, heterosexual women. The anti-essentialist and intersectionalist project has been to explore the ways in which race, class, sexual orientation, and other axes of subordination interplay with gender and to uncover the implicit, detrimental assumptions that have often been employed in feminist theory.

Men and Feminism

Since the 19th century, men have taken part in significant cultural and political responses to feminism within each "wave" of the movement. This includes seeking to establish equal opportunities for women in a range of social relations, generally done through a "strategic leveraging" of male privilege. Feminist men have also argued alongside writers like bell hooks, however, that *men's* liberation from the socio-cultural constraints of sexism and gender roles is a necessary part of feminist activism and scholarship.

History

Parker Pillsbury and other abolitionist men held feminist views and openly identified as feminist, using their influence to promote the rights of women and slaves respectively.

Pillsbury helped to draft the constitution of the feminist American Equal Rights Association in 1865, he served as vice-president of the New Hampshire Woman Suffrage Association. In 1868 and 1869 Parker edited *Revolution* with Elizabeth Cady Stanton.

Throughout the seventeenth and eighteenth centuries, the majority of pro-feminist authors emerged from France, including Denis Diderot, Paul Henri Thiry d'Holbach, and Charles Louis de Montesquieu. Montesquieu introduced female characters, like Roxana in *Persian Letters*, who subverted patriarchal systems, and represented his arguments against despotism. The 18th century saw male philosophers attracted to issues of human rights, and men such as the Marquis de Condorcet championed women's education. Liberals, such as the utilitarian Jeremy Bentham, demanded equal rights for women in every sense, as people increasingly came to believe that women were treated unfairly under the law.

In the 19th century, there was also an awareness of women's struggle. The British legal historian, Sir Henry Maine, criticized the inevitability of patriarchy in his *Ancient Law* (1861). In 1866, John Stuart Mill, author of *The Subjection of Women*, presented a women's petition to the British parliament, and supported an amendment to the 1867 Reform Bill. Although his efforts focused on the problems of married women, it was an acknowledgment that marriage for Victorian women was predicated upon a sacrifice of liberty, rights, and property. His involvement in the women's movement stemmed from his long-standing friendship with Harriet Taylor, whom he eventually married.

In 1840, women were refused the right to participate at the World Anti-Slavery Convention in London. Supporters of the women attending argued that it was hypocritical to forbid women and men from sitting together at this convention to end slavery; they cited similar segregationist arguments in the United States that were used to separate whites and blacks. When women were still denied to join in the proceedings, abolitionists William Lloyd Garrison, Charles Lenox Remond, Nathaniel Peabody Rogers, and Henry Stanton, all elected to sit silently with the women.

One argument against female participation, both at the World Anti-Slavery Convention, and commonly in the nineteenth century, was the suggestion that women were ill-constituted to assume male responsibilities. Abolitionist Thomas Wentworth Higginson argued against this, stating:

"I do not see how any woman can avoid a thrill of indignation when she first opens her eyes to the fact that it is really contempt, not reverence, that has so long kept her sex from an equal share of legal, political, and educational rights...[a woman needs equal rights] not because she is man's better half, but because she is his other half. She needs them, not as an angel, but as a fraction of humanity."

American sociologist Michael Kimmel categorized American male responses to feminism at the turn of the twentieth century into three categories: pro-feminist, masculinist, and antifeminist. Pro-feminist men, believing that changes would also benefit men, generally welcomed women's increased participation in the public sphere, and changes in the division of labour in the home; in contrast anti-feminists opposed women's suffrage and participation in public life, supporting a traditional patriarchal family model. Finally, the masculinist movement was characterized by men's groups, and developed as an indirect reaction to the perceived femininization of manhood.

Men's Liberation Movement

The men's liberation movement began in the early 1970s as consciousness-raising groups to help men free themselves from the limits of sex roles. Proponents of men's liberation argued that male bonding is a mechanism to conform men's identities to a single sense of masculinity, which reinforces patriarchy. In lieu of such bonding, the men's liberation movement called for open acknowledgment of the costs of masculinity: men's entrapment in their fixed role as the breadwinner of the nuclear family and the taboo against men expressing emotions. Most significantly, this movement intended to make it acceptable for men to be open about their emotions while maintaining their masculinity.

The link between the biological male sex and the social construction of masculinity was seen by some scholars as a limitation on men's collaboration with the feminist movement. This sharply contrasted with sex role theory which viewed gender as something determined by biological differences between the sexes. Other key elements of the men's liberation movement were the ideas that genders are relational and each cannot exist without the other, and that gender as a whole is a social construction and not a biological imperative. Thus, second-wave profeminist writers were able to explore the interactions between social practices and institutions, and ideas of gender.

Men's Rights Movement

In the early 1980's, the Men's rights campaign emerged in America in response to the men's liberation movement. Men's rights activists refer to themselves as "masculinists" or are labeled as such. It is considered by some feminists to be part of an antifeminist response.

Masculinists claim that feminist advances have not been balanced by elimination of traditional feminine privileges, and that they should empower themselves by revitalizing their masculinity. This argument was also echoed in religious circles with the Muscular Christianity movement.

A uniting principle was the belief that men's problems were awarded less attention than women's and that any previous oppression of women had turned, or was about to turn, into oppression of men. Men's rights activists cite men's economic burden of the traditionally male breadwinner role, men's shorter average life expectancy, and inequalities favoring women in divorce issues, custody laws, and abortion rights as evidence of men's suffering.

The campaign has generally had the most success achieving legal reform in family law, particularly regarding child custody. Activists argue that the American judicial system discriminates against fathers in child custody hearings since mothers are typically viewed as the main caregivers. They claim that the economic burden of the breadwinner role has made it more difficult for men to take part in child rearing, and that court decisions rarely account for this obstacle.

Some organizations, such as the National Coalition of Free Men (NCFM), have made efforts to examine how sex discrimination affects men. For instance, this group argues that custody rights in favor of women discriminate against men because they are based on the belief that women are naturally more nurturing and better caregivers than men. Also, in the belief that women are somehow less culpable than men, women receive gentler treatment by the justice system for the same crimes that men have committed. Thus, groups such as NCFM promote awareness, resources, support, and openings for discussion for these issues.

Male Feminism and Pro-feminism

As feminist writer Shira Tarrant has argued, a number of men have engaged with and contributed to feminist movements throughout history. Today, academics like Michael Flood, Michael Messner, and Michael Kimmel are involved with men's studies and pro-feminism.

There is debate within feminism over whether or not men can be feminists. Some feminists, like Simone de Beauvoir in her seminal text *The Second Sex*, argue that men cannot be feminists because of the intrinsic differences between the sexes, Separatist feminists also hold this view, arguing that only by rejecting the masculine perspective entirely can feminism allow women to define themselves on their own terms, and that the involvement of men in the feminist movement will inculcate the values of patriarchy into any social change. Some writers hold that men do not suffer the same oppression as women, and as such cannot comprehend women's experience, and as such cannot constructively contribute to feminist movements or concepts.

Others argue that men's identification with the feminist movement is necessary for furthering the feminist causes. A number of feminist writers maintain that identifying as a feminist is the strongest stand men can take in the struggle against sexism against women. They have argued that men should be allowed, or even encouraged, to participate in the feminist movement. For some, the participation of men in the feminist movement is seen as part of a process of the universalization of the feminist movement, necessary for its continued relevance. One challenge of motivating men to participate, or promoting their inclusion, in feminism has been linked to the disconnect between gender and intersecting components of identity. An example of this is demonstrated in that African American men have largely been unable to realize the connection between the civil rights movement and that to end sexist oppression. The bonds formed in the civil rights movement established valuable solidarity among African American women and men. This is an approach that should be transferable and equally useful to the feminist movement. Making these important connections understood by women and men will greatly benefit feminism. As described in the theory of strategic intersectionality, utilizing the experiences of one part of our identity that intersects with another provides insightful tools to further improve the available tactics of the feminist movement. Other female feminists argue that men cannot be feminists simply because they are not women, cannot understand women's issues, and are collectively members of the class of oppressors against women. They claim that men are granted inherent privileges that prevent them from identifying with feminist struggles and thus make it impossible for them to identify with feminists.

One idea supporting men's inclusion as 'feminists' is that excluding men from the feminist movement labels it as solely a female task, which could be argued to be sexist in itself. This idea asserts that until men share equal responsibility for struggling to end sexism against women, the feminist movement will reflect the very sexist contradiction it wishes to eradicate. The term 'profeminist' occupies the middle ground in this semantic debate, because it offers a degree of closeness to feminism without using the term itself. Also, the prefix 'pro' characterizes the term as more proactive and positive. There has been some debate regarding the use of the hyphen (identifying as a 'pro-feminist' as opposed to a profeminist) claiming that it distances the term too much from feminism proper.

Feminist Men in Popular Culture

In 2014, several high-profile events led to the continued presence of feminist issues in the media. These events included Bring Back Our Girls, HeForShe campaign, the Gamergate controversy,

Malala Yousafzai winning the Nobel Peace Prize, and sexual assault allegations against Jian Ghomeshi and Bill Cosby.

Justin Trudeau

In 2015 Canadian Prime Minister Justin Trudeau made international headlines for establishing the first gender-balanced cabinet in Canada. In response to a media question asking his reason for doing so, Trudeau said "Because it's 2015." At the World Economic Forum in 2016, Trudeau again made headlines when he spoke about raising his sons to be feminists and urged men not to be afraid of using the word 'feminist'. A few months later at a United Nations conference, Justin Trudeau said "I'm going to keep saying, loud and clearly, that I am a feminist. Until it is met with a shrug." He explained further what that meant for him:

"It shouldn't be something that creates a reaction. It's simply saying that I believe in the equality of men and women and that we still have an awful lot of work to do to get there. That's like saying the sky is blue and the grass is green."

—Justin Trudeau, United Nations conference, March 16th 2016

This is what a Feminist Looks Like

In October of 2014 ElleUk created shirt with the slogan "This Is What a Feminist Looks Like" with The Fawcett Society. A photo series featuring many A-list stars wearing the shirts was released. The production of the shirts was criticized for being anti-feminist due to sweat-shop labour. In spite of this criticism, the phrase became popular, it was quoted by President Barack Obama in a speech at the United State of Women Summit in 2016. In 2017 two photographers, Carey Lynne Fruth and Sophie Spinelle, launched a photo series with subjects holding signs bearing the slogan.

Equal Pay Support in Hollywood

Five original stars from The Big Bang Theory including four men (Jim Parsons, Johnny Galecki, Kunal Nayyar and Simon Helberg) decided to take a pay cut so that their two female co-stars who joined later can earn a higher wage for season 11 and 12. The current is wage gap sits at $900,000 with the original cast making one million dollars per episode while Mayim Bialik and Melissa Rauch earn $100,000 per episode.

Emmy Rossum from Shameless put production of season 8 on hold when she was renegotiating her contract for equal pay as her co-star William H. Macy. She also requested a little more money to make up for the years of work where she was making less. When confronted by TMZ with this reality, William H. Macy responded with It's about f--king time, don't you think?" and "She works as hard as I do, she deserves everything."

Bradley Cooper responded to his frequent co-star Jennifer Lawrence's "Why Do These Dudes Make More Than Me?" essay by vowing to share his salary information with his female co-stars during the preproduction negotiation stage in an effort to reduce the gender gap.

Men Supporting the Women's March 2017

John Legend attended the Women's March on Main Street Park City in Utah on January 21st 2017. In an interview he reveals that he joined the march to show solidarity with everyone marching all around the world and to raise awareness on equality to ensure that all the progress women and people of colour have made over the past century does not get diminished under the President Donald Trump administration.

Many male liberal leaders and politicians took part in the march as well. Among them, Bernie Sanders took the stage at the Vermont Women's March on January 21st 2017. He spoke in support of equal work for equal pay, health care, planned parenthood and unifying the country.Former Secretary of State John Kerry also joined the Women's March in Washington, D.C.

Pro-feminist Campaign

There is also the "Untied Nation women's solidarity movement for gender equality, which encourages boys and men to become equal partners with women. The HeForShe campaign changes the perspective of an dominate society and enlists everyone to do their part to reimagine an society through gender equality. Since the launch of HeForShe campaign in 2014, UN Women ambassadors alongside Emma Watson and thousands of men across the globe are committed to the goal of gender equality. Overall, Bell Hooks concludes that gender issues are not just for women as some men may believe, but it is for everyone. Therefore, the more we work together, the better our society will be. Emma Watson's moving speech at the Untied Nations about gender equality for the UN's HeForShe campaign demonstrates the first look at the notion "HeForShe".

Men's Studies

Masculinity scholars seek to broaden the academic discourse of gender through men's studies. While some feminists argue that most academic disciplines, except women's studies, can be considered "men's studies" because they claim that the content of the curriculum consists of primarily male subjects, masculinity scholars assert that men's studies specifically analyzes men's gendered experiences. Central to men's studies is the understanding that "gender" does not mean "female," the same way "race" does not mean "black." Men's studies are typically interdisciplinary, and incorporate the feminist conception that "the personal is political." Masculinity scholars strive to contribute to the existing dialogue about gender created through women's studies.

There are various arguments and movements that support the cause for gender equality as it relates to feminism. Jackson Katz, suggests that we have a responsibility to help youths to create a society that will prevent future generations from experiencing the level of issues that regards gender equality. Gender studies is often referred to as women issues. Women's issues are sometimes viewed as issues that men contribute to. Jackson Katz argues that women issues should be men issues as well. Jackson Katz views this as when both of the genders work together, there is a change that the next generation can use to avoid suffering similar tragedies.

"We owe it to young men. These boys didn't make the choice to be a man in a culture that tells them that manhood is a certain way. We, that have a choice, have an opportunity and a responsibility to them."

—Jackson Katz, TEDxFiDiWomen conference, November ,2012

Recent Polls

In 2001 a Gallup poll found that 20% of American men considered themselves feminist, with 75% saying they were not. A CBS Poll in 2009 found 24% of men in the United States claim the term "feminist" is an insult. Four in five men refuse to identify themselves as feminist, but when a specific definition is given the number fell to two in five. An increasing number of men said that feminism had improved their lives in comparison to polls taken in 1983 and 1999 with an unprecedented, but marginal plurality of 47% agreeing. 60% believe that a strong women's movement is no longer needed. However, a YouGov Poll of Britain in 2010 found that only 16% of men described themselves as feminist with 54% stating they were not and 8% specifically claiming to be antifeminist.

Recent Studies

In 2001, a qualitative study of men's perception of feminism showed pervasive patterns of linear reasoning. Researchers found that the participants identified two genres of feminism and two strains of feminists, and dubbed it the 'Jekyll and Hyde' binary. The participants would classify feminism and feminists as either "good" or "monstrous". In 2016 the study was repeated by a new team of researchers to find that the binary persisted, as "unreasonable feminism" and "fair feminism".

References

- Allum, Cynthia (9 April 2015). "82 percent of Americans don't consider themselves feminists, poll shows". The New York Times. Retrieved 26, August 2020

- Rohana Ariffin; Women's Crisis Centre (Pinang, Malaysia). Shame, secrecy, and silence: study on rape in Penang. Women's Crisis Centre. ISBN 978-983-99348-0-9. Retrieved 01, June 2020

- Peraino, Judith, Girls with Guitars and Other Strange Stories, in Journal of the American Musicological Society, vol. 54, no. 3 (2001), p. 693

- Phillips, Melanie (2004). The Ascent of Woman: A History of the Suffragette Movement and the Ideas Behind it. London: Abacus. pp. 1–370. ISBN 978-0-349-11660-0

- "The Long Way to Women's Right to Vote in Switzerland: a Chronology". History-switzerland.geschichte-schweiz.ch. Retrieved 2011-01-08

- Halse, C. & Honey, A. (2005). Unraveling ethics: Illuminating the moral dilemmas of research ethics. Journal of Women in Culture and Society, 30 (4), 2141–2162

- papermagazine (2016-02-18). "Emma Watson and bell hooks Talk Feminism, Confidence and the Importance of Reading". PAPERMAG. Retrieved 08, June 2020

- Gilligan, Carol "In a Different Voice: Women's Conceptions of Self and of Morality". Harvard Educational Review. 47 (4): 481–517. Retrieved 08, June 2020

- Hegarty, P.; Buechel, C. (2006). "Androcentric reporting of gender differences in APA journals:1965-2004". Review of General Psychology. 10 (4): 377–389. doi:10.1037/1089-2680.10.4.377

- Rosenberg, Jessica; Gitana Garofalo (Spring 1998). "Riot Grrrl: Revolutions from within". Signs. 23 (3 – Feminisms and Youth Cultures): 809. JSTOR 3175311. doi:10.1086/495289

- Peraino, Judith A. (2001). "Girls with guitars and other strange stories". Journal of the American Musicological Society. 54 (3): 692–709. doi:10.1525/jams.2001.54.3.692

- Rosenberg, Jessica; Gitana Garofalo. "Riot Grrrl: Revolutions From Within; Spring 1998". Signs. 23 (Feminisms and Youth Cultures; number 3): 809. doi:10.1086/495289

- Hennessy, Rosemary; Ingraham, Chrys. Materialist feminism: a reader in class, difference, and women's lives. London: Routledge. pp. 1–13. ISBN 978-0-415-91634-9

- Ogunyemi, Chikwenye Okonjo. "Womanism: The Dynamics of the Contemporary Black Female Novel in English". Signs: Journal of Women in Culture and Society. 11 (1): 63–80. JSTOR 3174287. doi:10.1086/494200

LGBTQ Community in Gender Studies

LGBT is an acronym which stands for lesbian, gay, bisexual and transgender people. An important critical theory which is associated with LGBT community is the queer theory. It studies gender and sexual practices which challenge heteronormativity. The diverse aspects of LGBT community as well as the history of LGBT movement have been thoroughly discussed in this chapter.

Homosexuality

Homosexuality is the same sex behaviour within the animal species. Nature has created clear distinction in higher animals in terms of male and female partners. The ultimate goal of life is to re-produce by means of which it is possible to give the continuity of race in nature. Based on this principle, animal behaviour is directed directly and indirectly to re-produce and maintain the gene pool.

The traditional belief of male and female partners and subsequent marriage in society was incorporated in society and different religion, which was directly challenged by homosexual interactions. The ethical and moral discussions were based on natural differences and religious understandings. There is a vast difference in opinions regarding homosexuality. Homosexuality in humans has been center of the broad discussions and widely accepted by many societies in the recent times.

There are different theories regarding the homosexual behaviour in humans. These theories incorporate chemical, social and personal reasons behind the same sex attractions. We have come up with many studies and findings to explain same sex behaviour and understand it. Some of them give convincing evidences with proper explanation of homosexuality, which helps us to broaden our knowledge and incorporate sexual minorities into mainstream social role-play.

H-Y Antigens and Fraternal Birth Order Defect

The rational of homosexuality is attributed with Y-linked minor histocompatibility antigens (H-Y antigens). The concurrent pregnancy with male fetus will immunize the mother with this antigen leading to production of antibodies that are capable of crossing into fetal circulation. Therefore increase in the number of the same sex siblings in male is associated with homosexual behaviour. This observation is supported by a hypothesis that fetus receives the anti-H-Y antibodies from mother, causing an alteration of sexual differential in the brain of these fetuses. This can be proven by a decrease in the observed weight of homosexual males with older brothers in comparison to heterosexual males. This behaviour of perceived likelihood of homosexual orientation with direct increase in same sex sibling count is referred as fraternal birth order defect. There is also direct link of right and left-handedness in homosexual behaviour. The presence of elder sibling will increase the chances of homosexual behaviour in right-handed males; probably due to insensitive nature of the non-right-handed males to the maternal antibodies or absence of these antibodies in mothers in these groups.

One of the probable reasons of fraternal homosexual behaviour is same sex play with male siblings. But this has not been proven and established in terms of same sex orientations in females, as samesex play have not been found to alter the sexual preference in them. In regard to this observation same-sex play hypothesis does not look convincing and needs further evidences. In regard to the fraternal homosexual behaviour, sibling sex ration was also noted. The sibling same-sex ratio of homosexual males and lesbian females were not found to be significantly elevated. The overall number of fraternal homosexual constitutes a minority, in homosexual community.

Stressful Childhood Experience (SCE) and Homosexuality

Many lesbian, gay, bisexual, and transgender (LGBT) people were found to have some sort of stressful childhood sexual experiences when comparison was made in between homosexual and heterosexual. In one of the study based on US, stressful childhood experience was directly linked with homosexuality in the respondents. SCE is directly associated with stress related traumatic childhood disorder and these group has a high predisposition to substance abuse. Stressful childhood experience also had different outcomes based on race and ethnicity. Latino and African-American had the highest risk of psychiatric problems followed by Asian and whites. But there is no conclusive evidence and controlled research to prove a relationship between SSC and homosexuality beside observational evidences. Therefore there is a warrant for definitive study in LGBT community to establish this causation in the near future.

Homosexuality and its Related Implications

Suicidal Ideation among Homosexuals

Same sex sexual orientation is still not recognized by many society and considered taboo in many section of societies and religious beliefs. It is misunderstood as an alternative form of psychiatric problems and the negative attitude towards them is highly prevalent. Homosexual persons are likely to experience more violence and marginalization due to their sexual orientation. This negative behaviour targeted to them range from bullying to social discrimination, physical violence and psychological torture. Due to this adverse social behaviour directed towards homosexual males, there is higher incidence of suicide attempt and suicide related deaths amongst MSM. This increase in likelihood of suicidal ideation is partly contributed to the high-risk health behaviour and practices in homosexual related with substance abuse, sexually transmitted infections (STI) and Human immunodeficiency virus/ acquired immune deficiency syndrome (HIV/AIDS). Relationship breakup within gay partners and self-perception of the homosexuality, unavailability of gay partners and unexpected sudden abuse towards the belief by strangers are some others mentionable causes of the suicidal reasons.

Suicidal ideation and behaviour along with substance abuse is clearly higher in bisexuals and transsexuals, for some unknown reason, one of them might be due to high-risk behaviour and practices. In certain countries homosexual males totals more than 50% of suicidal attempters. One of the main reasons of suicidal ideation and attempt is depression. Homosexual and bisexual males suffer from depression more than other people in the community. These reasons completely coinciding with homosexual behaviour. Addressing social stigmata and change in the attitude against the vulnerable groups is an effective way to decrease the overall incidence of suicide rate in Sexual Minorities (SM).

Psychosocial Determinants

LGBT community has an increased risk of psychiatric problems. These psychiatric problems range from anxiety disorder, depression, suicidal tendencies and substance abuse in particular. Sexual minorities clearly show higher incidences of psychiatric problem and its related co-morbidities. The older same sex couples had a higher rate of psychological distress and functional disability associated with it in comparison to younger groups. Various factors can be implicated for the sexual problems in LGBT. All of these sexual minorities are at increased risk of depression; bisexual men have the highest rate of psychiatric problems. Negative perception of sexual behaviour by the community and negative attitude with social isolation is one of the most important determinate for increased rate of psychosocial problems in LGBT.

The effect of sexual orientation in alcohol consumption is skewed with higher incidences in lesbians and bisexual women. These homosexual and bisexual men and women spend considerable time in the bars as compared to the heterosexual counterpart. The time laps have a significant effect in drinking behaviour in females with higher incidences of alcohol consumption.

Risk of Sexually Transmitted Infections (STI)

STI are common determinants among homosexual community. There is a very high incidence of Human immunodeficiency virus/ acquired immune deficiency syndrome (HIV/AIDS) in young males who have sex with males (MSM). In US, black males were found to have higher prevalence's of HIV amongst MSM. Contrary to these findings, there was not much difference in blacks, whites or Hispanics in school age males <18 years age groups. These groups have higher chances of contracting STI due to their unpreparedness for the sexual encounter and lack of proper safety measures. Human Papilloma Virus (HPV) is common among the MSM community. HPV is capable of causing anal cancer, penile cancer and oro-pharyngeal cancer. There are reported cases of high Shigella transmission in MSM. Homosexual men also have an increased risk of Gonococcal and Chalmydial infection with higher chances of prostate cancer in homosexuals as compared with heterosexuals.

Pre-exposure prophylaxis (PrEP) among homosexual males having anal sex is directed towards preventive approach for HIV transmission. The pre-exposure prophylaxis has been tried with different drug combinations in the recent time. Among many combinations, emtricitabine and tenofovir disoproxil fumarate (FTC-TDF) has shown a promising efficacy in decreasing HIV transmission. Oral TDF is as effective as combination prophylactic antiretroviral regimen of FTC-TDF in high-risk individuals. PrEP in high risk sexual behaviour in male and females with daily oral regimen of antiretroviral medication is also an effective way to reduce overall HIV transmission. The overall transmission rate does depend on adherence to the regimen and behaviour modification in due consideration to all these factors.

Challenges

Sexual racism is the biggest challenge faced by LGBT community since the evolution of mankind. With the modernization and growing trend of technological advancement, sexual racism has taken its roots in the form of hate crimes delivered through electronic medium. Violence against LGBT community has drastically increased in the recent times. These increased in violence can be attributed to ultra-orthodox thoughts and religious belief. There are several incidences of hate crimes targeted against sexual minority in every corner of the world. Sexual minorities still face biggest challenge to establish themselves firmly in society and to be accepted in every forms of it.

Homophobia and HIV

Homophobia is "the irrational hatred, intolerance, and fear" of lesbian, gay, bisexual and transgender (LGBT) people. These views are expressed through homophobic behaviours such as negative comments, bullying, physical attacks, discrimination and negative media representation.

As well as the actions of individuals, homophobia may be expressed through actions of the state, such as punitive laws, as well as other social institutions. Some LGBT people may internalise negative attitudes towards same-sex attraction, this is called self-stigma.

Homophobia continues to be a major barrier to ending the global AIDS epidemic. The global HIV epidemic has always been closely linked with negative attitudes towards LGBT people, especially men who have sex with men (sometimes referred to as MSM); a group that is particularly affected by HIV and AIDS.

At the beginning of HIV epidemic, in many countries gay men and other men who have sex with men were frequently singled out for abuse as they were seen to be responsible for the transmission of HIV. Sensational reporting in the press, which became increasingly homophobic, fuelled this view. Headlines such as "Alert over 'gay plague'", and "'Gay plague' may lead to blood ban on homosexuals" demonised the LGBT community.

LGBT people face specific challenges and barriers, including violence, human right violations, stigma and discrimination. Criminalisation of same-sex relationships, cross-dressing, sodomy and 'gender impersonation' feeds into 'social homophobia' — everyday instances of discrimination — and both factors prevent LGBT people from accessing vital HIV prevention, testing, and treatment and care services. As a result, some LGBT people are unknowingly living with HIV or being diagnosed late when HIV is harder to treat.

Moreover, research has shown that men who have sex with men may exhibit less health-seeking behaviour and have greater levels of depression, anxiety and substance misuse because of stigma they face For example, a study published in 2016 on men who have sex with men in China found that depression experienced by Chinese men who have sex with men due to community norms and feelings of self-stigma around homosexuality directly affected HIV testing uptake.

A global study in 2013 found that young men who have sex with men experience higher levels of homophobia than older men who have sex with men, and also face greater obstructions to HIV services, housing and employment security. The loss of these forms of security often lead young men who have sex with men to adopt behaviour that puts them at risk of HIV (such as injecting drugs or exchanging sex for money).

Yet the percentage of young men who have sex with men who are able to access cheap condoms, information about how to prevent HIV and other sexually transmitted infections (STIs), HIV and

STI treatment is extremely low. Nearly half of the study's young respondents who were living with HIV were not on antiretroviral treatment, compared to 17% of older respondents.

In 2014, MSMGF (the Global Forum on men who have sex with men and HIV) conducted its third biennial Global Men's Health and Rights Study of just under 5,000 men who have sex with men from countries across the world. The results, published in 2016, indicate significant gaps in HIV prevention and treatment for both HIV-negative and HIV-positive men who have sex with men. It found perceptions and experiences of sexual stigma and discrimination to be associated with lower access to HIV services and lower odds of viral suppression, which is when treatment has successfully reduced the level of HIV in someone's body to such a low level they are in good health and are unlikely to pass the virus on to someone else. Interestingly, participants in the study who reported higher levels of engagement with the gay community were significantly more likely to have had an HIV test and received the result; to have participated in HIV prevention programmes and, for those living with HIV, were significantly more likely to be retained in care, giving them higher odds of viral suppression.

Similarly, a study of men who have sex with men in Tijuana, Mexico found that self-stigma, or what the study describes as 'internalised homophobia' caused by cultural norms of machismo and homophobia, was strongly associated with never having tested for HIV, while testing for HIV was associated with identifying as homosexual or gay and being more 'out' about having sex with men. The study cites evidence of HIV-positive men who have sex with both men and women yet avoid affiliation with the LGBT community out of fear of homophobia. It argues that innovative strategies are needed to engage non-gay-or-bisexual-identifying men who have sex with men in HIV testing programmes without exacerbating experiences of stigma and discrimination.

A large proportion of men who have sex with men in both West and Central Africa and East and Southern Africa also engage in heterosexual sex, often with wives or other long-term female partners. For example, a 2015 study of men who have sex with men in Abidjan, Côte d'Ivoire found the most widespread sexual orientation among men who have sex with men to be bisexuality. The HIV epidemic among men who have sex with men is therefore interlaced with the epidemic in the wider population in these regions.

How Homophobia Affects HIV Service Provision

The provision of HIV services that are specific to the needs of LGBT people remains inadequate in many countries, as the needs of people from these groups are not given priority by governments. HIV data relating to LGBT people is also grossly under-reported, inconclusive or not reported at all. For example, while Ukraine's National Target Program calls for tolerance and less discrimination towards people living with HIV, it does not specifically mention stigma against men who have sex with men or transgender people. As a result, these groups have very limited access to specialised programmes, even in comparison with other key populations such as people who inject drugs and sex workers. In addition, many programmes are typically focused on medical interventions and do not take into account human rights issues.

Homophobia around the World

Despite the important number of countries repealing laws that discriminate against LGBT people, same-sex sexual acts were illegal in 73 countries and five entities as of June 2016. This is a decrease from 92 in 2006. Homosexual acts are punishable by death in 13 states (or parts of) including Sudan, Iran, Saudi Arabia, Nigeria and Somalia, an increase from 9 countries in 2006. Such criminalisation can deter men who have sex with men from seeking out HIV prevention, testing, treatment and other services when they need them.

Societal opinions about the acceptance of homosexuality vary between regions, with acceptance prominent in North America, Western Europe and most of Latin America. Rejection was reported in Muslim nations, Africa, parts of Asia, Central and Eastern Europe and Russia. Secular countries, as opposed to religious countries, are more accepting of homosexuality.

In 2016, the International Lesbian, Gay, Bisexual, Trans and Intersex Association began a yearly global attitudes survey to gather credible data on public attitudes to LGBTI people on every continent. The first year findings included responses from 54 countries and revealed strong regional differences. For example, to the question of 'How would you feel if your neighbour were gay, lesbian or bisexual?', less than half (43%) of African respondents and just 50% of Asian respondents said they would feel 'no concern'. More than three quarters of respondents answered positively in the Americas (81%), Europe (74%) and Oceania (83%). It is notable that 39% of respondents in Africa and 28% of respondents in Asia would be 'very uncomfortable'. The North African states of Egypt (26%), Morocco (33%) and Algeria (34%) displayed the least level of 'no concern' in Africa, and Indonesia (26%), Jordan (27%), Saudi Arabia (32%) in Asia.

Interestingly, more than 50% of participants from each of the countries included in the survey responded favourably to the statement: 'Human rights should be applied to everyone, regardless of whom they feel attracted to or the gender they identify with'. Algeria was the lowest at 50%, and both Ireland and Italy were the highest at 78%. This suggests that many people living in countries with regressive legal and policy frameworks have attitudes that contradict their government's stance.

The Economic Cost of Homophobia

As well as having a very real human cost, homophobia is also damaging to a country's economy. This is because stigma and discrimination based on sexual orientation and identity can result in fewer earnings, and fewer employment opportunities, for people who are LGBT, which results in less money going towards a country's gross domestic product (GDP). The barriers to health care faced by people who are LGBT, coupled with violence and mental health issues experienced by this population due to homophobia, can also cut short the number of years LGBT people are able to work, which again affects GDP.

To highlight this, UNAIDS included findings from the global Homophobic Climate Index (HCI) in its 2016 Prevention Gap Report. The HCI takes into account a country's laws on homosexuality, as well as its levels of 'social homophobia'. The closer the HCI is to 1.0, the higher the homophobia in that country.

The HCI found homophobic laws and social norms could be costing the world up to US $119.1 billion of global GDP each year. It found the highest total cost of homophobia to be in Asia and the Pacific at US $88.3 billion annually, although the region with the highest cost of homophobia as a share of GDP was the Middle East and North Africa, reaching 0.59% of GDP or US $16.92 billion.

The lowest cost of homophobia as a share of GDP was in Western and Central Europe and North America, at 0.13% of GDP, although this was still estimated to be costing the region US $50 billion each year. Homophobia was estimated to be costing Latin America and the Caribbean up to US $8.04 billion, Eastern Europe and Central Asia up to US $10.85 billion and sub-Saharan Africa up to US $4.9 billion.

What Factors put Men who have Sex with Men at Risk of HIV?

The fact that HIV prevalence among men who have sex with men is so high in many countries means that members of this group have an increased chance of being exposed to the virus. This is mainly due to having unprotected sex. However, there are other factors that put men who have sex with men at heightened risk of HIV.

Biological Factors

One of the key reasons for high vulnerability to HIV among this group is that unprotected anal sex carries a higher risk of transmission than vaginal sex. This is because the walls of the anus are thin and more easily torn, creating an entry point for HIV into the bloodstream.

Having a sexually transmitted infection (STI) also makes a person more susceptible to HIV infection. STI rates among men who have sex with men are high and have been rising for the last 20 years. Despite these heightened biological risks, HIV testing and sexual health check-up frequency remains relatively low among this group.

Various studies in different countries have found that men who have sex with men are fearful of experiencing discrimination, moral judgment, mistreatment and confidentiality breaches in healthcare settings. As a result, many men who have sex with men are living with an undiagnosed STI which may put them at higher risk of HIV.

There is a particularly high risk of HIV being transmitted if someone has unprotected sex with a person who has recently become infected. For example, a study in London, United Kingdom (UK) reported that 27% of infections among men who have sex with men were from a partner recently infected with HIV. However, many men who have sex with men who engage in casual sex are unaware of this.

Behavioural Factors

Having multiple sexual partners is common among men who have sex with men, yet many men engaging in casual sex do not use condoms consistently. In 33 countries less than 60% of men who have sex with men had reported using a condom at last anal sex, and only 15 countries had rates higher than 80%.

Data on other STIs among men who have sex with men are further evidence of inconsistent condom use. Access to HIV testing services among men who have sex with men is also varied. In several European and North American cities, men who have sex with men are approaching or have exceeded the 90-90-90 targets, with over 90% of men who have sex with men aware of their HIV status. Yet studies conducted in Kenya, Malawi and South Africa have found that only one in three HIV-positive men who have sex with men were aware of their status, and in Mozambique it was fewer than 10%. A study in India found that only 30% of a cohort of more than 1,000 men who have sex with men living with HIV were aware of their status.

Not testing for HIV means that many men who have sex with men are unaware of their HIV status and may be unaware of the need to take protective measures to prevent onward transmission to others. Alcohol and drugs are a common part of socialising in some communities of men who have sex with men. Being under the influence of drugs or alcohol can make it more likely that people will have unprotected sex and a higher number of sexual partners, increasing the risk of HIV transmission. For instance, a study conducted in India among men who have sex with men found a link between alcohol, increased sexual risk behaviour and HIV acquisition.

In Asia and the Pacific, and North America and Western Europe, evidence is growing that some men who have sex with men are participating in group sex most commonly known as 'chemsex' (also referred to as 'party and play' or 'PNP') under the influence of psychoactive and performance-enhancing drugs. The drugs being used, namely GHB (gamma-hydoxybutyrate), methamphetamine and methedrone, facilitate prolonged sexual sessions and usually involve multiple partners. Data from 2014 suggests around 3 in 10 gay men in the UK engaged in chemsex in the previous year.

Healthcare professionals are particularly concerned with the high-risk behaviours that these drugs induce; a lack of physical inhibition and awareness often means a participant is exposed to multiple partners without protection or to shared drug taking equipment which increases the risk of HIV transmission. In cases where sexual activity is prolonged there is also a concern that participants living with HIV may forget to take ART medication, or that those who are HIV-negative will miss the 72-hour window to be eligible for receiving post-exposure prophylaxis (PEP) after suspected exposure to HIV.

Men in this group often become HIV-positive while still young. Estimates suggest that 4.2% of young men (under-25) who have sex with men are living with HIV. This is more common in countries where HIV prevalence among the whole men who have sex with men population is relatively high. One study carried out in Bangkok found HIV incidence was more than twice as high among men aged 18 to 21 years compared to men over 30 years of age.

Where race intersects with age and sexuality, HIV risk can also be affected. For example, in the USA, young black men (aged between 13 and 24) who have sex with men are around three times more likely to have HIV than white men who have sex with men of the same age.

Young men who have sex with men often find it harder to access HIV services, due to age of consent laws or unsociable opening times. HIV testing and status awareness in 2014 was lower among young men who have sex with men (36%) than among this group as a whole (43%). Data from more than 9,000 USA-based men who have sex with men who took part in an online survey found being young, from a black or ethnic minority, and having a low level of education were all significantly associated with not being aware of HIV status.

Legal Factors

As of 2019, 67 countries criminalised same-sex conduct, affecting the rights of men who have sex with men and other members of the LGBTQ community. In eight countries including Iran, Sudan, Saudi Arabia, Yemen and parts of Nigeria and Somalia, homosexuality is punishable by death. As a result, men who have sex with men are far less likely to access HIV services for fear of their sexual orientation and identity being revealed.

As of 2019, 32 countries restricted people's freedom to express their sexual identity. Some have laws that ban content that 'promote' homosexuality or 'non-traditional' sexual relations. Around 41 countries have laws that restrict non-government organisations (NGOs) that work on LGBTQ issues.

For example, Russia has an anti-propaganda law that it uses to prevent NGOs delivering HIV services to men who have sex with men. Its influence in the region is such that similar laws have also been introduced in Lithuania and Belarus and are also periodically being proposed, then challenged in Ukraine. Parliaments in Kyrgyzstan, Kazakhstan, Poland, Romania, Tajikistan, Azerbaijan, and Armenia have also attempted to pass anti-propaganda laws but none have been successful yet.

Social and Cultural Factors

Many men who have sex with men have experienced homophobic stigma, discrimination and violence. This drives men who have sex with men to hide their identity and sexual orientation. Many fear a negative reaction from healthcare workers. As a result, men who have sex with men are less likely to access HIV services than heterosexuals.

Men who have sex with men are more likely to experience depression due to social isolation and being disconnected from health systems. This can make it harder to cope with aspects of HIV such as adherence to medication.

HIV Prevention Programmes for Men who have Sex with Men

It is evident that prevention strategies are failing to reach this group due to high HIV prevalence in communities around the world. For example, HIV infections among men who have sex with men in Asia are rising and prevalence is 5% or higher in 10 countries in the region. The countries reporting the highest prevalences among MSM are Indonesia (25.8%), Malaysia (21.6%) and Australia (18.3%). Rates among younger men who have sex with men (15-24 years) are especially high.

In Africa, the Middle East, Eastern Europe and Central Asia, government-run HIV services for men who have sex with men are extremely limited, yet hostile legal, policy and social environments sometimes make it difficult for NGOs to fill the service gap.

Reports from 20 countries between 2009 and 2013 show that the percentage of men who have sex with men reached by HIV prevention programmes fell from 59% to 40%. However, access varies greatly between regions and within countries. For example, men who have sex with men on a higher income are more likely to be able to afford, and therefore access, prevention initiatives than those on a low income.

When men who have sex with men are targeted by HIV prevention campaigns they can be extremely effective. It is important that a combination of prevention programmes are available.

In recognition of this, in 2015, a group of international agencies and non-governmental organisations (NGOs) released a tool for use by public health officials, HIV and STI programmes officials, NGOs (both international and community-based) and health workers. The tool, Implementing Comprehensive HIV and STI Programmes with Men Who Have Sex with Men, provides recommendations for HIV prevention, testing and treatment for men who have sex with men and is based on successful community-led approaches.

Condoms and Lubricants

One of the most important prevention responses is to make high-quality condoms, along with water-based lubricants, available and accessible to men who have sex with men. In some countries, gay bars and other known meeting places for men who have sex with men, such as bathhouses, provide and promote condoms and lubricants. For example, the Blue Sky Club in Vietnam is a civil society group that provides 'edutainment' events in local bars and clubs, combining HIV education and condom distribution with entertainment, which are well received by local men who have sex with men. In many settings, providing condoms and lubricants in gay-friendly places is much more effective than expecting men who have sex with men to purchase them from pharmacies, or healthcare settings that they may be fearful of visiting.

Community Empowerment

Some of the most successful HIV programmes aimed at men who have sex with men are community-based and community-led initiatives. These are services and interventions that are designed and led by men who have sex with men, delivered to and for men who have sex with men in locations that people feel comfortable in.

In Sub-saharan Africa, studies have shown how community-based HIV services have seen the greatest response and uptake. One of the main reasons for this is that delivering services outside clinical settings avoids the risk of men who have sex with men having their sexual orientation exposed, which could lead to stigma and discrimination, abuse, violence and arrest.

Training men who have sex with men to educate their peers on HIV prevention including providing prevention commodities such as condoms and lubricants, campaigning for better access to services, and linking people to MSM-friendly HIV services has been shown to effectively reach and engage this population and significantly reduce HIV transmission rates.

This prevention strategy works on the basis that there is an elevated sense of trust between men who have sex with men and their peers, lowering fears of stigma. Organisations staffed by men who have sex with men are also more credible and accessible to recipients.

Peer Training in the Philippines

In the Philippines, one initiative attempted to help civil society engage with local government in the HIV response. Eighteen community-based groups were set up and 200 men who have sex with men and transgender people were trained in sexual health and rights.

After three years, community leadership led to dialogue with local government officials on HIV, gender and human rights issues. One outcome of this process was an anti-discrimination ordinance in the city of Cebu in 2012 which prohibits discrimination on the basis of sexual orientation, gender identity and health status (including HIV).

HIV Testing Initiatives

Two of the most effective ways to encourage HIV testing among men who have sex with men is to permit home-based testing and provide community-based testing.

Community-based testing is HIV testing carried out at local pop-up clinics or mobile vans in an area that men who have sex with men feel comfortable in. This removes the need to test in clinics where men who have sex with men may experience discrimination and mistreatment. Home-based testing has the benefit of the person testing for HIV being able to avoid identification by healthcare workers. The privacy of conducting an HIV test alone at home makes this an appealing option for many men who have sex with men. One study in Brazil found that 90% of men who have sex with men participants would use self-testing kits, although concerns included receiving the result alone and being able to read the result properly.

Another study conducted in Australia found that HIV self-testing doubled frequency of testing among men who have sex with men at high risk of HIV, and quadrupled the frequency among non-recent testers, compared with standard care. It also showed that the availability of self-testing kits did not reduce the frequency of facility-based HIV testing. A study conducted in Myanmar on self-testing found the majority of men who have sex with men expressed a preference for this type of testing compared to testing carried out by community-based organisations.

HIV self-testing should be made more widely available to help increase testing and earlier diagnosis. Men who have sex with men should be educated about the use of self-testing kits, to heighten their confidence in using one as an alternative to testing at regular healthcare settings. For example, an HIV self-test kit vending machine designed with the input of gay men has been installed at various gay venues in the UK, including saunas, bars, clubs, pharmacies, university campuses and train stations. The first machine was installed in Brighton, and eight times more men took up testing via the vending machine compared to testing offered by community outreach workers at the same venue during the same period.

PrEP

PrEP is a single pill taken every day by people who are at risk of HIV exposure. Research has shown that pre-exposure prophylaxis (PrEP) can reduce HIV transmission among men who have sex with men by 92%. WHO states that if its use is scaled up, an estimated 20% to 25% of new HIV infections among this population could be prevented?

Despite expanding evidence of its effectiveness in HIV prevention, access to PrEP remains limited. As of 2018, 46 countries had regulatory approval for PrEP. It is being introduced nationally in 10 countries, and a further 29 have smaller-scale PrEP projects, some of which include men who have sex with men.

There are indications that, where individuals have been able to access it, PrEP has had considerable success in preventing new HIV infections among men who have sex with men, even in countries where it is not available within national healthcare systems. For example, in 2016, sexual health clinics in London reported a 40% drop in the number of new HIV diagnoses among men who have sex with men. Several clinics have attributed this to the purchasing of generic PrEP online, as the decline in new infections coincided with a rapid increase in the number of men buying PrEP online. In 2017, the UK made PrEP available to 10,000 men who have sex with men across 200 UK clinics.

In order for PrEP to provide effective prevention it must be taken correctly and consistently. Men who have sex with men should be counselled and informed about the correct use of PrEP before it is offered. PrEP does not provide protection against STIs, and if not taken consistently is much less effective, so does not replace other prevention options like condoms.

There have been concerns that PrEP use could lead to a reduction in condom use, however these have been refuted by studies, including the PROUD study in the UK. A 2019 evidence review analysing 20 PrEP studies and trials found high rates of STIs among men who have sex with men who use PrEP. However, this does not necessarily mean PrEP use is causing STI rates to rise.

A study published in 2018 points to the fact that STI rates among men who have sex with men have been rising for the past 20 years, which means PrEP alone cannot explain the increase. Results suggest that there are other behavioural factors to consider, such as changes in mixing patterns within risk groups, use of smartphone dating applications, group sex, recreational drug use, and access to healthcare.

PEP

Post-exposure prophylaxis (PEP) is taken after potential exposure to HIV. WHO recommends offering PEP to men who have sex with men as part of a package of prevention options. It must also be coupled with counselling about the importance of finishing the treatment course. One study found that an average of just 67% of men who have sex with men completed the 28-day course, limiting the effectiveness of PEP.

However, French study among men who have sex with men who had taken previously taken PEP found many reported negative experiences. These included 'awkward' encounters when trying to access PEP at a health clinic, experiencing uneasiness and shame when accessing PEP at a hospital, unpleasant interactions and judgements from medical staff, side effects, and prevention messages that were 'inconsistent with real life'. This highlights the possible barriers to PEP men who have sex with men experience, which may compromise uptake.

Bible and Homosexuality

For Christians to whom the Bible is God's very written word, it is widely understood that God produced its contents through inspired human authors to tell the story of God's creation, how sin entered the world, and the redemption that is found through Jesus Christ and his salvation.

In this light, the Bible is often seen as the primary source that helps us figure out how the people of God should live. It is important to point out though that being God's word doesn't mean we come to understand what is right or wrong through reading isolated passages. Rather, most Christians make these difficult determinations by studying what the whole of Scripture says regarding a specific topic, exploring the linguistic, historical and cultural context within which the words were written, and then putting these discoveries in conversation with what we know to be true of the character of God more broadly. While the book of Hebrews affirms that "Jesus Christ is the same yesterday, today and forever," our ability to understand and apply the Bible's teachings changes and deepens as we grow in our faith and learn more about the world.

What is Biblical Interpretation?

Whenever any person opens the Bible, they begin a process of interpretation. Individuals attracted to others of the same sex are regularly told they are 'elevating' their experience over Scripture when they come to affirming conclusions about their relationships and identities. They are often told this is a direct rejection of the Bible's authority in their lives. But, the question is begged, is this a fair and accurate assessment? Are there such things as neutral interpretations? Is there one true or correct way to interpret the Bible, and if so, who determines that?

The study of biblical interpretation is called hermeneutics, and helps us to address these kinds of questions. Hermeneutics is what we do when we take a text and ask not just "what does this say," but "what does this mean?" In asking, "What does the Bible say about homosexuality" (or more appropriately stated, "what does the Bible say about attraction to someone of the same sex,") our task is to explore what the relevant biblical passages on the topic meant in their original context and what they mean for us today. More specifically, we are seeking to determine if the biblical writers were condemning specific practices related to sexuality in the ancient world, or were they indeed condemning all same-sex relationships of any kind for the rest of time?

Troubling the Waters of Exclusionary Interpretations

For many evangelicals and other conservative Christians, the answer to this question is 'yes'. Their interpretation is that same-sex relationships are not able to reflect God's creative intent. Their reasoning includes, but is not limited to:

- What they were always taught was an "unbiased" interpretation of the relevant passages.

- A core belief that sex differentiation is an indispensable part of Christian marriage.

The latter being of tremendous importance, because according to the New Testament, marriage is a primary symbol of the love between Christ and his beloved "bride," the church..To them, same-sex couples (and single people for that matter) are uniquely excluded from participation in this symbol on the basis of a failure to perform one or more dimensions of an often vague category referred to as 'gender complementarity.'

While gender complimentarity is indeed rooted in passages from Genesis 1 and 2, it is worth noting that these stories say God began by creating human beings of male and female sex (defined as the complex result of combinations between chromosomes, gonads, genes, and genitals) but there is nothing that indicates in Scripture that God only created this binary. This account says little to nothing about gender, (the social and cultural norms and practices corresponding to what is considered masculine and feminine.) Two dimensions of the text that become important in considering the biblical affirmation of intersex, transgender, non-binary, and other gender diverse people. To further complicate the argument against same-sex relationships, Scripture doesn't suggest that respecting biblical authority means Christians should reject experience as a teacher. In fact, what Jesus said in the Sermon on the Mount about good trees bearing good fruit and bad trees bearing bad fruit (Matthew 7:17-18) indicates experience should inform how we learn God's truth. This was what allowed the first Christians to decide to include gentiles who were not keeping the Old Testament law in the early church (Acts 15:1-19). It also was the basis for the Christian arguments that put an end to slavery and has supported movements for women's equality throughout church history as well.

The call to reform Christian teaching in these instances didn't suggest that human experience should be held over Scripture. What they did suggest was that the obvious exclusion, injustice and destructive outcomes of widely held beliefs should take Christians back to the text to consider a different perspective, one which might better reflect the heart of God. While some Christians say that the Bible presents a variety of hard teachings as well as promising suffering for followers of Jesus (Matthew 16:24), it never endorses oppression. In order for suffering to be Christ-like, it must be redemptive. Redemptive suffering does not uphold oppressive forces but always expresses resistance against them. For all of these reasons and more, Christians have a moral imperative to reconsider their interpretation of what the Bible says about LGBTQ identities.

So then what are those Passages talking about?

While the six passages that address same-sex eroticism in the ancient world are negative about the practices they mention, there is no evidence that these in any way speak to same-sex relationships of love and mutuality. To the contrary, the amount of cultural, historical and linguistic data surrounding how sexuality in the cultures of the biblical authors operated demonstrates that what was being condemned in the Bible is very different than the committed same-sex partnerships we know and see today. The stories of Sodom and Gomorrah (Genesis 19) and the Levite's concubine (Judges 19) are about sexual violence and the Ancient Near East's stigma toward violating male honor. The injunction that "man must not lie with man" (Leviticus 18:22, 20:13) coheres with the context of a society anxious about their health, continuing family lineages, and retaining the distinctiveness of Israel as a nation. Each time the New Testament addresses the topic in a list of vices (1 Corinthians 6:9, 1 Timothy 1:10), the argument being made is more than likely about the sexual exploitation of young men by older men, a practice called pederasty, and what we read in the Apostle Paul's letter to the Romans is a part of a broader indictment against idolatry and excessive, self-centered lust that is driven by desire to "consume" rather than to love and to serve as outlined for Christian partnership elsewhere in the Bible.

While it is likely that Jews and Christians in the 1st century had little to no awareness of a category like sexual orientation, this doesn't mean that the biblical authors were wrong. What it does mean, at a minimum, is that continued opposition toward same-sex relationships and LGBTQ identities must be based on something other than these biblical texts, which brings us back to a theology of Christian marriage or partnership.

If neither Sex Differentiation nor Gender Complementarity are the Basis for Christian Partnership, then what is?

While the work to undo the decades-long, dominant and exclusionary interpretations of these passages are important, its emphasis over and against the affirming dimensions of Christian theology for LGBTQ people has stifled exploration of a deeper meaning of sexuality for everyone. From Genesis 2, to Matthew 19, to Ephesians 5, what these passages make explicit (and is echoed throughout the rest of Scripture): marriage is sacred for Christians because it can represent the enduring love between Christ and the Church. Christian partnership creates an opportunity to live out God's love. While some kind of difference seems to be important in embodying this metaphor, understanding that all our differences can lead to empathy, compassion, good listening, sacrifice, and what it means to "love our neighbor as ourselves," there is scant evidence that it is our biology or our views of gender that are the required difference.

Anyone who has ever been in an intimate relationship of any kind can testify to the range of differences (and resulting conflicts) that are an inherent part of any two personalities attempting to integrate their lives. And remember, those who are not married but are not LGBTQ, like single people or people whose spouses have passed, are embraced as Christians. The larger point here is that God's design for Christian partnership is about reflecting the truest and sweetest love that anyone could know; that is the self-giving, ever-enduring, liberating love between God and creation made possible for us through Christ. A tall order, but nevertheless something countless LGBTQ individuals and couples have been living into and continue to live into today.

LGBT Terminology

The words we use to talk about lesbian, gay, bisexual and transgender (LGBT) people and issues can have a powerful impact on our conversations. The right words can help open people's hearts and minds, while other words can create distance or confusion.

Designed for new allies who often face a confusing array of terminology and descriptions, this short guide offers an overview of essential vocabulary to use and avoid. For messages and approaches that can be used to talk about various issues.

Gay, Lesbian and Bisexual

Terms to Use	Usage Examples	Terms to Avoid	Explanation
• gay (adj.) • lesbian (n. or adj.) • bisexual, bi (adj.)	"gay people" "gay man/men" "lesbian couple" "bisexual people" "He is gay." / "She is a lesbian." / "He is bisexual."	• "homosexual" • "gay" (n.) (as in, "He is a gay.")	Gay is an adjective, not a noun; it is sometimes used as a shorthand term encompassing gay, lesbian and bisexual orientations (though not transgender people or gender identity). Also, while many lesbians may identify as gay, the term lesbian(s) is clearer when talking only about a woman or women. Opponents of LGBT equality often use words like "homosexual" to stigmatize gay people by reducing their lives to purely sexual terms.
being gay/lesbian/bisexual	"She talked about being gay/a lesbian/ bisexual." "He discussed being bisexual."	• "homosexuality" • "lesbianism" • "That's so gay." (a hurtful slur)	Talking about a person's "homosexuality" can, in some cases, reduce the life of that person to purely sexual terms. Talk about being gay/lesbian/ bisexual instead. Also, the term "lesbianism" is considered pejorative, as is using "gay" as an insult or slur.
• lesbian, gay, bisexual and transgender (on first usage) • gay and transgender (on repeated subsequent references, as needed for brevity, TV or radio ads, etc.) • LGBT (with LGBT and allied audiences; in longer written documents such as reports, after defining)	"people who are lesbian, gay, bisexual or transgender" "laws that protect gay and transgender people" "Only 29% of LGBT adults in the United States report they are thriving financially, compared to 39% of non-LGBT adults.	• "LGBT" (with those who are not yet strong supporters)	Reference both sexual orientation and gender identity when talking about issues pertaining to the entire LGBT community. The abbreviation LGBT is commonly used within the LGBT movement and is essential when talking with LGBT and strongly supportive audiences; however, it can confuse people who are unfamiliar with its meaning and alienate those who aren't yet strong supporters. When talking to mainstream media

			and audiences, try to use lesbian, gay, bisexual and transgender on first reference for clarity and inclusion—but if there is a need for brevity in repeated subsequent references, shorten to gay and transgender rather than "LGBT." Use LGBT in longer written documents such as reports after the abbreviation is defined.
• sexual orientation • orientation	"a person's sexual orientation" "Sexual orientation can be a complex topic. A person's orientation is..."	• "sexual preference" • "gay/lesbian/ bisexual lifestyle" • "same-sex attractions" • "sexual identity"	The term "sexual preference" is used by opponents to suggest that being gay, lesbian or bisexual is a choice, and therefore can be changed or "cured." Similarly, the term "lifestyle" is used to stigmatize LGBT people and suggest that their lives should be viewed only through a sexual lens. Just as one would not talk about a "straight lifestyle," don't talk about a gay, lesbian or bisexual "lifestyle."

Transgender

The term transgender refers to people whose gender identity (the sense of gender that every person knows inside) or gender expression is different from their sex at birth. At some point in their lives, transgender people decide they must live their lives as the gender they have always known themselves to be, and often transition to living as that gender.

Terms to Use	Usage Examples	Terms to Avoid	Explanation
• transgender (adj.)	"transgender person" "transgender man" "transgender woman" "transgender advocate" "protecting people who are transgender"	• "transgendered" • "a transgender" (n.) • "transgenders" (n.) • "transvestite" • "tranny"	Transgender is an adjective, not a noun. Be careful not to call someone "a transgender." Do not add an unnecessary "-ed" to the term ("transgendered"), which connotes a condition of some kind. Always use a transgender person's chosen name. Also, a person who identifies as a certain gender should be referred to using pronouns consistent with that gender. If it isn't possible to ask what pronoun a person would prefer, use the pronoun that is consistent with the person's appearance and

	"I'm a transgender man. I was born and raised as a girl, but inside I always knew I was male. Many years ago I transitioned from female to male, and now I live life as the man I've always known myself to be."		gender expression. The term trans, often used within the LGBT community, may not be understood by unfamiliar audiences. While terms like transgender man and transgender woman are commonly used, they are not universally understood. Unfamiliar audiences often think, for example, that a transgender man is a man who identifies as a woman. Consider pairing these terms with a reference to a person's direction of transition. Not everyone who is transgender identifies that way. Because transgender men are men, and transgender women are women, some transgender people may simply identify as male or female, without modifiers.
• gender identity • gender expression	"fair and equal treatment based on gender identity and expression.	• "sexual identity" (the correct term is gender identity)	The terms gender identity (one's internal sense of gender) and gender expression (how a person outwardly expresses that gender) are not interchangeable. These terms can be unfamiliar and confusing to many people; referring to transgender people is often clearer.
• transition	"A transgender woman grows up knowing she's a girl, even though she was born and raised as a boy. So later in life she transitions to live as a woman."	• "sex change" • "sex-change operation" • "pre-operative" / "post-operative"	Transition is the accurate term that does not fixate on a person's anatomy or on surgeries, which many transgender people do not or cannot undergo. It can also be helpful to clarify a person's direction of transition (for example, from female to male) when first referencing that a person is transgender.
• people who are not transgender	"transgender people and non-transgender people alike"	• "cisgender" (with those who are not yet strong supporters)	The term "cisgender" tends to confuse and alienate unfamiliar audiences. Use everyday language that is clear and relatable instead.
• someone who doesn't identify as either male or female	"Most people know from childhood that they're male or female. But some people don't fit into either gender, and don't identify as either male or female."	• "nonbinary"/ "gendernonconforming"/ "genderqueer" (with those who are not yet strong supporters)	Terms like "non-binary" and "gender non-conforming," while comfortable and familiar for many in the LGBT community, tend to confuse and alienate unfamiliar, conflicted audiences and are seen as insider-speak or talking over their heads. Instead, use everyday language that describes these concepts in more relatable, non-insider ways.

Talking about LGBT Issues

Talking about LGBT issues Conversations about LGBT people and equality are most effective when we can talk in genuine, emotionally compelling ways that connect with the values of our audience. Showing people how they can support LGBT people and equality in a way that is consistent with their beliefs and values can help people work through any inner conflict they may feel. It also makes it more difficult to ignore or dismiss the discrimination and other harms that LGBT people face.

When talking about equality for LGBT people, use language that emphasizes our common values, beliefs, hopes and dreams— and which reminds people that LGBT people are everyday Americans who live everyday lives.

Terms to Use	Usage Example	Terms to Avoid	Explanation
• fair, equal treatment • treating people fairly and equally	"Everyone, including LGBT people, should be treated fairly and equally by the laws of our state."	• "rights" • "civil rights" • "gay rights"/"LGBT rights"	Don't talk about "rights," "civil rights," or make direct comparisons between different kinds of discrimination, especially when it comes to discrimination based on race. Such comparisons can alienate many African Americans and others, creating unnecessary distance where there would otherwise be common ground.
• discrimination • rejection • exclusion • unfairness	"Protecting people from discrimination is about treating others as we want to be treated. It's not for me to judge."	• "hate"/"haters"/ • "hatred" "bigot"/"bigots"/ • "bigotry" "prejudice"	Don't descend into name-calling. Calling anti-LGBT opponents "bigoted" or "hateful" can alienate those who are honestly wrestling with the issues. Instead, use language that is measured and relatable to create empathy and a sense of how discrimination hurts LGBT people and their families.
• anti-gay/antitransgender/antiLGBT activists • opponents	"the hurtful rhetoric of anti-gay activists" "those who oppose protecting LGBT people from discrimination"	• "anti-gay religious extremists/ extremism" • "anti-gay Christian groups"	Many religious people and faith traditions support LGBT people. Avoid language that unfairly paints an entire religious tradition or denomination, or religion more broadly, as being anti-LGBT or extremist.

History of LGBT Movements

Social movements, organizing around the acceptance and rights of persons who might today identify as LGBT or queer, began as responses to centuries of persecution by church, state and medical authorities. Where homosexual activity or deviance from established gender roles/dress was banned by law or traditional custom, such condemnation might be communicated through sensational public trials, exile, medical warnings and language from the pulpit. These paths of persecution entrenched homophobia for centuries—but also alerted entire populations to the existence of difference. Whether an individual recognized they, too, shared this identity and were at risk, or dared to speak out for tolerance and change, there were few organizations or resources before the scientific and political revolutions of the 18th and 19th centuries. Gradually, the growth of a public media and ideals of human rights drew together activists from all walks of life, who drew courage from sympathetic medical studies, banned literature, emerging sex research and a climate of greater democracy. By the 20th century, a movement in recognition of gays and lesbians was underway, abetted by the social climate of feminism and new anthropologies of difference. However, throughout 150 years of homosexual social movements (roughly from the 1870s to today), leaders and organizers struggled to address the very different concerns and identity issues of gay men, women identifying as lesbians, and others identifying as gender variant or nonbinary. White, male and Western activists whose groups and theories gained leverage against homophobia did not necessarily represent the range of racial, class and national identities complicating a broader LGBT agenda. Women were often left out altogether.

What is the pre-history of LGBT activism? Most historians agree that there is evidence of homosexual activity and same-sex love, whether such relationships were accepted or persecuted, in every documented culture. We know that homosexuality existed in ancient Israel simply because it is prohibited in the Bible, whereas it flourished between both men and women in Ancient Greece. Substantial evidence also exists for individuals who lived at least part of their lives as a different gender than assigned at birth. From the lyrics of same-sex desire inscribed by Sappho in the seventh century BCE to youths raised as the opposite sex in cultures ranging from Albania to Afghanistan; from the "female husbands" of Kenya to the Native American "Two-Spirit," alternatives to the Western male-female and heterosexual binaries thrived across millennia and culture. These realities gradually became known to the West via travelers' diaries, the church records of missionaries, diplomats' journals, and in reports by medical anthropologists. Such eyewitness accounts in the era before other media were of course riddled with the biases of the (often) Western or white observer, and added to beliefs that homosexual practices were other, foreign, savage, a medical issue, or evidence of a lower racial hierarchy. The peaceful flowering of early trans or bisexual acceptance in different indigenous civilizations met with opposition from European and Christian colonizers.

In the age of European exploration and empire-building, Native American, North African and Pacific Islander cultures accepting of "Two-Spirit" people or same-sex love shocked European invaders who objected to any deviation from a limited understanding of "masculine" and "feminine" roles. The European powers enforced their own criminal codes against what was called sodomy in the New World: the first known case of homosexual activity receiving a death sentence in North America occurred in 1566, when the Spanish executed a Frenchman in Florida. Against the emerging backdrop of national power and Christian faith, what might have been learned about same-sex love or gender identity was buried in scandal. Ironically, both wartime conflict between emerging nations and the departure or deaths of male soldiers left women behind to live together and fostered strong alliances between men as well. Same-sex companionship thrived where it was frowned upon for unmarried, unrelated males and females to mingle or socialize freely. Women's relationships in particular escaped scrutiny since there was no threat of pregnancy. Nonetheless, in much of the world, female sexual activity and sensation were curtailed wherever genital circumcision practices made clitoridectomy an ongoing custom.

Where European dress—a clear marker of gender—was enforced by missionaries, we find another complicated history of both gender identity and resistance. Biblical interpretation made it illegal for a woman to wear pants or a man to adopt female dress, and sensationalized public trials warned against "deviants" but also made such martyrs and heroes popular: Joan of Arc is one example, and the chilling origins of the word "faggot" include a stick of wood used in public burnings of gay men. Despite the risks of defying severe legal codes, cross-dressing flourished in early modern Europe and America. Women and girls, economically oppressed by the sexism which kept them from jobs and economic/education opportunities designated for men only, might pass as male in order to gain access to coveted experiences or income. This was a choice made by many women who were not necessarily transgender in identity. Women "disguised" themselves as men, sometimes for extended periods of years, in order to fight in the military (Deborah Sampson), to work as pirates (Mary Read and Anne Bonney), attend medical school, etc. Both men and women who lived as a different gender were often only discovered after their deaths, as the extreme differences in male vs. female clothing and grooming in much of Western culture made "passing" surprisingly easy in certain environments. Moreover, roles in the arts where women were banned from working required that men be recruited to play female roles, often creating a high-status, competitive market for those we might today identify as transwomen, in venues from Shakespeare's theatre to Japanese Kabuki to the Chinese opera. This acceptance of performance artists, and the popularity of "drag" humor cross-culturally, did not necessarily mark the start of transgender advocacy, but made the arts an often accepting sanctuary for LGBT individuals who built theatrical careers based around disguise and illusion.

The era of sexology studies is where we first see a small, privileged cluster of medical authorities begin promoting a limited tolerance of those born "invert." In Western history, we find little formal study of what was later called homosexuality before the 19th century, beyond medical texts identifying women with large clitorises as "tribades" and severe punishment codes for male homosexual acts. Early efforts to understand the range of human sexual behavior came from European doctors and scientists including Carl von Westphal, Richard von Krafft-Ebing and Havelock Ellis. Their writings were sympathetic to the concept of a homosexual or bisexual orientation occurring naturally in an identifiable segment of humankind, but the writings of Krafft-Ebing and Ellis also labeled a "third sex" degenerate and abnormal. Sigmund Freud, writing in the same era, did not consider homosexuality an illness or a crime and believed bisexuality to be an innate aspect beginning with undetermined gender development in the womb. Yet Freud also felt that lesbian desires were an immaturity women could overcome through heterosexual marriage and male dominance. These writings gradually trickled down to a curious public through magazines and presentations, reaching men and women desperate to learn more about those like themselves, including some like English writer Radclyffe Hall who willingly accepted the idea of being a "congenital invert." German researcher Magnus Hirschfeld went on to gather a broader range of information by founding Berlin's Institute for Sexual Science, Europe's best library archive of materials on gay cultural history. His efforts, and Germany's more liberal laws and thriving gay bar scene between the two World Wars, contrasted with the backlash, in England, against gay and lesbian writers such as Oscar Wilde and Radclyffe Hall. With the rise of Hitler's Third Reich, however, the former tolerance demonstrated by Germany's Scientific Humanitarian Committee vanished. Hirschfeld's great library was destroyed and the books burnt by Nazis on May 10, 1933.

In the United States, there were few attempts to create advocacy groups supporting gay and lesbian relationships until after World War II. However, prewar gay life flourished in urban centers such as New York's Greenwich Village and Harlem during the Harlem Renaissance of the 1920s. The blues music of African-American women showcased varieties of lesbian desire, struggle and humor; these performances, along with male and female drag stars, introduced a gay underworld to straight patrons during Prohibition's defiance of race and sex codes in speakeasy clubs. The disruptions of World War II allowed formerly isolated gay men and women to meet as soldiers and war workers; and other volunteers were uprooted from small towns and posted worldwide. Many minds were opened by wartime, during which LGBT people were both tolerated in military service and officially sentenced to death camps in the Holocaust. This increasing awareness of an existing and vulnerable population, coupled with Sen. Joseph McCarthy's investigation of homosexuals holding government jobs during the early 1950s outraged writers and federal employees whose own lives were shown to be second-class under the law, including Frank Kameny, Barbara Gittings, Allen Ginsberg and Harry Hay. Awareness of a burgeoning civil rights movement (Martin Luther King's key organizer Bayard Rustin was a gay man) led to the first American-based political demands for fair treatment of gays and lesbians in mental health, public policy and employment. Studies such as Alfred Kinsey's 1947 Kinsey Report suggested a far greater range of homosexual identities and behaviors than previously understood, with Kinsey creating a "scale" or spectrum ranging from complete heterosexual to complete homosexual.

The primary organization for gay men as an oppressed cultural minority was the Mattachine Society, founded in 1950 by Harry Hay and Chuck Rowland. Other important homophile organizations on the West Coast included One, Inc., founded in 1952, and the first lesbian support network Daughters of Bilitis, founded in 1955 by Phyllis Lyon and Del Martin. Through meetings and publications, these groups offered information and outreach to thousands. These first organizations soon found support from prominent sociologists and psychologists. In 1951, Donald Webster Cory published "The Homosexual in America", asserting that gay men and lesbians were a legitimate minority group, and in 1953 Evelyn Hooker, PhD, won a grant from the National Institute of Mental Health to study gay men. Her groundbreaking paper, presented in 1956, demonstrated that gay men were as well-adjusted as heterosexual men, often more so. But it would not be until 1973 that the American Psychiatric Association removed homosexuality as an "illness" classification in its diagnostic manual. Throughout the 1950s and 60s, gay men and lesbians continued to be at risk for psychiatric lockup as well as jail, losing jobs, and/or child custody when courts and clinics defined gay love as sick, criminal or immoral.

As the civil rights movement won new legislation outlawing racial discrimination, the first gay rights demonstrations took place in Philadelphia and Washington, D.C., led by longtime activists Frank Kameny and Barbara Gittings. The turning point for gay liberation came on June 28, 1969, when patrons of the popular Stonewall Inn in New York's Greenwich Village fought back against ongoing police raids of their neighborhood bar. Stonewall is still considered a watershed moment of gay pride and has been commemorated since the 1970s with "pride marches" held every June across the United States. Recent scholarship has called for better acknowledgement of the roles that drag performers, people of color, bisexuals and transgender patrons played in the Stonewall Riots.

The gay liberation movement of the 1970s saw myriad political organizations spring up, often at odds with one another. Frustrated with the male leadership of most gay liberation groups, lesbians influenced by the feminist movement of the 1970s formed their own collectives, record labels, music festivals, newspapers, bookstores, and publishing houses, and called for lesbian rights in mainstream feminist groups like the National Organization for Women (NOW). Gatherings such as women's music concerts, bookstore readings and lesbian festivals well beyond the United States were extraordinarily successful in organizing women to become activists; the feminist movement against domestic violence also assisted women to leave abusive marriages, while retaining custody of children became a paramount issue for lesbian mothers.

Expanding religious acceptance for gay men and women of faith, the first out gay minister was ordained by the United Church of Christ in 1972. Other gay and lesbian church and synagogue congregations soon followed. Parents and Friends of Lesbians and Gays (PFLAG), formed in 1972, offered family members greater support roles in the gay rights movement. And political action exploded through the National Gay and Lesbian Task Force, the Human Rights Campaign, the election of openly gay and lesbian representatives like Elaine Noble and Barney Frank, and, in 1979, the first march on Washington for gay rights. The increasing expansion of a global LGBT rights movement suffered a setback during the 1980s, as the gay male community was decimated by the AIDS epidemic, demands for compassion and medical funding led to renewed coalitions between men and women as well as angry street theatre by groups like AIDS Coalition to Unleash Power (ACT UP) and Queer Nation. Enormous marches on Washington drew as many as one million gay rights supporters in 1987 and again in 1993. Right wing religious movements, spurred on by beliefs that AIDS was God's punishment, expanded via direct mail. A New Right coalition of political lobby groups competed with national LGBT organizations in Washington, seeking to create religious exemptions from any new LGBT rights protections. In the same era, one wing of the political gay movement called for an end to military expulsion of gay, lesbian and bisexual soldiers, with the high-profile case of Col. Margarethe Cammermeyer publicized through a made-for- television movie, "Serving in Silence." In spite of the patriotism and service of gay men and lesbians in uniform, the uncomfortable and unjust compromise "Don't Ask, Don't Tell" emerged as an alternative to decades of military witch hunts and dishonorable discharges. Yet more service members ended up being discharged under DADT.

During in the last decade of the 20th century, millions of Americans watched as actress Ellen DeGeneres came out on national television in April 1997, heralding a new era of gay celebrity power and media visibility—although not without risks. Celebrity performers, both gay and heterosexual, continued to be among the most vocal activists calling for tolerance and equal rights.

Milestones in LGBT Rights Movement

1. December 10, 1924: The Society for Human Rights is founded by Henry Gerber in Chicago. The society is the first gay rights organization as well as the oldest documented in America. After

receiving a charter from the state of Illinois, the society publishes the first American publication for homosexuals, Friendship and Freedom. Soon after its founding, the society disbands due to political pressure.

2. 1948: Biologist and sex researcher Alfred Kinsey publishes Sexual Behavior in the Human Male. From his research Kinsey concludes that -homosexual behavior is not restricted to people who identify themselves as homosexual and that 37% of men have enjoyed homosexual activities at least once. While psychologists and psychiatrists in the 1940s consider homosexuality a form of illness, the findings surprise many conservative notions about sexuality.

3. November 11, 1950: In Los Angeles, gay rights activist Harry Hay founds America's first sustained national gay rights organization. In an attempt to change public perception of homosexuality, the Mattachine Society aims to "eliminate discrimination, derision, prejudice and bigotry," to assimilate homosexuals into mainstream society, and to cultivate the notion of an "ethical homosexual culture."

4. December 15, 1950: A Senate report titled "Employment of Homosexuals and Other Sex Perverts in Government" is distributed to members of Congress after the federal government had covertly investigated employees' sexual orientation at the beginning of the Cold War. The report states since homosexuality is a mental illness, homosexuals "constitute security risks" to the nation because "those who engage in overt acts of perversion lack the emotional stability of normal persons."

Over the previous few years, more than 4,380 gay men and women had been discharged from the military and around 500 fired from their jobs with the government. The purging will become known as the "lavender scare."

4. April, 1952: The American Psychiatric Association lists homosexuality as a sociopathic personality disturbance in its first publication of the Diagnostic and Statistical Manual of Mental Disorders. Immediately following the manual's release, many professionals in medicine, mental health and social sciences criticize the categorization due to lack of empirical and scientific data.

5. April 27, 1953: President Dwight Eisenhower signs Executive Order 10450, banning homosexuals from working for the federal government or any of its private contractors. The Order lists homosexuals as security risks, along with alcoholics and neurotics.

6. September 21, 1955: In San Francisco, the Daughters of Bilitis becomes the first lesbian rights organization in the United States. The organization hosts social functions, providing alternatives to lesbian bars and clubs, which are frequently raided by police.

August 30, 1956: American psychologist Evelyn Hooker shares her paper "The Adjustment of the Male Overt Homosexual" at the American Psychological Association Convention in Chicago. After administering psychological tests, such as the Rorschach, to groups of homosexual and heterosexual males, Hooker's research concludes homosexuality is not a clinical entity and that heterosexuals and homosexuals do not differ significantly. Hooker's experiment becomes very influential, changing clinical perceptions of homosexuality.

8. January 13, 1958: In the landmark case One, Inc. v. Olesen, the United States Supreme Court rules in favor of the First Amendment rights of the lesbian, gay, bisexual and transgender (LGBT)

magazine "One: The Homosexual Magazine." The suit was filed after the U.S. Postal Service and FBI declared the magazine obscene material, and it marks the first time the United States Supreme Court rules in favor of homosexuals.

9. January 1, 1962: Illinois repeals its sodomy laws, becoming the first U.S. state to decriminalize homosexuality.

10. July 4, 1965: At Independence Hall in Philadelphia, picketers begin staging the first Reminder Day to call public attention to the lack of civil rights for LGBT people. The gatherings will continue annually for five years.

11. April 21, 1966: Members of the Mattachine Society stage a "sip-in" at the Julius Bar in Greenwich Village, where the New York Liquor Authority prohibits serving gay patrons in bars on the basis that homosexuals are "disorderly." Society president Dick Leitsch and other members announce their homosexuality and are immediately refused service.

Following the sip-in, the Mattachine Society will sue the New York Liquor Authority. Although no laws are overturned, the New York City Commission on Human Rights declares that homosexuals have the right to be served.

12. August, 1966: After transgender customers become raucous in a 24-hour San Francisco cafeteria, management calls police. When a police officer manhandles one of the patrons, she throws coffee in his face and a riot ensues, eventually spilling out onto the street, destroying police and public property.

Following the riot, activists established the National Transsexual Counseling Unit, the first peer-run support and advocacy organization in the world.

13. June 28, 1969: Patrons of the Stonewall Inn in Greenwich Village riot when police officers attempt to raid the popular gay bar around 1am. Since its establishment in 1967, the bar had been frequently raided by police officers trying to clean up the neighborhood of "sexual deviants."

Angry gay youth clash with aggressive police officers in the streets, leading to a three-day riot during which thousands of protestors receive only minimal local news coverage. Nonetheless, the event will be credited with reigniting the fire behind America's modern LGBT rights movement.

14. June 28, 1970: Christopher St. Liberation Day commemorates the one-year anniversary of the Stonewall riots. Following the event, thousands of members of the LGBT community march through New York into Central Park, in what will be considered America's first gay pride parade.

In the coming decades, the annual gay pride parade will spread to dozens of countries around the world.

15. December 15, 1973: The board of the American Psychiatric Association votes to remove homosexuality from its list of mental illnesses.

16. January, 1974: Kathy Kozachenko becomes the first openly gay American elected to public office when she wins a seat on the Ann Arbor, Michigan City Council.

17. June 7, 1977: Singer and conservative Southern Baptist Anita Bryant leads a successful campaign with the "Save Our Children" Crusade to repeal a gay rights ordinance in Dade County, Florida. Bryant faces severe backlash from gay rights supporters across the U.S. The gay rights ordinance will not be reinstated in Dade County until December 1, 1998, more than 20 years later.

18. November 8, 1977: Harvey Milk wins a seat on the San Francisco Board of Supervisors and is responsible for introducing a gay rights ordinance protecting gays and lesbians from being fired from their jobs. Milk also leads a successful campaign against Proposition 6, an initiative forbidding homosexual teachers.

A year later, on November 27, 1978, former city supervisor Dan White assassinates Milk. White's actions are motivated by jealousy and depression, rather than homophobia.

19. May 21, 1979: Dan White is convicted of voluntary manslaughter and is sentenced to seven years in prison. Outraged by what they believed to be a lenient sentence, more than 5,000 protesters ransack San Francisco's City Hall, doing hundreds of thousands of dollars' worth of property damage in the surrounding area. The following night, approximately 10,000 people gather on San Francisco's Castro and Market streets for a peaceful demonstration to commemorate what would have been Milk's 49th birthday.

20. October 14, 1979: An estimated 75,000 people participate in the National March on Washington for Lesbian and Gay Rights. LGBT people and straight allies demand equal civil rights and urge for the passage of protective civil rights legislature.

21. July 8, 1980: The Democratic Rules Committee states that it will not discriminate against homosexuals. At their National Convention on August 11-14, the Democrats become the first major political party to endorse a homosexual rights platform.

22. July 3, 1981: The New York Times prints the first story of a rare pneumonia and skin cancer found in 41 gay men in New York and California. The CDC initially refers to the disease as GRID, Gay Related Immune Deficiency Disorder.

When the symptoms are found outside the gay community, Bruce Voeller, biologist and founder of the National Gay Task Force, successfully lobbies to change the name of the disease to AIDS.

23. March 2, 1982: Wisconsin becomes the first U.S. state to outlaw discrimination on the basis of sexual orientation.

24. March 10, 1987: AIDS advocacy group ACT UP (The AIDS Coalition to Unleash Power) is formed in response to the devastating affects the disease has had on the gay and lesbian community in New York. The group holds demonstrations against pharmaceutical companies profiteering from AIDS-related drugs as well as the lack of AIDS policies protecting patients from outrageous prescription prices.

25. October 11, 1987: Hundreds of thousands of activists take part in the National March on Washington to demand that President Ronald Reagan address the AIDS crisis.

Although AIDS had been reported first in 1981, it is not until the end of his presidency that Reagan speaks publicly about the epidemic.

26. May - June, 1988: The CDC mails a brochure, Understanding AIDS, to every household in the U.S. Approximately 107 million brochures are mailed.

27. December 1, 1988: The World Health Organization organizes the first World AIDS Day to raise awareness of the spreading pandemic.

28. August 18, 1990: President george Bush signs the Ryan White Care Act, a federally funded program for people living with AIDS. Ryan White, an Indiana teenager, contracted AIDS in 1984 through a tainted hemophilia treatment. After being barred from attending school because of his HIV-positive status, Ryan White becomes a well-known activist for AIDS research and anti-discrimination.

29. 1991: Created by the New York-based Visual AIDS, the red ribbon is adopted as a symbol of awareness and compassion for those living with HIV/AIDS.

30. December 21, 1993: The Department of Defense issues a directive prohibiting the U.S. Military from barring applicants from service based on their sexual orientation. "Applicants... shall not be asked or required to reveal whether they are homosexual, " states the new policy, which still forbids applicants from engaging in homosexual acts or making a statement that he or she is homosexual. This policy is known as "Don't Ask, Don't Tell."

31. May 20, 1996: In the case of Romer v. Evans, the United States Supreme Court decides that Colorado's 2nd amendment, denying gays and lesbians protections against discrimination, is unconstitutional, calling them "special rights."

32. September 21, 1996: President Clinton signs the Defense of Marriage Act into law. The law defines marriage as a legal union between one man and one woman and that no state is required to recognize a same-sex marriage from out of state.

33. April 1, 1998: Coretta Scott King, widow of civil rights leader Martin Luther King, Jr., calls on the civil rights community to join the struggle against homophobia. She receives criticism from members of the black civil rights movement for comparing civil rights to gay rights.

34. April 26, 2000: Vermont becomes the first state in the U.S. to legalize civil unions and registered partnerships between same-sex couples.

35. June 26, 2003: In Lawrence v. Texas the U.S. Supreme Court rules that sodomy laws in the U.S. are unconstitutional.

36. May 18, 2004: Massachusetts becomes the first state to legalize gay marriage. The court finds the prohibition of gay marriage unconstitutional because it denies dignity and equality of all individuals.

In the following six years, New Hampshire, Vermont, Connecticut, Iowa and Washington D.C. will follow suit.

37. August 9, 2007: Sponsored by the Human Rights Campaign, the Logo cable channel hosts the first American presidential forum focusing specifically on LGBT issues, inviting each presidential candidate. Six Democrats participate in the forum, including Hillary Clinton and Barack Obama, while all Republican candidates decline.

38. November 4, 2008: California voters approve Proposition 8, making same-sex marriage in California illegal. The passing of the ballot garners national attention from gay-rights supporters across the U.S. Prop 8 inspires the NOH8 campaign, a photo project that uses celebrities to promote marriage equality.

39. June 17, 2009: President Obama signs a Presidential Memorandum allowing same-sex partners of federal employees to receive certain benefits. The memorandum does not cover full health coverage.

40. October 28, 2009: The Matthew Shepard Act is passed by Congress and signed into law by President Obama on October 28th. The measure expands the 1969 U.S. Federal Hate Crime Law to include crimes motivated by a victim's actual or perceived gender, sexual orientation, gender identity or disability.

Matthew Shepard was tortured and murdered near Laramie, Wyoming on October 7, 1998 because of his sexual orientation.

41. August 4, 2010: A federal judge in San Francisco decides that gays and lesbians have the constitutional right to marry and that Prop 8 is unconstitutional. Lawyers will challenge the finding.

42. December 18, 2010: The U.S. Senate votes 65-31 to repeal "Don't Ask, Don't Tell" policy, allowing gays and lesbians to serve openly in the U.S. Military.

43. February 23, 2011: President Obama states his administration will no longer defend the Defense of Marriage Act, which bans the recognition of same-sex marriage.

44. June 24, 2011: New York State passes the Marriage Equity Act, becoming the largest state thus far to legalize gay marriage.

Queer Theory

Historically, the term queer has been used to silence, suppress, and shame practices, identities, and values located outside of perceived social boundaries. To be referred to as queer meant a person was a symbol of perversion, disdain, sickness, and absurdity. Queer then becomes defined against what is considered normal in social practices, identities, and values. The goal here is to establish social regulation so that people govern themselves (and each other) according to what is right/wrong, good/bad, and so forth. The recent reclamation of the term queer represents a resistance movement, largely led by academics and activists, to transform the oppressive nature of the term into a positive, political, and preferable depiction of the self, especially for differently gendered individuals. The deployment of queer in this manner is also an attempt to move beyond the hegemonic and historic practice of institutionalized systems using identity-categories (e.g., a "homosexual" identity) to shame, regulate, and eradicate same-sex sexual behavior.

If the term queer becomes a marker of a resistance, then "queer theory" forms the theoretical pulse to the movement. The term queer theory originated as part of de Lauretis' scholarly work on lesbian and gay male sexualities. Queer theory is a conceptual framework that "conveys a double emphasis—on the conceptual and speculative work involved in discourse production and on the necessary critical work of deconstructing our own discourses and their constructed silence". Queer theory problematizes fixed and stable identity-categories, including male/female, masculine/feminine, and lesbian/gay/straight distinctions, and re-thinks notions of plurality, intersectionality, and fluidity in discourse production. Queer theory posits these categories of "lesbian and gay" or the use of "heterosexual/homosexual" as binary to display heterodominance are social constructions and that they are, as such, artificial. Queer theory attempts to break down the continual use of categories and labels that stereotype and harms those who are in marginalized positions, such as lesbian, gay, bisexual, and transgender (LGBT) people. Queer theory "re-presents" a more fluid concept of gender and sexuality to enhance understanding of human diversity. Noting how most indigenous cultures do not have a historical practice of naming and categorizing sexual identities is one example where we question how we have to come to adhere to the use of sexual identity in Western contexts.

In an alternate view, Queer theory brings sexuality and desire to the fore and engages with a queer pedagogy that examines our positionalities, representations, relations, and needs in relation to a "re-structured self" The introduction of queer theory into educational contexts works to "challenge the reproduction of sameness, of difference, of patriarchy. In different ways we work to teach the same(sexed) as the exemplification, the solidification and mobilization of difference" To integrate queerness into the learning experience means to end silence of sexual identities, knowledge, and values that have long been oppressed in society.

Queer theory introduces the concept of heteronormativity, which is a powerful discourse that structures human relations according to heterosexuality. Scholars say that a whole field of social relations becomes intelligible as heterosexuality, and this privatized sexual culture bestows on its sexual practices a sense of rightness and normalcy. This sense of rightness—embedded in things and not just in sex—is what we call heteronormativity.

Heteronormativity interferes in individual psyches and social institutions, practices, and knowledge systems as a means to position heterosexuality as the dominant sexuality. For example, heteronormative discourses embedded in training systems lead one to believe that identities (e.g., clients, participants), ideas (e.g., curricula, policy), and relationships (e.g., notions of "family") are exclusively heterosexual, which, concomitantly, silences sexual and gender-difference.

Another hallmark of queer theory is Butler's notion of performativity. Through enlisting gender as the basis for her points, Butler put forth (a) the notion of "performativity" as it relates to the expression of identity and (b) a radical critique of category-generating terms that manage identity. First, Butler drew attention to social practices and rules involved with being and becoming (an individual). Through these social practices and rules, difficulties arise for subjects trying to develop a sense of agency, resistance, and subjectivity around their gender identity. These rules decenter and dismiss individual autonomy and demand that they be adhered to. Gender identity then becomes "performative," whereby individuals "perform" their gender according to these social rules and practices.

Encounters with performativity in this sense suggest that gender identity-categories are fluid and not fixed. Butler and others "trouble" the hegemonic nature of these social rules and practices by exposing them and interrogating the ways in which they construct and bind gender. For example,

Researchers suggested the notion of "hegemonic masculinity," which asserts that male masculinity is constructed as dominant through social, institutional, and influential rules and that femininity and subordinated masculinity are inferior. It is clear through this work that when people disturb such binding practices around (gender) identity, they then open up political possibilities that break from the constraints of social regulation.

In sum, the notions of heteronormativity and performativity as hallmarks of queer theory may be useful in interrogating power structures and "the way that things are done" in the workplace. Recently, queer theory has been critiqued as being too Western in scope, and, as a result, has evolved to include aspects of transnationalism in light of globalized societies. This critique has been useful in illustrating how queer theory can be employed as an analytic strategy to destabilize and deconstruct discourse, such as exploring how intersecting notions of "race," citizenship, gender, class, and sexuality are constructed differently in various settings.

References

- Understanding-Homosexuality-Challenges-and-Limitations-320010405: researchgate.net, Retrieved 27, April 2020

- Homophobia, hiv-social-issues: avert.org, Retrieved 10, February 2020

- Men-sex-men, key-affected-populations, hiv-social-issues: avert.org, Retrieved 16, June 2020

- What-does-the-bible-say-about-homosexuality: hrc.org, Retrieved 28, August 2020

- Allys-guide-to-terminology: lgbtmap.org, Retrieved 02, March 2020

- Stonewall-milestones-american-gay-rights-movement, American-experience: pbs.org, Retrieved 14, July 2020

Permissions

Index

Lightning Source UK Ltd.
Milton Keynes UK
UKHW052034220922
409258UK00002B/57

9 781639 875740